TECHNOLOGY POLICY AND AMERICA'S FUTURE

*Also published by St. Martin's Press
in association with the Henry L. Stimson Center*

NAVAL ARMS CONTROL: A Strategic Assessment
Barry M. Blechman, William J. Durch, W. Phillip Ellis
and Cathleen S. Fisher

THE POLITICS OF ARMS CONTROL TREATY RATIFICATION
Edited by Michael Krepon and Dan Caldwell

OPEN SKIES, ARMS CONTROL, AND COOPERATIVE SECURITY
Edited by Michael Krepon and Amy Smithson

THE EVOLUTION OF UN PEACEKEEPING:
Case Studies and Comparative Analysis
Edited by William J. Durch

TECHNOLOGY POLICY AND AMERICA'S FUTURE

∞

Steven M. Irwin

St. Martin's Press
New York

AQC 5476-4/2

Scholarly & Reference Division,
St. Martin's Press,
175 Fifth Avenue,
New York, N.Y. 10010

First published in the United States of America in 1993

Printed in the United States of America

ISBN 0-312-09961-4

Library of Congress Cataloging-in-Publication Data

Irwin, Steven M.
    Technology policy and America's future / Steven M. Irwin.
        p. cm.
    Includes index.
    ISBN 0-312-09961-4 : $39.95
    1. Technology and state—United States. 2. High technology
industries—United States. I. Title.

    T21.I76 1993
    338.9'7306—dc20   93-952
                                                       CIP

Contents

List of Figures

List of Tables

Preface

After more than a decade of debate, the United States is poised to launch a new, more activist federal policy designed to promote the fortunes of America's high technology companies. With the election of Bill Clinton and Al Gore, many of the ideological barricades to increased governmental intervention in the economy have suddenly collapsed, leaving a path open for policymakers to redress what many consider to be fatal flaws in the US approach to research and development.

The end of the Cold War and the strong political impetus provided by the massive restructuring of America's defense sector has also persuaded many that a radically new approach to US technology policy is required. Policies and regulations which perpetuate the relative isolation of the US defense research establishment from the commercial economy are clearly in need of overhaul. Similarly, the changing structure of the world economy and the increasing dependence of military systems on commercial technologies alone force policymakers to reconsider their long-held conceptions of the American defense industrial base.

Policies which seek selectively to promote "critical" technologies and "strategic" industries are already taking shape. Similarly, efforts to integrate defense and civilian technology bases through the targeted spending of defense dollars on "dual use" technologies promise to gain momentum. In the years ahead, such programs will likely command an increasing share of the nation's tax dollars as federal technology grants, subsidies, and tax credits are extended to more and more American industries.

While these changes constitute a healthy reexamination of some of the more rigid ideological tenets of the past twelve years, they carry with them considerable risks. In too many cases, technology policy recommendations focus on the symptoms of America's competitiveness problems without asking more basic questions about the underlying causes. Indeed, the overemphasis on technology as both the source of, and the solution to, America's economic problems draws attention away from more fundamental challenges facing the US economy. Increasing the nation's saving and investment rates, improving the quality of the country's educational system, and controlling the costs of health care all promise greater returns than even the most ambitious and well-conceived technology strategy. Technology alone cannot solve the United States' economic ills.

The limitations of technology policy are certainly not due to a shortage of creative policy alternatives. Indeed, if anything, the technology policy debate of the past decade has produced an excess of recommended approaches. Specific policies have been proposed to address the competitive challenges of virtually every high technology industry in America. What has been missing, unfortunately, has been an overall vision of how these various policies can be integrated into a coherent approach which promises to actually improve the economic well-being of the nation.

Instead, the limits of current technology policy proposals stem from their failure to focus on the more basic question of what federal policy is seeking to achieve. The issue is not how to make a particular industry more competitive given the conditions prevailing in today's business environment. Rather, it is to identify the systemic reasons that firms are not developing the technologies necessary to compete.

This study represents a modest effort to integrate some of the current thinking about technology policy, American competitiveness, and the changing global technological environment into a more unified approach to these issues. Rather than setting forth yet another laundry list of detailed proposals, I have tried to place these issues in context and to return to some fundamental questions about the purposes and potential implications of various policy alternatives. Hopefully, this reexamination will help stimulate a fuller discussion of the ways in which the American technology development system can be improved.

This book is the result of a project sponsored by the John D. and Catherine T. MacArthur Foundation.

I want to thank Michael Krepon and the Henry L. Stimson Center for providing a congenial home for me during my work on this project. I also want to express my gratitude to Barry Blechman for his insightful comments, careful editing, and unwarranted patience throughout this entire effort. Thanks also to Scott Hamilton for his editing assistance, Jane Dorsey for formatting the final text, and Jay Korman for his research and editing assistance during the final phases of the book. I also want to thank Dr. Theodore Moran and Dr. Ellen Frost for their helpful comments on an earlier version of this manuscript.

Finally, I want to express my deepest gratitude to my wife Bernadine. Despite the miles that separated us, her love, support, and smiling voice carried me through each day and this project. To her, I dedicate this book.

1

Introduction

F or much of the cold war, America's predominant economic and technological position in the world allowed policymakers largely to ignore the critical relationship between military security and economic vitality. However, the abrupt disintegration of the Soviet Union, the steadily rising economic challenge posed by America's European and Asian allies, and a decade of fiscally irresponsible government policies have rendered this approach untenable. For the foreseeable future, America's national security will be intertwined with its ability to reconstruct and revitalize its economy. Unless the United States is able to pursue a coherent strategy of increased investment, greater productivity growth, and renewed innovation, it will be unable to reap the hard-won rewards of four decades of cold war confrontation. In sum, continued poor macroeconomic management and underinvestment in human and physical resources will settle, to our dismay, the nagging question of whether or not the United States is a nation in decline.

With the end of the cold war, the world has entered a period of tremendous promise and substantial change. However, the continued sluggish economic performance of the United States poses a direct threat to continued American leadership in world affairs. Efforts to settle disputes throughout the world by a more active United Nations, to reenergize the global trading system, and to address pressing challenges of environmental degradation would all benefit from strong and vigorous American leadership. Whether future American presidents will have the resources to offer that leadership depends critically on new initiatives to redress the nation's macroeconomic woes and to foster increased productivity growth throughout the economy. Failure to act aggressively will result in an unmistakably weaker, less-respected America unable to seize the opportunities created by years of steadfast leadership and sacrifice.

Already, the burdens of America's domestic economic difficulties have influenced the conduct of US foreign policy. America's bold stance in the Persian Gulf was only possible politically because of the largesse of America's more financially secure allies. And while the nations of Eastern Europe and the former Soviet

Union struggle to transform their economic and political systems, the United States has been able to offer only token assistance, sadly pointing to an empty wallet and a domestic polity unwilling to assist fledgling democracies abroad when Americans themselves are facing economic adversity. Finally, policymakers contemplating foreign arms sales have been forced to consider disagreeable trade-offs between broad foreign policy objectives and the more parochial concerns of domestic manufacturers. The 1992 campaign-year decisions to sell advanced fighters to Taiwan and Saudi Arabia, despite the potential negative implications for US foreign policy objectives in Asia and the Middle East, provide ample evidence of the constraints placed on American policymakers by the nation's economic difficulties.

Rebuilding US economic strength depends on the ability of American companies and workers throughout the country to become more productive. Productivity rates are the single most important factor in determining the nation's standard of living and its ability to pursue a broad range of foreign and domestic policies. While policymakers and citizens may be distracted by concerns about the international competitiveness of individual industrial sectors, negative foreign trade balances, job losses, and short-term movements in the country's overall growth rate, these phenomena are merely transitory symptoms of deeper problems. In contrast, changes in the nation's productivity levels translate directly into changes in the nation's economic well-being.

The rate at which productivity increases, in turn, is dependent on three basic factors: (1) how much the country devotes to expanding the capital stock through savings and investment; (2) how much the productivity of individual workers is increasing due to improved skills and education; and, (3) how much more efficient the country is in using its resources as a result of technical and managerial innovations. Though interdependent, these three factors are driven by different forces. A nation's savings and investment patterns are determined largely by the incentive systems prevailing in the country's capital markets and the opportunities for profitable investment available in the economy. The skill levels of its workers depend on the quality of its educational system and the incentives for employers to make available, and for workers to take advantage of, continued training throughout an individual's career. Finally, innovation depends on the availability of skilled individuals, market opportunities, adequate resources, and sufficient incentives.

In recent years, numerous reports on the US economy have noted problems in all three of these areas that have hindered efforts to improve America's international competitiveness.[1] The US capital market is handicapped by short-sighted fiscal mismanagement by the federal government and by systemic flaws which create perverse incentives and discourage investments in areas critical to the country's long-term productivity growth. The US education system is widely seen as inadequate to the task of equipping citizens with the skills necessary to succeed in today's job market. Moreover, the system provides few incentives to encourage employers or workers to continue to invest in training over the course of a person's career.

Even more troubling, America's technological competitiveness is increasingly being called into question, with critics citing problems at every stage of the innovation process. In aggregate terms, the United States invests a considerably smaller share of its gross domestic product in commercial research and development than its economic rivals. Instead, the United States devotes an enormous amount to the development of new military technologies, within a system that makes the transfer of technology between military and commercial laboratories exceedingly difficult. Finally, even when American firms do invest in innovation, they tend to concentrate disproportionately on short-term, product-oriented research rather than on longer-term projects and process improvements. This underinvestment in less tangible

---

1. The list of reports on US competitiveness is lengthy. Some of the more noteworthy include: US Congress, Office of Technology Assessment, *Making Things Better: Competing in Manufacturing*, OTA-ITE-443 (Washington, D.C.: US Government Printing Office, February 1990); Michael L. Dertouzos, Richard K. Lester, and Robert M. Solow, *Made in America: Regaining the Productive Edge* (Cambridge, Mass.: The MIT Press, 1989); Thomas H. Lee and Proctor P. Reid, editors, *National Interests in an Age of Global Technology* (Washington, D.C.: National Academy Press, 1991); Carnegie Commission on Science, Technology, and Government, *Technology and Economic Performance: Organizing the Executive Branch for a Stronger National Technology Base* (New York: Carnegie Commission, September 1991); Competitiveness Policy Council, *First Annual Report to the President & Congress: Building a Competitive America* (Washington, D.C.: Competitiveness Policy Council, March 1, 1992); Council on Competitiveness, *Gaining New Ground: Technology Priorities for America's Future* (Washington, D.C.: Council on Competitiveness, 1991); National Science Board, Committee on Industrial Support for R&D, *The Competitive Strength of US Industrial Science and Technology: Strategic Issues* (Washington, D.C.: National Science Foundation, August 1992); and Michael Porter, *Capital Choices: Changing the Way America Invests in Industry* (Washington, D.C.: Council on Competitiveness, 1992).

areas offering significant, though not easily measurable, rewards is often noted as a critical shortcoming. In particular, failures within the technological infrastructure of US companies appear to be a serious barrier to the translation of laboratory breakthroughs into successful products in the marketplace.

These problems are particularly disconcerting because, in many ways, the creation, dissemination, and application of new technologies play a disproportionate role in fostering increased productivity growth. Analyses of past economic growth demonstrate that technological progress, broadly defined, is the single most important determinant of future productivity growth, and, by extension, of the nation's standard of living. While other paths toward economic growth are possible, these do not ensure that the country's standard of living will improve.

For the purposes of this study, technology will be defined broadly to encompass skills and innovations in products, processes, and organization. Edward Denison, in writing about the sources of economic growth, used the term "advances in knowledge," rather than "technology," to emphasize the fact that productivity growth requires advances in both physical technologies and organizational structures. In Denison's words,

> The term "advances in knowledge" must be construed comprehensively. It includes what is usually defined as technological knowledge—knowledge concerning the physical properties of things, and of how to make, combine, or use them in a physical sense. It also includes "managerial knowledge"—knowledge of business organization and of management techniques construed in the broadest sense. Advances in knowledge comprise knowledge originating in this country and abroad, and knowledge obtained in any way: by organized research, by individual research workers and inventors, and by simple observation and experience.[2]

A new semiconductor chip design, improvements in machine tools, and the concept of "Total Quality Management" would all be included under the heading of advances in knowledge. Indeed, given the American focus on Japanese management techniques, it could be argued that American firms have been challenged more by advances in Japanese managerial practices than by any specific technological accomplishment.

After studying the forty-year period beginning in 1929, Denison found that such advances in knowledge represented the single

---

2. Edward F. Denison, *Accounting for United States Economic Growth 1929-1969* (Washington, D.C.: The Brookings Institution, 1974), 79.

largest contributor to US economic expansion, amounting to almost 27 percent of all growth.[3] When he calculated the contribution of advances in knowledge to labor productivity, Denison found that technical progress accounted for roughly 48 percent of the growth in productivity per employed worker between 1929 and 1969, making it the single most important factor in US labor productivity growth.

The Debate on US Technology Policy

The end of the cold war has inspired a reappraisal of America's national priorities and policies, a reappraisal which has focused on the need to reenergize the nation's economy to cope with the economic challenges that lie ahead. The end of 45 years of superpower confrontation promises to release considerable resources for use in improving America's economic position in the world. Moreover, the 1991-92 recession and the turbulence buffeting the country's defense industry and its workers have conspired to give additional political weight and legitimacy to calls for the federal government to play a more active role in the economy.[4] These calls have also been given shape by the evident technological success of America's armed forces during the Gulf War and the widespread perception that, when it wished, the United States could develop the most advanced technologies in the world. This military success stood in contrast to the difficulties US companies experienced in the commercial realm, where the technological achievements of the country's economic rivals and the apparent

---

3. Denison, *Accounting for Growth*, 128.
4. Cut backs in defense spending have also led to a range of studies on how the US defense development and acquisition process should be restructured to cope with budget reductions and the growing importance of commercial technologies. For example, see US Congress, Office of Technology Assessment, *Holding the Edge: Maintaining the Defense Technology Base*, OTA-ISC-420 (Washington, D.C.: US Government Printing Office, April 1989), *Redesigning Defense: Planning the Transition to the Future US Defense Industrial Base*, OTA-ISC-500 (Washington, D.C.: US Government Printing Office, July 1991), and *Building Future Security: Strategies for Restructuring the Defense Technology and Industrial Base*, OTA-ISC-530 (Washington, D.C.: US Government Printing Office, June 1992); Carnegie Commission on Science, Technology, and Government, *New Thinking and American Defense Technology* (New York: Carnegie Commission, August 1990); and John A. Alic, et al., *Beyond Spinoff: Military and Commercial Technologies in a Changing World* (Boston, Mass.: Harvard Business School Press, 1992).

willingness of foreign governments to intervene in their economies seemed to place US firms at a severe competitive disadvantage. These developments have manifested themselves in a
widespread and vocal movement to enact a federal *technology*
policy, designed to promote high-technology products and to
improve the competitive status of American industry.

While there have been occasional deviations from such a policy,
since World War II the US government has generally refrained
from promoting purely commercial technologies, preferring instead to invest in mission-oriented research and development
(primarily defense) and to support basic scientific research without great regard to its direct commercial potential. The success
of this approach is evident. The United States possesses the most
diverse and capable scientific research establishment in the
world, while its armed forces are unquestionably the world's most
technologically sophisticated.

Although the United States could also claim to be the clear
technological leader in the commercial realm for much of the
postwar era, the increasing technical capabilities of Japan and
Western Europe have undermined America's position of technological preeminence. While the erosion of the United States'
technological hegemony was perhaps inevitable given the recon-
struction of Japan and Europe after the war and the inherent
dynamics of technology transfer between leader and follower
nations, this development has nonetheless caused considerable
unease in the United States and has inspired a heated debate over
the formulation of an American technology policy.

The debate on technology policy draws together a diverse community of interests. In some contexts, technology policy is presented as a natural extension of federal science policy, justified
by the growing complexity of technology development and by new
models of innovation which suggest that distinctions between
basic and applied research are overstated. By inference, this link
also offers the comfort of a strong political consensus which
already accepts the appropriateness of federal support for basic
scientific research. In other contexts, technology policy is tied to
concerns about national defense and the ability of the United
States to continue to field the most sophisticated armed forces in
the world. References to the need to protect the nation's security
lend legitimacy to arguments for expanding the federal role in
technology development, helping to overcome the deep-rooted
American tendency to reject direct government intervention in
the commercial marketplace.

The most prevalent rationale now being offered for an enhanced federal role is the oft-cited contribution that an activist technology policy supposedly could make to strengthening the global competitiveness of US industry. Policy proposals often call for the development of specific technologies in order to leverage the federal investment and maximize the economic benefits for the nation. In essence, this makes the technology policy debate a more nuanced extension of the industrial policy proposals of the early 1980s. Recent technology policy proposals have been less ambitious, however, seeking more to assist companies in pursuing markets and technologies of their own choosing than to determine the specific path private industry should follow. Aided by concerns over the nation's economic future, this more measured approach has attracted considerable political support.

As their emphasis shifts toward industry- and technology-specific strategies, however, these proposals for federal technology policy raise fundamental issues concerning the purpose, justification, nature, and limitations of various recommendations. Although much work has been done developing portraits of key technological areas and detailing areas suitable for greater federal intervention, all too often the underlying goals are ill-defined and the ultimate effectiveness of such efforts are taken as a matter of faith. Without a clear understanding of these basic issues, no policy proposal will ever live up to its promise. More importantly, policies which are premised on fundamental changes in the American political process and ideology stand little chance of surviving over the long-term. An American technology strategy must conform to the country's basic values in order to survive and succeed.

Toward an American Technology Strategy

In the commercial realm, private companies and individuals should and will continue to play the central role in funding the development of new technologies. The complexity of the market, the rapid pace of technological change, and the constant need to balance cost and performance dictate that decisions regarding which technologies are developed and which are abandoned remain in private hands. The urgent need to conform to the discipline of the market ensures that company decision-makers will be better attuned to the changing economic tides than even the most astute government official. Moreover, given the vastness of the US economy, there is simply no feasible alternative to continued reliance on free markets as the primary decision-making mechanisms.

Still, the incentives and disincentives which drive private sector decisions can often be influenced by government policy. By changing the structure within which company decision-makers operate, a well-conceived federal technology strategy could promote better outcomes for the economy as a whole. For example, there is ample evidence that market mechanisms alone are unlikely to produce the socially ideal level of investment in research and development. As a result, government efforts to compensate for the differences between public and private returns from R&D investment could lead to improved economic conditions for all. Also, given the rules governing America's capital markets, firms tend to underinvest in technologies which promise significant returns through increased productivity. Public policy changes in the conditions under which company officials make their investment decisions offer a viable means of encouraging greater attention to innovation and technical advancement. In fact, a rigorous argument for government support of technology development and diffusion can be made that should attract broad support from across the ideological spectrum.

However, the case for selective support of specific technologies and industries is more suspect, relying more on intuition and speculation than on solid analysis. The temptation to focus federal technology policy on the specific problems of individual industrial sectors is understandable. Yet, the lack of a sound and unbiased methodology for directing federal funding to specific sectors, and the nature of the American political system itself, make the chances of implementing a successful, targeted technology policy remote. This raises the very real possibility that the incremental benefits derived from a more proactive government stance would be offset by the negative economic consequences of excessive federal intervention and support of uncompetitive sectors. Without clear measures of need, or indicators of success, the tendency to allocate resources preferentially to politically astute companies in the districts of well-placed legislators will likely remain the norm. As a result, narrow segments of the economy will be likely to benefit at the expense of the overall economic health of the nation.

While improvements in technology hold substantial promise, by themselves they are insufficient to effect a permanent change in American economic well-being. Technological advancement and innovation depends on simultaneous improvements in investment and educational levels. Without a firm base of sound macroeconomic policies and investment in human resources, isolated advances in technology will yield little economic benefit. New technologies can only be introduced to the marketplace and the manufacturing floor if sufficient investment capital is available. By the same token, technological advancement will be hindered if the country lacks a large pool of technically capable workers with the skills necessary to maximize the return on the country's investment in research and development. The introduction of technology is only one step in the process of innovation, with a significant portion of the benefits resulting from the organizational innovations that result directly from those same technical advancements.

Finally, substantial increases in national productivity growth rates hinge on technological progress throughout the economy. Even large improvements in the performance of a narrow set of high-profile, high-technology industries will do little to significantly improve the productivity of the nation as a whole. Instead, innovation must be encouraged in all sectors of the economy, with particular emphasis placed on improving the performance of labor-intensive operations which have thus far been resistant to large productivity gains. In the end, the real benefits from innovation will be achieved only if all industries are encouraged to apply advanced technologies to their operations, organization, and products.

The task thus becomes one of defining the proper goals for a new American strategy for technology promotion while imposing the necessary limits to ensure that the benefits of government assistance are not consumed through pork barrel political decisions. Establishing the proper objectives will require US policymakers to look beyond immediate concerns and focus on the fundamental determinants of economic growth. This will also require that the United States adopt a long-term strategy that encourages productivity growth, establishing objectives and policies that are likely to be sustained for decades. While the pendulum of opinion in the United States may from time to time swing between support for direct governmental intervention in the economy and a position of benign neglect, the ideological debate over the adoption of an industrial policy for the United States is unlikely to disappear. As a result, success will only be achieved if US technology policies are constructed on a firm foundation of broad consensus.

Constructing the necessary limits on policy will be even more difficult. In a political culture renowned for its short-term perspective and parochial interests, establishing policies that seek long-term goals across the entire economy will obviously be problematic. Instead, the natural tendency will be to focus on specific challenges and industries, offering assistance to those sectors best able to make a convincing case for why they deserve special attention. While such a strategy may make political sense, it promises no economic rewards to the nation. Instead, any successful technology policy will have to be structured so as to channel political influences toward national objectives while minimizing the possibility that programs will be captured by special interests. Fortunately, the experimental efforts already undertaken at the federal, state, and local levels offer some guidelines to suggest how such a balancing act can be accomplished.

Study Objectives and Outline

The objective of this book is to address systematically the simple but fundamental issues that must be considered when attempting to formulate a coherent and sustainable technology policy. It aims to place the various technology policy alternatives now being considered in their proper economic, technological, military, and political context, identifying the potential risks and benefits of different courses of action. Next, it seeks to develop specific guidelines for federal action that are designed to promote both economic prosperity and military security and to remain consistent with enduring American political realities. In brief, this study seeks to address the following issues:

First, what are the technological and competitive challenges confronting the United States? Despite the fact that the 1980s were a period of unprecedented economic expansion, many have grown concerned that the United States has somehow lost its ability to compete in international markets. At the extreme, these doubts raise the specter of a nation in permanent and irreversible decline. Regardless of whether one accepts such a judgment, it is clear that the US economy is undergoing a substantial change, both in its structure and its relative position in the world. Moreover, a number of studies have indicated serious weaknesses in the manner in which firms pursue new technologies, weaknesses which, if remedied, could yield real gains for the United States as a whole.

Second, how have global economic and technology relationships changed in recent years, and what are the implications of these changes for US policy? The growing sophistication of America's trading partners suggests that technological capabilities are spreading more rapidly around the globe, eliminating one of the key competitive advantages enjoyed by US corporations since World War II. At the same time, evidence indicates that major corporations are globalizing their technical operations, further accelerating the pace of technology transfer and greatly complicating the formulation of a *national* technology strategy in a global economy.

Third, how has US policy for technology development evolved in the half-century since World War II, and what national objectives should govern a reformulation of that policy? Over much of the past four decades, the federal government has concentrated R&D funding on defense, space, and basic scientific research. This strategy grew out of the experience of World War II and has provided the basis for US science and technology policy ever since. However, over the course of the 1980s and early 1990s, many, particularly in Congress, have pushed for a revision of this strategy and for the introduction of numerous programs to support commercial technology development directly. But, while a reformulation of US technology policy is desirable, it should be premised on a clear understanding of the objectives it is designed to serve.

Fourth, why is technological progress important to the economy, and what justification exists for government intervention to support commercial technology development? Evidence indicates that technological progress is essential for the long-term health of the economy. While this would seem to argue for a greater federal role in promoting development of advanced technologies, any successful technology policy will have to aim at remedying cases of market failure while simultaneously avoiding economic distortions that might lead to increased inefficiencies.

Fifth, what influence can domestic political and cultural factors be expected to play in the formulation of a comprehensive federal policy on commercial technology? The forces operating in the political system differ significantly from those in the commercial economy, raising numerous challenges to the implementation of an effective long-term federal technology strategy. Programs may be captured by private interest groups, hamstrung by concerns over fairness and accountability, rendered irrelevant under the dragging weight of bureaucratic process, or redirected to serve the unique goals of the implementing agencies. At the same time, policies must build a strong enough political constituency to compete effectively in the annual budget battles without becoming so vulgarized that broader goals are sacrificed. In the short run, these difficulties might be overcome by a combination of a driving national consensus and high-level leadership in the Congress and the White House. Unfortunately, such high-level attention is unlikely to be maintained over time, dictating that more subtle steps be pursued that help reshape the American business environment.

Sixth, how should funding for defense research be adjusted to cope with an era of uncertain threats, lower defense spending, and increasing reliance on commercial technologies? These developments highlight three interrelated trends in defense research and development: (1) the growing irrelevance of defense-specific R&D to the commercial marketplace; (2) the increasing reliance of military systems on commercial components and technologies; and (3) the greater use of foreign-supplied products in US military systems. These trends raise important and perplexing dilemmas for defense planners and policymakers. Should the military concentrate on defense-specific R&D or fund development of dual-use technologies? How can the United States maintain its technological edge during a period of fiscal austerity? How should the United States respond to the latent threat posed by reliance on foreign suppliers and the globalization of the defense industrial base? While there are few satisfying answers to these challenges, they establish a clear choice for US defense policymakers between a neomercantilist strategy and a commitment to transnational integration.

Finally, the question of where technology fits within the larger policy and business context must be addressed. Even assuming that any proposed policy succeeds beyond all expectations, it still constitutes only one element of a broader "competitiveness" agenda. Other factors, including the quality of American managers, the education of the work force, and the overall rate of productive investment could be far more significant to the nation's long-term economic health. An emphasis on technical "quick fixes" over more fundamental reforms is understandable, but certainly not desirable. Although beyond the scope of this study, these issues must be recognized so that the contribution of technology policy can be analyzed within its proper framework. Similarly, the pursuit of a more assertive technology policy must be reconciled with America's other policy objectives. This is particularly important given the effect that such efforts might have on the country's trade policy and its long-term commitment to a global free-trade regime. Policies which assume a neomercantilist stance risk inviting foreign retaliation, perhaps offsetting any positive returns from the original effort. While a firm US position against foreign trade barriers is essential, efforts to copy the subsidy practices of other governments may undermine American arguments that such measures are detrimental to the promotion of free trade and global economic prosperity.

In short, this study confirms the need for a broad, national effort to upgrade the technological capabilities of all US-based industries. The development and application of new technologies offers perhaps the brightest hope for America's long-term economic future and for sustained improvement in the standard of living of all Americans. While the United States is certainly not on the road to technological ruin, as is so often proclaimed, it does engage in practices which negatively impact American economic performance. In any event, business and government leaders have gradually reached a broad consensus on the importance of technological development to the nation's future. The growing constituency favoring a renewed emphasis on technology as an engine of economic growth offers policymakers and business executives a unique opportunity to make fundamental improvements in the US economy.

Unfortunately, attention is being diverted from fundamental national concerns to the specific problems faced by politically powerful industrial sectors. Rather than designing policies to improve the nation's overall economic condition, many of the proposals now being circulated concentrate on specific industries or technologies, with scant reference to the national interest. Such "common sense" approaches—supporting this or that high-tech industry—are often intuitively appealing. Regrettably, these narrow solutions to specific problems could lead to irrational national policies. If we are to answer effectively that "nagging question" with which this study began, we must develop a more far-sighted program that is at one and the same time compatible with America's tremendous economic and technical strengths, geared to the reality of a truly global marketplace, and clearly intended to improve the lives of all Americans. In order to endure, such a program must concentrate on enhancing America's technological capabilities across the board by establishing sustainable *processes* to promote innovation. Simply developing the next generation of technology is not enough. Instead, the United States must implement policies designed to promote the constant upgrading of the US economy, its businesses, and the skills of its workers.

Part One
The Context for Policy

2

American Competitiveness: Fire Bells and False Alarms

A t times, the calls for the United States to adopt a more assertive federal technology policy have grown apocalyptic, warning of permanent and irreversible economic decline unless drastic actions are taken. Armed with a welter of statistics and anecdotes to prove their case, critics of the United States' traditional "hands-off" approach to the economy point to the competitive failure of sector after sector of US industry and to the rise of foreign competition in high technology industries as evidence of the economy's fatal misdirection. To these observers, the persistent US merchandise trade deficit, relatively slow productivity growth rates, and foreign penetration of key high-technology industries are signals of impending disaster.[1] Given these realities, some would argue for a new paradigm, a new economic nationalism, to replace what they view as the outdated and dangerous policy of laissez-faire.

While such hyperbole is perhaps inevitable given the economic challenges of the past decade, it obscures the more complex realities of America's competitive position in the world economy. It also offers an overly simplified image of the technological challenges facing American business in the 1990s. Unquestionably, there are real weaknesses in the US economy, weaknesses which could at least partially be remedied by more responsible and proactive federal policies. Indeed, many of the oft-identified problems with the US economy—low savings and investment rates, a chronic failure to invest in human resources, federal fiscal mismanagement—pose very real threats to the nation's well-being. In all of these areas, the government's failure to respond threatens the country's long-term economic welfare.

---

1. For two notable examples of such "declinist" literature, see Office of Technology Assessment, *Competing Economies: America, Europe, and the Pacific Rim* (Washington, D.C.: US Government Printing Office, October 1991) and Lester Thurow, *Head to Head: The Coming Economic Battle Among Japan, Europe, and America* (New York: William Morrow, 1992).

However, the economy also possesses considerable strengths which must not be overlooked in the rush to reinvigorate government policy. The United States remains the most productive and diverse economy in the world. In fact, recent evidence suggests that US industry maintained or extended its productivity lead over its foreign rivals during the 1980s. The United States retains leadership in a range of high technology sectors—from biotechnology to software—and has integrated advanced technologies into a substantially larger portion of its industries than have other countries. While foreign competitors have gained markedly in selected areas of manufacturing, other parts of their economies often remain woefully unproductive and uncompetitive. Moreover, according to most observers, the United States remains uniquely able to nurture the development of new companies, industries, and technologies, quickly shifting resources to promising fields well ahead of our foreign rivals. Although these strengths offer no basis for complacency, they do suggest that a more carefully reasoned and less emotional approach to improving America's long-term technological competitiveness is in order.

This chapter reviews briefly the evidence of America's still competitive position in the world economy in order to provide a more complete context for the policy discussions which follow. It also provides an overview of aggregate trends in US and foreign investment in research and development. The subsequent chapter focuses more specifically on the perceived technological shortcomings of US firms and the growing trend toward the internationalization of high-technology enterprises and activities. More than anything else, these two chapters paint a picture of an economy undergoing tremendous change—change which is unsettling for many because it is altering fundamentally the domestic and international patterns of economic life that have prevailed in the United States for the past five decades. This change has already resulted in the disappearance of many factories, companies, and even entire industries. And, of course, the vast economic changes of the past decade have brought about the dislocation of thousands upon thousands of workers. However, the same economic disruptions have also opened doors to new jobs, technologies, and industries. Most importantly, these changes offer opportunities for long-term economic gains that will benefit the entire United States.

A critical distinction to be kept in mind throughout this discussion is the difference between relative and absolute economic decline. One of the most striking features of the postwar era has been the rapid economic growth of America's allies in Europe and Asia. Despite the tremendous technological head start enjoyed by the United States after World War II and four decades of heavy US government investment in advanced technology, many signs now point toward a convergence of technological capabilities among the leading nations of the industrialized world. The strength of Japanese companies in the international markets for dynamic random access memory semiconductors, consumer electronics, machine tools, and automobiles—markets once dominated by US firms—provides ample evidence of the diffusion of technological capabilities around the globe. Of course, given the sheer size of the American economy, and the nation's unsurpassed investment in research and development, for the foreseeable future, no single nation is likely to be in a position to compete with the United States across the entire technological spectrum. However, companies from several nations have matched or surpassed their American counterparts in a number of high-profile, high-technology industries. When taken together, the advanced industrialized nations of Europe and Japan have reached a point where they can challenge the long-held image of America as a technological hegemon.

While there is no single indicator of the state of a country's technical prowess and its relative economic competitiveness, a composite picture can be drawn from measures of national R&D spending levels, employment patterns, national productivity trends, and trade figures. These indices suggest that the United States remains a powerful producer of advanced technologies and that it continues to lead the world in a broad range of technical fields. However, these indicators also demonstrate the growing capacity of a number of America's economic rivals to compete with US industry on the cutting edge of science and technology. Measured in relative terms against the size of their individual economies, these nations' investment in R&D and their level of scientific and technical production have climbed steadily to levels comparable with, and in some cases, superior to, those of the United States. Moreover, in absolute terms, these countries have achieved remarkable increases in their productivity levels, standards of living, and shares of world high-technology trade.[2]

---

2. For a valuable discussion of the globalization of technology and the rising technological capabilities of the rest of the industrialized world, see Thomas H. Lee and Proctor Reid, eds., *National Interests in an Age of Global Technology* (Washington, D.C.: National Academy Press, 1991), 14-44.

However, close examination of the accomplishments of America's industrial rivals indicates that they are unevenly distributed. While they may have made substantial gains in selected industries, in others—particularly in the service sector—their performance falls far short of that found in their counterparts in the United States. Moreover, US-based companies continue to hold a commanding position in a wide range of industries, and remain internationally competitive even in those sectors where foreign gains have been most pronounced. Even some industrial sectors, once written-off as hopeless victims of foreign competition, have shown surprising signs of renewed strength after sometimes painful adjustment processes.[3] Though none of this diminishes the accomplishments of European or Japanese high technology companies, it does suggest that an overly selective examination of the competitive position of US industry, as well as simplistic projections of future performance based on trends that emerged during the early- and mid-1980s, can be highly misleading.

Macroeconomic Developments in the US Economy

In macroeconomic terms, the 1980s were a turbulent decade for the United States—a period of tremendous growth, but also one marked by significant, and often negative, developments in a number of sectors and economic indicators. By most measures, economic growth over the decade was substantial, making the 1980s witness to the longest peacetime expansion on record. However, as the economy expanded, the US trade deficit with the rest of the world grew sharply as US export growth stalled and foreign, particularly Japanese, imports into the United States grew at a steady pace. Moreover, the 1981-82 recession and its severe impact on US manufacturing triggered grave concerns over the health of America's industrial sector, concerns which were kept alive by the growing foreign share of the US market for manufactured goods and the continued decline in manufacturing employment in the United States. The continued distress of certain segments of the manufacturing sector, including high technology manufacturing, has inspired much of the current support for a more assertive industrial policy.

3. Steven Lohr, "High-Tech Goliaths, Taking Pains to Act Small," *The New York Times*, December 30, 1992, D1.

Aggregate US Trade Performance

Perhaps more than any other indicator, the US trade deficit has served as a shorthand index of the declining competitiveness of American industry during the public debate of the 1980s and early 1990s over US technology policy. Indeed, a cursory review of the evidence seems alarming. For example, the United States has not enjoyed a trade surplus since 1975, and trade deficits in the mid-1980s regularly exceeded $100 billion per year. Moreover, the US trade imbalance with Japan has been particularly severe, rising from a deficit of $121 billion in 1980 to $445 billion by 1990. Even more ominous is the fact that the US balance of trade in high-technology products, always an area of American strength, dipped temporarily into deficit for the first time ever in 1986. In automobiles, semiconductors, machine tools, and consumer electronics, foreign manufacturers penetrated the US market to an unprecedented degree while US exports lagged. In many cases, the pressures of foreign competition proved too much for indigenous US manufacturers, driving some American companies out of business entirely and pushing surviving firms to move their manufacturing facilities overseas, in order to reduce costs. Moreover, whereas foreign competition had previously only affected producers of relatively low-technology goods such as textiles and simple manufactured products, the 1980s witnessed a significant rise in foreign competition in leading edge sectors such as electronics and aerospace. Whereas many were willing to accept as a necessary part of economic progress the decline of labor-intensive, low technology industries such as textile production, foreign challenges to America's high technology sectors seemed to raise more fundamental questions about the technological competitiveness of US products, workers, and companies.

While America's trade troubles over the past decade have been at times alarming, the implications of the nation's declining trade position are more complex than often indicated in discussions of the country's industrial competitiveness. In fact, real growth in US exports has been substantial in recent years, particularly beginning in 1986-87, when the effects of lower exchange rates and improved product quality began to yield real returns in terms of export growth. Between 1986 and 1991, US exports grew in real terms by 83 percent, two to three times the growth rates experienced by the other G-7 nations.[4] This rapid increase in US exports was by no means an aberration. In fact, US export growth

4. Council on Competitiveness, *Competitiveness Index* (Washington, D.C.: Council on Competitiveness, 1992), 3.

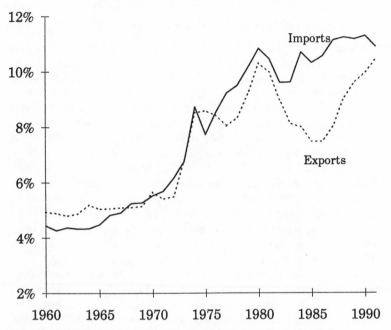

Source: *National Income Product Accounts*, Aggregate Data. Revised February 13, 1992.

Figure 2.1. US Exports and Imports as a Percentage of GDP, 1960-1991.

for the past two decades has been impressive, rising in real terms by over 220 percent. Only export-oriented Japan, with real export growth of 322 percent, turned in a stronger performance over the same 20-year period.

Nevertheless, the US trade position did indeed suffer greatly during the early 1980s. As Figure 2.1 indicates, beginning in 1982, US imports and exports diverged dramatically. Exports fell from their high of nine percent of GDP in 1980 to just over six percent by 1985. In contrast, growth in imports to the United States remained strong throughout the 1980s. As exports recovered during the later half of the decade, this gap between imports and exports began to narrow, with the 1991 trade deficit standing at only $27 billion, compared to the $132 billion deficit recorded in 1986.[5]

---

5. *National Income Product Accounts*, Aggregate Data, February 13, 1992.

Using aggregate trade balances as a measure of the nation's economic competitiveness offers an imperfect perspective at best. Simply stated, changes in the overall American trade position during the last decade says almost nothing about the state of US industry. The rapid rise in the US trade deficit which began in the early 1980s, was far more the product of macroeconomic developments in the American economy than of any real change in the competitiveness of the US industrial sector. This is hardly surprising, considering that it would be remarkable for a nation so suddenly to lose its ability to compete internationally because of real changes in the productivity of its major industries. The deteriorating US trade position of the 1980s reflected policy choices made early in the Reagan administration. Its decision to simultaneously cut taxes and federal revenues while sharply increasing defense spending contributed to record US federal budget deficits. Naturally, these deficits raised US interest and exchange rates, making American products less attractive overseas and imports relatively more attractive at home. This produced disastrous results for America's exporters and a boon for American consumers. US exporters suddenly faced a 40 percent cost disadvantage due to the run-up in the dollar's value.[6] Once President Reagan accepted the 1985 Plaza Agreement to intervene in the currency markets to push down the value of the dollar, US exports rebounded sharply, largely erasing the overall US trade deficit which had grown during the first half of the decade.

While these aggregate developments are reassuring in that they suggest that many of the problems experienced by US firms trying to compete in the international marketplace during the 1980s were the product of macroeconomic conditions rather than competitiveness failures, to many, trends in world trade shares for high-technology manufactured products would indicate that something more fundamental is wrong.

Over the course of the 1980s, America saw its share of high-technology trade deteriorate significantly. Figure 2.2 shows the shares of the world export market for technology-intensive products over the period 1965 to 1987. While European trade shares have remained relatively stable, the Japanese portion of global high-technology trade more than doubled over the two decades, largely at the expense of US industries. The United States' share of world high-technology exports declined significantly over the two decades, from roughly 28 percent in 1965 to 21 percent in

---

6. I.M. Destler, *American Trade Politics*, 2nd Edition (Washington, D.C.: Institute for International Economics, June 1992), 57.

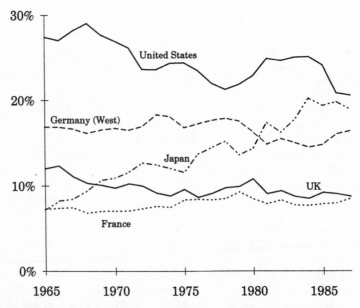

Source: National Science Foundation, *International Science and Technology Data Update: 1991* (NSF-91-309) (Washington, D.C. : National Science Foundation, April 1991).

Figure 2.2. Export Shares of Technology-Intensive Products, 1965-1987.

1987. Sector trends confirm these aggregate developments. In computers, US exports fell from 39 percent of the world total in 1980 to 24 percent in 1989; in telecommunications, from 11 to 9 percent; in scientific instruments, from 28 to 25 percent; and in aerospace, from 48 percent to 46 percent.[7]

While the declining market share of US high-technology products is worrisome, negative trends in macroeconomic conditions most likely played a major role in driving these markets during the 1980s. During the last decade, the US balance of trade in electronics, for example, followed a path similar to that of the overall trade balance. In 1983, the US electronics trade balance slipped into deficit as exports stagnated and imports continued to grow. This gap widened sharply during the middle of the decade.

7. National Science Board Committee on Industrial Support for R&D, *The Competitive Strength of US Industrial Science and Technology: Strategic Issues* (NSB-92-138) (Washington, D.C.: National Science Foundation, August 1992), 71.

However, by the end of the decade, as the effects of exchange rate changes took hold, the US electronics trade picture improved markedly. The $14.6 billion deficit recorded in 1987 shrank to $5.2 billion by 1991. Even in the highly controversial area of solid state components (e.g., semiconductors), the $1.4 billion deficit recorded in 1987 became a $1.4 billion surplus by 1991.[8]

Moreover, using trade statistics as measures of US technological competitiveness has other limitations. Despite the substantial increase in both US exports and imports over the past two decades, international trade continues to represent only a small share of the US economy when compared to its trading partners. Manufacturing exports, for example, represented only 5.7 percent of total GDP in 1991 compared to 9.2 percent for Japan, 15.5 percent for France, and 23.5 percent for Germany.[9] Moreover, the composition of America's exports is changing, with service exports growing in significance. In 1975, service exports accounted for just 15 percent of all US exports. By 1990, this figure had climbed to 26 percent, or roughly $138 billion. In fact, in 1990, the net trade surplus in services largely offset the trade deficit incurred in merchandise trade.

Trends in Income per Capita

A second popular measure of the nation's well-being is the level of income per capita. By most accounts, the United States remains the most productive nation in the world, and American citizens continue to enjoy the highest standard of living (in economic terms) in the industrialized world. However, the US lead in gross domestic product (GDP) per capita has eroded steadily beginning in the 1950s as Europe and Japan have rebuilt their economies and raised their national incomes. Starting from an initial disadvantage following the war, these countries have enjoyed per capita income growth far greater than that experienced in the United States. By one measure, for the period 1972 to 1991, per capital gross domestic product increased in real terms by only 28 percent in the United States, compared to 87 percent in Japan and 65 percent in Italy.[10] On average, real GDP per capita increased by 63 percent for the non-US members of the Group of Seven (G-7), a considerably faster pace than that experienced by the United States.

8. Electronic Industries Association, *1992 Electronic Market Data Book* (Washington, D.C.: Electronic Industries Association, 1992), 112-113.
9. Council on Competitiveness, *Competitiveness Index*, 3.
10. Council on Competitiveness, *Competitiveness Index*, 1.

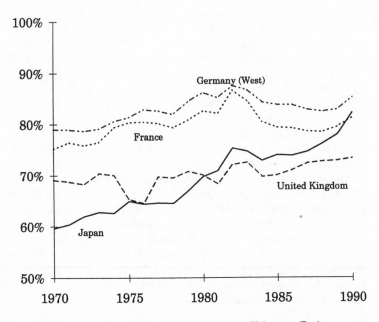

Source: OECD, *National Accounts: Main Aggregates, Volume 1* (Paris: OECD, 1992)

Figure 2.3. Real Gross Domestic Product Per Capita, 1970-1990 (US=100).

What disturbs many is the prospect that the rapidly growing economies of Europe and Asia will continue expanding at their current rate, matching, and eventually surpassing, the standard of living levels of the United States. Such a projection from past trends is likely to miss the mark, however. In fact, between 1980 and 1990, there was no discernable improvement in the GDP per capita ratios for Germany, France or the United Kingdom relative to those of the United States (see Figure 2.3). In 1990, income per capita for these countries was between 14 and 25 percent lower than that of the United States. Japan did improve its position relative to the United States over the same period, however, with income per capita growing from 70 percent of US levels in 1980 to 82 percent by 1990. If Japan were able to sustain these rates of increase indefinitely, it would surpass the United States by the end of the century.[11] As will be discussed, however, there are

11. Organization for Economic Cooperation and Development, Department of Economics and Statistics, *National Accounts: Main Aggregates,*

strong reasons to suspect that Japan will find it increasingly difficult to further close the income gap with the United States. In any event, while GDP per capita is a useful measure of a nation's overall standard of living, it offers little insight into the efficiency of the economy or the competitiveness of its industries.

Trends in Productivity Growth

A better measure of the efficiency of a nation's industries is its productivity level. In simple terms, productivity is the ratio of output per unit of input. Labor productivity therefore measures the output generated per unit of labor (e.g., per full-time employee, per hour worked, etc.). Total Factor Productivity (TFP) measures the efficiency with which output is generated from all inputs. As productivity increases, a country becomes better able to translate its resources, human and physical, into usable outputs. Unfortunately, precise measures of productivity are difficult, meaning that analysts typically rely on a number of different measures to provide a better picture of reality. Moreover, current productivity measures are incapable of adequately capturing improvements in quality which are not reflected in higher prices. Despite these measurement problems, the importance of productivity growth to the long-term health and well-being of the nation cannot be overstated.

Despite a general sense that the US position among industrialized nations has been slipping over the past decade, evidence on national productivity rates indicates a somewhat more complicated picture. At the broadest level, trends in productivity reveal a steady narrowing of the lead that the United States opened up following World War II. In many ways, such a development is to be expected, however, particularly given the terrible destruction wrought by the war in Europe and Asia and the unusual economic advantages enjoyed by the United States following the war.

The war's transformation of the global balance of technical power was unprecedented. Total factor productivity shifted dramatically as a result of the war. In 1938, US productivity was twice that of Japan, 41 percent higher than Germany's, and 14 percent higher than that of Britain. After the war, in 1950, US productivity was almost *five* times that of Japan, over twice that of Germany, and 38 percent higher than the United Kingdom's. The tremendous differences were the product of renewed US productivity growth (up over 54 percent between 1938 and 1950) and the dismal performance of the war-ravaged economies of

Germany and Japan, where productivity dropped by 6.5 and 34 percent, respectively, and of the United Kingdom, where productivity rose by only 26 percent.[12]

Moreover, after the war, the US government did not simply take the country's continued economic prosperity and technological superiority for granted. Instead, it embarked on new policies toward science and technology that vastly increased public support for research and development. These policies were largely responsible for the creation of the R&D infrastructure which exists today in the United States. In contrast, during the late 1940s and 1950s, neither Europe nor Japan were in the position to match the United States' commitment to increased R&D spending.

With their post war productivity levels severely depressed, and having the United States to serve as a model for advanced economic development, Western Europe and Japan naturally experienced higher average growth rates than the United States in the five decades following the war. These countries benefitted from well-educated and technically capable populations, a history, particularly in Europe, of industrial achievement comparable to that of the United States, and a forward-looking US policy that specifically sought to rebuild these economies through free access to the US market and massive infusions of much-needed capital. As a result, a rapid convergence in national productivity rates among the industrialized world was inevitable.

Figure 2.4 tracks real GDP per employed person for the four top industrialized nations over the past forty years against that of the United States. All of these countries have made substantial gains in their labor productivity rates, most sharply during the 1950s and 1960s, and then more slowly during the 1970s and 1980s. By 1989, according to one estimate, Japan's productivity level per employed person stood at roughly 73 percent of US levels, making its workers only slightly more productive than workers in Britain, where productivity levels were 72 percent of those in the United States. Germany and France enjoy much higher productivity levels, measuring 82 and 86 percent of US rates.[13]

If one attempts to take into account differences in hours worked, the achievements of France and Germany become even

---

12. William J. Baumol, Sue Anne Batey Blackman and Edward N. Wolff, *Productivity and American Leadership: The Long View* (Cambridge, Massachusetts: The MIT Press, 1989), 335.
13. National Science Foundation, *International Science and Technology Data Update*, 113.

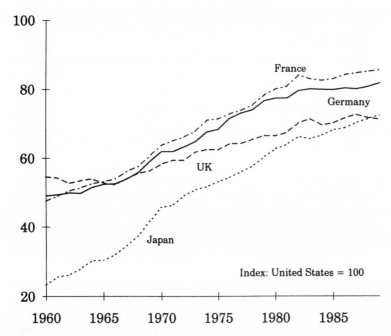

Source: National Science Foundation

Figure 2.4. Real Gross Domestic Product per Employed Person, 1950-1989.

more impressive, with labor productivity actually exceeding US levels. In contrast, Japan's productivity rates become less striking when hours worked are considered, reflecting the Japanese tendency to put in much longer hours than their European or American counterparts.[14]

These aggregate measures of productivity suffer a number of flaws, however. Most importantly, they include output from sectors in which productivity is either impossible to measure or meaningless. These "non-market" parts of the economy include government, health care, education, non-profit organizations, and real estate. The size of these non-market sectors are significant, ranging from 19 percent of the economy in Japan to thirty

---

14. McKinsey Global Institute, *Service Sector Productivity* (Washington, D.C.: McKinsey & Company, October 1992), Exhibit 1-3, 1-4. While consideration of work hours should give a better indication of actual productivity levels, caution is in order because of the difficulties involved in collecting consistent data on actual hours worked.

percent in the United States. Employment in these sectors is also considerable, from 11 percent in Japan to 29 percent in the United States.[15]

When these segments of the economy are excluded, productivity rates for all countries fall in comparison with those of the United States. Data for 1988 indicates that French labor productivity per full-time employee drops from 91 percent of US levels to just 84 percent when non-market segments are excluded. Germany's productivity falls from 86 percent to 80 percent, while Japan's declines from 72 to 61 percent of US levels. These figures suggest that aggregate productivity rates in the United States is depressed somewhat by the poor relative performance of the non-market segments of the economy. This would seem to lend credence to the widely held perception that inefficient government operations and the health care system in the United States constitute a drag on the overall economy.

The relatively poor productivity performance of Japan's market economy seems inconsistent with the dominant image of Japan as an economic superpower and its success in international trade. Indeed, Japanese gains in automobiles, machine tools, consumer electronics, and microelectronics are a driving force behind many of the efforts to improve American productivity levels. However, when one examines the Japanese economy in its entirety, it becomes clear that productivity performance varies significantly among Japanese business sectors. Clearly, Japanese companies in a select number of manufacturing industries have achieved world-class status and enjoy productivity levels equal or superior to those of American firms. These manufacturing firms constitute only a small share of Japan's total economy, however. In contrast, many other Japanese industries, manufacturing and non-manufacturing alike, have very low productivity rates. This is particularly true in the Japanese service sector, which lags behind US and European performance significantly.

While static measures indicate that the United States remains the most productive economy in the world, data on productivity growth rates has often been cited as reason for alarm. While US productivity grew at a healthy pace following World War II, it was far lower than growth rates abroad, particularly in Japan and Germany. As suggested previously, this was to be expected given the destruction wrought by the war and the effects of rapidly rebuilding these economies. More disconcerting has been the slowdown in productivity growth beginning in 1973. Whereas

---

15. McKinsey, *Service Sector Productivity*, 3-4. Data is for 1988.

industrial productivity in the United States grew by an average annual rate of 2.2 percent between 1950 and 1973, it slowed to just 1.1 percent for the time period 1973 to 1987. Although more difficult to measure, productivity rates for services also declined substantially, falling from 1.4 percent to just 0.2 percent per year.[16]

In contrast, Japan's industrial productivity increased by 9.5 percent per year between 1950 and 1973, while Germany's grew at an annual rate of 5.6 percent. While productivity growth has remained stronger in these countries than in the United States since 1973, their growth rates have nevertheless declined significantly. Japan's industrial productivity growth dropped to 3.9 percent per year, while Germany's fell to 2.0 percent. These rates are well above comparable US rates, but represent a substantial slowdown from the heady expansion of the 1950s and 1960s.

However, as Figure 2.5 demonstrates, the rate at which America's industrialized allies are closing the productivity gap with the United States has steadily declined since the late 1960s. For example, whereas Japan was increasing its GDP per employed person relative to the United States at a rate of around eight percent per year around 1970, by the late 1980s the rate of closure had fallen to one to two percent. Major European economies showed a similar, if less pronounced, slowdown. This points to a growing convergence of productivity rates within the industrialized world.

The fact that all nations in the industrialized world suffered a slowdown in productivity growth after 1973 suggests more general factors are at work. While there is no agreement on the exact causes for the lower post-1973 growth rates, it seems likely that the unprecedented expansion during the 1950-73 time period served to compensate for the lower-than-normal growth rates of the 1930s and 1940s.[17] In turn, the economic troubles of the early 1970s probably triggered the permanent end to this period of higher-than-average growth.

Manufacturing Productivity Although no other nation has yet achieved overall productivity rates equal to those of the United States, European and Japanese manufacturing companies have substantially closed the gap between themselves and their

---

16. Angus Maddison, *Dynamic Forces in Capitalist Development: A Long-Run Comparative View* (New York: Oxford University Press, 1991), 150.
17. William J. Baumol, et al., *Productivity and American Leadership*, 68-71.

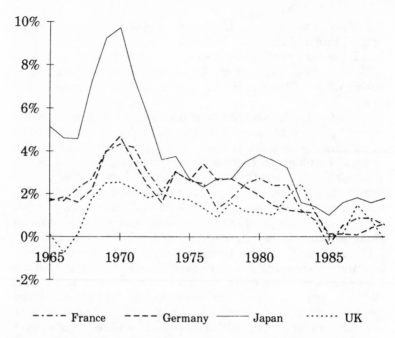

----- France   ---- Germany   ——— Japan   ······ UK

Source: National Science Foundation

Figure 2.5. Annual Percentage Gain in Real GDP per Employed Person Relative to the United States, Three-Year Moving Average, 1965-1989.

American counterparts. Germany, Japan, and the United States now dominate the world's output of manufacturing products. In 1988, they produced roughly 54 percent of the free world's manufactured goods. They also accounted for 35 percent of the international trade in manufactured goods among capitalist countries.

A recent study on manufacturing production and efficiency suggest that German and Japanese gains in manufacturing have been uneven.[18] In terms of their overall levels of output, the German manufacturing sector was approximately 28 percent the size of that of the United States, while Japan's was 59 percent in 1987. In addition to being smaller, these countries' manufacturing sectors differ markedly from that of the United States in terms of their composition. Most obviously, the machinery, elec-

18. Dirk Pilat and Bart van Ark, "Productivity Leadership in Manufacturing: Germany, Japan and the United States, 1973-1989," unpublished paper, University of Groningen, March 1992.

trical, and transport equipment industries comprised a far larger share of total Japanese manufacturing as compared to the United States. In 1987, these industries represented only about one-third of total US manufacturing output. In contrast, they constituted roughly half of all manufacturing output in Japan in the same year. In fact, in absolute terms, this part of Japan's manufacturing sector was larger than that of the United States. German manufacturing is similarly concentrated, with these sectors representing 45 percent of all German industrial output. The US manufacturing sector is more varied, with food processing, textile production, paper and wood manufacturing, and chemical production comprising a greater share of overall manufacturing output than is the case in either Germany or Japan.

Turning to manufacturing productivity levels, data indicate that the United States continues to hold a significant advantage in overall manufacturing productivity. In 1989, US manufacturing industries were 20 percent more efficient than those of Germany or Japan. More surprising are the trends in relative productivity rates for the period 1973 to 1989. Germany, which is often perceived as a more efficient producer than the United States, in fact did not significantly close the gap with the United States in terms of manufacturing productivity. German productivity first reached 80 percent of the US level in 1974. Through the late 1970s and early 1980s, it gained steadily on the United States. Since then, however, Germany's relative productivity has declined. In fact, from 1979 to 1989, German manufacturing productivity grew more slowly than did that of the United States, rising at only 1.1 percent per year as compared to 3.5 percent for the United States.

Japan's manufacturing industries have fared better, making substantial progress in closing the productivity gap with their US counterparts over the past 20 years. In 1973, Japanese manufacturing productivity stood at roughly 56 percent of US levels. By 1981, it had reached 77 percent of US levels. Since then, however, progress has been extremely slow, with productivity rising only three percentage points relative to the United States over eight years. While Japan's productivity growth rates still outpaced those of the United States, they did so only marginally. For the ten years between 1979 and 1989, manufacturing productivity in Japan grew by 4.6 percent per annum, 1.1 percentage points faster than in the United States. At this rate, it would take Japan nearly 20 years to make up the remaining difference with the United States.

While aggregate measures of US manufacturing productivity might belie the widely held notion that America's manufacturing sector is uncompetitive, analysis of individual manufacturing sectors indicates that the US position varies significantly by industry. As could be expected, in those industries where Germany and Japan are most competitive internationally, productivity levels approach or exceed those of the United States. In particular, Japanese productivity rates for machinery, electrical engineering, and transportation equipment exceeded those of the United States in 1989, helping explain the prominence of Japan's automobile, electronics, and machine tool industries in global markets. Japanese auto makers, for example, enjoy a substantial, though declining, cost advantage over their US counterparts due to their higher productivity rates. Productivity rates in Japan's basic metals and metal products industries also nearly match those found in the United States.

In other manufacturing areas, however, productivity levels abroad pale in comparison to those of the United States. Japan's food processing and textile industries, for example, were all far less competitive than their American counterparts. Typically, these industries do not trade internationally and are relatively protected from outside competition, helping to explain their failure to reach international competitive standards. Germany's productivity levels were more even throughout its manufacturing industries, although certain sectors, such as food processing, are significantly less productive than German manufacturing industries as a group.

While the productivity and international competitiveness of Japan's transportation, machinery, and electronics sectors are of obvious concern to US companies, the relative threat posed by these sectors must be put in perspective. In 1988, the combined output from all manufacturing, utilities, and construction industries represented approximately 27 percent of total US GDP, or 39 percent of all market sector GDP. In terms of employment, these industries accounted for roughly 22 percent of total employment, as compared to 46 percent for the market service sector. Given that the machinery, electrical engineering, and transport equipment sectors account for about one-third of all manufacturing in the United States, this means that these industries account for only about one-tenth of the entire output of the American economy.[19]

---

19. McKinsey, *Service Sector Productivity*, 3.

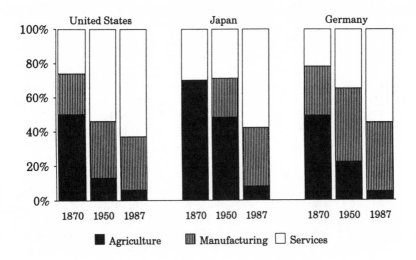

Note: Services includes government. Manufacturing also includes construction, mining, and utilities.

Source: Angus Maddison, *Dynamic Forces in Capitalist Development: A Long-Run Comparative View* (New York: Oxford University Press, 1991).

Figure 2.6. US, Japanese, and German Employment Structure, 1870, 1950, 1987 (Percent).

Moreover, manufacturing employment in the United States, which grew sharply from the beginning of the industrial revolution through the 1950s, has begun to decline as a share of total employment. By one estimate, in 1870, agricultural employment accounted for half of all American jobs, with manufacturing (24 percent) and services (26 percent) comprising the other half.[20] By 1950, manufacturing employment had grown to roughly 33 percent of the total workforce, while agricultural employment had dropped to just 13 percent. Service employment exploded during this same period, growing to 54 percent by 1950. By 1987, however, agriculture employed only six percent of the nation's workforce, and total industrial employment accounted for 31 percent of total jobs. Over the same period, service sector employment continued its steady growth, rising to 63 percent of total employment by 1987. (See Figure 2.6).

---

20. Maddison, *Dynamic Forces in Capitalist Development*, 248-249.

Germany has followed a similar pattern as seen in the United States, with industrial employment growing sharply between 1870 and 1950, then declining as a percentage of total employment as jobs shifted to the country's service sector. Germany and the United States industrialized at roughly the same time, helping to explain the similar trends in employment composition and suggesting that declining manufacturing employment is not the same as a declining manufacturing sector. Certainly, there is little correlation between the health of the US agricultural sector and the employment levels in farming. In fact, to the degree that labor productivity outpaces increases in demand, total employment in any industry can be expected to decline.

In contrast, Japan came late to the modern era, possessing virtually no manufacturing capability in 1870. Since then, manufacturing employment has grown steadily, accounting for one-third of total employment by 1987. As the Japanese economy matures, however, it can be expected to follow a path similar to that of the United States and Germany. Already, the size of the Japanese service sector has increased substantially, while the percentage of the workforce engaged in farming has declined. Recent slowdowns in Japanese manufacturing growth and the first, tentative steps toward layoffs suggest that Japan may in fact be moving toward a more service-oriented employment structure.

Trends in Service Sector Productivity Although certain American manufacturing sectors have been severely challenged by foreign competition, it is important to remember the importance of other sectors of the US economy to the nation's overall economic well-being. Though often dismissed as a sector that simply offers low-wage, low-skill jobs, America's service sector is largely responsible for the nation's continued lead in overall productivity levels. Given the size of the US service sector and its large share of total US employment, productivity increases in services can have a substantially larger effect on national productivity rates than can improvements in manufacturing efficiency. Moreover, the efficiency of the service sector has a direct effect on the productivity of a country's manufacturing industries. By one estimate, 23 percent of the value of industrial sector sales in the United States are the product of service sector increases.[21] As a result, the greater efficiency of America's service industries

---

21. McKinsey, *Service Sector Productivity*, 11.

translates directly into a cost advantage for US manufacturing firms competing in the international marketplace.

Unfortunately, service sector productivity is particularly hard to quantify. Difficulties in measuring inputs and output, accounting for qualitative differences, and obtaining accurate data have made sectorial analyses problematic. Case studies, however, backed by the analysis of overall productivity rates given above, suggest that America's service sector is significantly more productive that those of Europe or Japan. For example, labor productivity in Germany's state-owned telecommunications sector is estimated to be roughly one-half of that found in America's private, competitive telecommunications markets. Similarly, Japan's overregulated retailing industry was found to be only 44 percent as productive as its US counterpart. Studies have found that the United States also enjoys advantages in the retail banking and airline industries. Moreover, American companies generally offer a broader range of services than their foreign counterparts. US airlines offer more flights, telephone companies a wider range of telephone services, and retail banks a broader array of financial service options than their foreign counterparts.

Service sector productivity in the United States, like productivity in the manufacturing sector, chiefly benefits from a highly competitive environment relatively free from governmental interference and protection. In contrast, foreign service industries are often strictly regulated or, more damagingly, protected from foreign competition. As a result of the highly competitive domestic environment, American companies are often better organized, more adept at utilizing advances in technology, and more responsive to market pressures than their foreign counterparts.

This review of US productivity rates suggests that while there is certainly no basis for complacency, actual developments in US productivity over the past decade are perhaps less alarming than has sometimes been reported. Certainly, the slowdown in productivity growth rates after 1973 is disturbing. However, this dropoff was a universal development. Moreover, while Europe's major economies and that of Japan have managed to narrow significantly the productivity gap with the United States, they continue to lag the United States by a substantial margin. Their rates of improvement have slowed in recent years, pointing more toward a convergence of productivity rates among the industrialized world than to an eclipse of the United States.[22] Moreover, while

---

22. On the subject of convergence of productivity rates among the United States and the rest of the industrialized world, see William J. Baumol,

the competitive pressures posed by foreign advances in certain manufacturing sectors have caused great distress in segments of the US manufacturing base, these industries represent a relatively small, though certainly not unimportant, part of the overall US economy.

Investment in Science and Technology

While the above analysis of the overall economic position of the United States is in many ways reassuring, trends in research and development investment are ambiguous at best. By almost any measure, the United States spends heavily on research and development. In 1988, the United States invested more in R&D and employed more scientists and engineers than Japan, Germany, France, the United Kingdom, Sweden, and Italy combined. The sheer size of the US technical enterprise is staggering. Currently, the United States spends approximately $150 billion each year on research and development, employs roughly four million scientists and engineers, and produces more than one-third of the world's scientific literature. Moreover, industry and government funding for research and development has grown substantially since the 1950s, increasing in *real* terms by 475 percent between 1953 and 1990.[23]

The federal contribution to this effort is significant, reflecting the continuing consensus that the nation has a basic interest in utilizing public resources to promote scientific and technological progress. In 1990, for example, federal R&D funding represented 46 percent ($69 billion) of all monies spent on R&D in the United States. Moreover, federal R&D spending has grown considerably since the 1950s, almost quadrupling in real terms between 1953 and 1990. Of this, defense remains the largest component by far, absorbing roughly $42 billion (64 percent) in 1990.[24]

Despite these impressive figures, there are indications of serious problems with the US research and development system. Heavy government spending on defense research yields relatively

Productivity and American Leadership, 85-113 and Angus Maddison, *Dynamic Forces*, 128-165.
23. National Science Foundation, *National Patterns in R&D Resources: 1990* (NSF 90-316) (Washington, D.C.: National Science Foundation, May 1990), 43; National Science Foundation, *International Science and Technology Data Update: 1991* (NSF 91-309) (Washington, D.C.: National Science Foundation, April 1991), 25, 89.
24. National Science Foundation, *National Patterns*, 56.

few benefits for the economy as a whole. Moreover, the large federal share serves to mask relatively low levels of R&D investment by US private industry. Despite significant increases in private R&D expenditures over the last decade, American companies still invest relatively less than their rivals overseas. In fact, US high-technology companies, in particular, are consistently outspent by their overseas competitors. Given the immense importance of private, product-oriented R&D to the nation's competitiveness, these trends do not bode well for America's competitive future.

Aggregate Investment in Research and Development

Although the United States continues to outspend its rivals in absolute terms, America invests relatively less of its gross domestic product in research and development than either Germany or Japan. Figure 2.7 highlights the trends in total national R&D spending as a percentage of GNP for the United States, Japan, Germany, France, and Britain since 1961 (the earliest date for which data are available). In 1961, the United States spent a greater percentage of its GNP on research and development (2.7 percent) than did any other industrialized nation. Only the

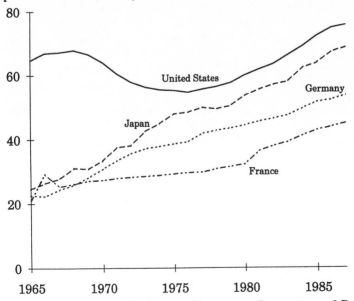

Figure 2.7. Total R&D Expenditures as a Percentage of Gross National Product by Country.

United Kingdom, at 2.5 percent, approached the US spending level. Others, most notably Japan, spent far less, from between 1.2 to 1.4 percent of GNP.[25]

By 1990, however, the situation had changed significantly. Although total R&D spending still amounted to 2.7 percent of GDP in the United States, it had risen to 2.8 percent in West Germany and 3.1 percent in Japan. More striking still, US spending levels lagged despite immense government spending on military research and a boom in company-funded commercial R&D during the 1980s. While increased federal and corporate spending helped the nation to rebound from the fall-off in R&D spending which occurred during the 1970s, the increases essentially served only to restore spending levels to what they were in the 1960s. In contrast, the increases in Germany's and Japan's R&D spending levels have been more consistent, yielding increasing technical capabilities and wealth for both of these economies.

The disparities between relative R&D spending are even more striking when defense research is removed from the equation. Figure 2.8 shows non-defense R&D as a percentage of GDP for the five major industrialized nations. Excluding defense, the United States spent just 1.9 percent of its GDP on R&D in 1990, as compared to 3.0 percent for Japan and 2.7 percent for Germany. The rapid growth of both the Japanese economy and the share of Japanese income devoted to R&D has caused Japan's total research expenditures to rise dramatically. In 1972, for example, non-defense Japanese R&D spending was roughly 35 percent of US spending. By 1989, this figure had risen to just under 60 percent of US non-defense spending and showed no signs of declining.[26]

It is important to note that total research and development spending in the United States is driven far more by government spending than is the case in either Germany or Japan. While the governments of these countries offer various incentives to encourage private sector R&D spending, they fund relatively little R&D directly. In contrast, the federal government in the US funds roughly half of all R&D in the United States, and a large share of the R&D undertaken by US industry is funded by the federal government.

25. National Science Foundation, *International Science and Technology Data Update*, 4-5.
26. National Science Foundation, *International Science and Technology Data Update*, 9.

Moreover, the focus of US government-funded R&D efforts is significantly different than that found in either Germany or Japan. As noted, US defense research accounts for roughly 60 percent of all government-funded R&D. This is roughly comparable to the amount spent by Europe's major military powers, Britain (55 percent) and France (42 percent), but far exceeds levels found in Germany (19 percent) or Japan (9 percent). Other areas which receive considerable funding in the US are health (13 percent), space (7 percent), and, to a lesser degree, energy (4 percent). In contrast, Germany's spending is distributed between defense (19 percent), industrial development (19 percent), and energy (9.5 percent). Japan, with its limited domestic natural energy resources, devotes the lion's share of its government R&D budget to energy research (39 percent), and, to a much more limited extent, civilian space. Interestingly, Japan spends only a small share (8 percent) of its relatively smaller government R&D

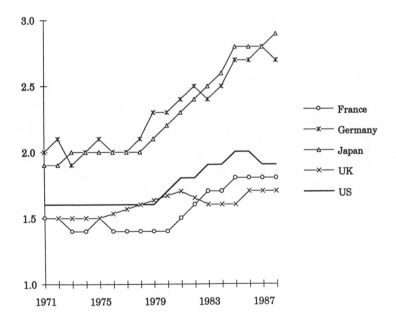

Source: National Science Foundation

Figure 2.8. Non-Defense R&D Expenditures as a Percentage of Gross National Product by Country.

budget on industrial development. The Japanese government relies more on low-interest loans and tax incentives than on direct R&D subsidies to encourage firms to invest in R&D.[27]

Of course, the United States spends virtually nothing directly on industrial research and development. Those that are undertaken, such as Sematech and the VLSI program, are typically justified on national security grounds. While these federal research programs may have contributed to US industrial competitiveness, the growing divergence of government and commercial technical requirements and commercial procedures, combined with the haphazard nature of the technology transfer process, have reduced the economic effectiveness of even these limited federal R&D efforts.[28]

In any event, despite the fact that the US federal government plays a far more direct role in determining overall national R&D spending levels, US spending on commercial technology development lags that of other countries. Increasing the federal share of R&D spending even more offers one alternative for improving America's technological position. Stimulating additional R&D investment by private industry represents another possibility.

Changes in American Industrial R&D Spending

In 1991, US industry spent approximately $76 billion on research and performed another $30 billion worth of R&D that was funded by the federal government. This made industry the leading performer, by far, of research and development in the United States, accounting for close to three-quarters of all R&D performed. By comparison, colleges and universities and the federal government performed respectively only 15 and 11 percent of the research carried out in the United States; the non-profit sector accounted for just three percent.[29]

During the late 1970s and early 1980s, industry funding for research and development grew sharply, increasing in real terms by 6.1 percent between 1975 and 1980 and by 7.3 percent between 1980 and 1985. These increases in R&D spending brought about a sharp rise in R&D intensity during the 1980s. R&D intensity,

27. National Science Foundation, *International Science and Technology Data Update*, 11.
28. For a discussion of these issues, see John M. Alic, et al., *Beyond Spinoff: Military and Commercial Technologies in a Changing World* (Boston, Mass.: Harvard Business School Press, 1992).
29. National Science Board Committee on Industrial Support for R&D, *The Competitive Strength of US Industrial Science and Technology*, 9-11.

calculated as the ratio of company-funded R&D to net sales, remained steady throughout the 1970s at around 2.0 percent. Beginning in 1981, however, this ratio climbed sharply, rising to over three percent by 1986. This increase marked an important improvement in technological competitiveness of US companies, and no doubt contributed to the renewed strength of many industries during the late 1980s and early 1990s.

Beginning in the mid-1980s, however, the high rates of R&D spending growth experienced during the previous decade slowed significantly, with industry-funded research and development barely keeping up with inflation. Between 1985 and 1992, industry R&D grew in real terms by only 0.4 percent. Virtually every major sector of the economy that performs R&D experienced a similar reduction in real R&D growth after 1985, with only the automobile industry increasing its spending during the latter half of the decade.[30] Moreover, the R&D intensity of US industry levelled off around three percent.

The slowdown in R&D spending has been ascribed to a number of factors, including the 1991–92 US recession, declining sales and profits, increasing high-technology competition from abroad, corporate restructuring, and the effects of the mergers and acquisitions that occurred in the latter half of the 1980s. Certainly, the debt load incurred by many US firms as a result of the mergers and acquisitions of the 1980s negatively affected their ability to perform research and development.[31] The move to support externally performed R&D by universities, non-profit consortia, and foreign laboratories has also been blamed for the slowdown. Finally, legislative changes that reduced the value of the research and development tax credit have also been cited as contributing to slower industrial R&D investment.[32] Regardless of the specific

---

30. The National Science Board found that R&D by service corporations increased six-fold during the 1980s, lead by growth in the software and telecommunications sectors. Service sector R&D represents approximately nine percent of all corporate R&D. Because of the difficulties in collecting data on R&D in service corporations, however, this data is necessarily suspect. National Science Foundation, *The Competitive Strength of US Industrial Science and Technology*, 10.
31. Bronwyn Hall, "The Impact of Corporate Restructuring on Industrial Research and Development," *Brookings Papers on Economic Activity: Microeconomics: 1990*, 85-136.
32. Martin Neil Baily and Robert Z. Lawrence, "Tax Incentives for R&D: What Do the Data Tell Us?" in US Congress, House Ways and Means Committee, *Permanent Extension of Certain Expiring Tax Provisions* (Washington, D.C.: US Government Printing Office, 1992), 383-408.

cause, the stagnation of industry-funded R&D is clearly disturbing.

Technical Employment in US Industry

The overall increase in research and development spending by US firms during the early 1980s resulted in a faster-than-average growth in relative employment levels of scientists and engineers. Between 1984 and 1990, employment levels for such technical workers increased from 40 per thousand employees to 49 per thousand. Technical employment growth in the manufacturing sector was even more pronounced, expanding from 39 per thousand in 1980 to 51 per thousand by 1989. For those industries performing the greatest share of R&D over the past decade, technical employment levels have increased across the board. Between 1980 and 1990, technical workers per thousand employees increased by 66 percent in the electrical equipment sector, 73 percent in the chemicals industry, 77 percent in the machinery industry, and 99 percent in the computer sector.[33]

A country's pool of scientific and technical talent represents a key component of its overall technical capabilities. Those directly engaged in research and development work represent the leading edge of the work force, and are essential to the creation of new technologies and the diffusion of technical know-how throughout the economy. In 1965, the United States enjoyed a marked advantage in terms of the percentage of its work force consisting of scientists and engineers directly engaged in research and development. At roughly 65 per 10,000 in the labor force, US levels were almost three times those of West Germany (with 22.6 per 10,000) and over two-and-a-half times Japan's (24.6 per 10,000).

Even with the increases in US technical employment levels during the 1980s, however, this US advantage has declined substantially as France, Germany, and, particularly, Japan have steadily increased the number of scientists and engineers engaged in research and development (Figure 2.9). By 1987, Japan's employment levels for R&D professionals per laborer had reached 90 percent of US figures. The US lead in total nonacademic technical personnel (including scientists and engineers not working on R&D activities), remains somewhat greater, with the United States employing 30 percent more than its closest rival, Japan, in the mid-1980s. Nevertheless, the trend toward a more

---

33. National Science Foundation, *The Competitive Strength of US Industrial Science and Technology*, 69.

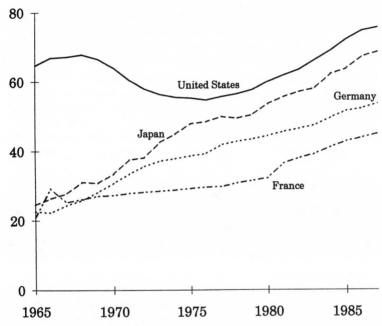

Source: National Science Foundation.

Figure 2.9. Scientists and Engineers Engaged in R&D per 10,000 Labor Force by Country.

equal distribution of scientific and technical talent around the world is clear.[34]

Trends in Technological Leadership

The rising level of foreign investment in high technology and the steady increases in the number of technical personnel employed abroad has led to tremendous strides in Europe and Asia in a wide range of industrial sectors. Sectorial studies indicate foreign gains led to a relative decline in US technological leadership in a number of important manufacturing industries. In some sectors, observers generally agree that foreign firms now hold an advantage in cutting edge technologies, while in others, US firms continue to hold the lead, although their relative positions have been eroded significantly.

---

34. National Science Foundation, *International Science and Technology Data Update*, 46-47.

During the early 1990s, a number of attempts were made to identify important technologies and evaluate the position of US industry relative to companies in Europe and Japan. For example, the Department of Commerce, the Department of Defense, and the Office of Science and Technology Policy all sponsored reports, at Congress' request, to identify critical technologies which were considered essential to the country's economic future and military security. Private groups, including the Council on Competitiveness and a number of industry trade associations, also produced evaluations of the relative US technological position in key sectors.

These reports documented the steady relative technological decline of US companies, despite the encouraging trends in overall productivity and economic growth rates over the past decade. For example, the 1991 Council on Competitiveness report, *Gaining New Ground*, identified 94 important technologies deemed crucial to competitiveness in the next century (see Table 2.1). In 15 of these, the Council concluded that US industry was losing badly or had lost its position to foreign competitors. US companies were considered weak in 18 additional technical areas. While US corporations were considered competitive or strong in the remaining 61, the Council warned that the relative US position was still eroding. In no areas was the United States actually gaining on its competitors.[35]

The Department of Commerce also concluded that the United States was losing its technological lead over Japan. In ten of thirteen emerging technologies identified, Japan was gaining rapidly or had surpassed the United States (see Table 2.2). Commerce went on to project that these trends, if they were to continue, would result in Japanese superiority in all thirteen technologies by the year 2000, and that even the European Community would supplant the United States in a number of areas. Among the technologies where the United States was "losing" or "losing badly" were advanced semiconductors, sensor technologies, medical devices, high-performance computing, biotechnology, and advanced materials[36]

35. Council on Competitiveness, *Gaining New Ground: Technology Priorities for America's Future* (Washington, D.C., 1991.)
36. US Department of Commerce, *Emerging Technologies: A Survey of Technical and Economic Opportunities* (Washington, D.C.: Department of Commerce, 1990. The National Critical Technologies Panel came to a similar conclusion. *Report of the National Critical Technologies Panel* (Washington, D.C.: Office of Science and Technology Policy, March 1991).

Table 2.1. Council on Competitiveness Assessment of the US Competitive Position in Critical Technologies.

Technologies in which the United States is Strong	Technologies in which the United States is Competitive
Materials and Associated Processing Technologies Bioactive/Biocompatible Materials Bioprocessing Drug Discovery Techniques Emissions Reduction Genetic Engineering Recycling/Waste Processing	**Materials and Associated Processing Technologies** Catalysts Chemical Synthesis Magnetic Materials Metal Matrix-Composites Net Shape Forming Optical Materials Photoresists Polymers Polymer Matrix Composites Process Controls Superconductors
Engineering and Production Technologies Computer-Aided Engineering Systems Engineering	
Electronic Components Magnetic Information Storage Microprocessors	**Engineering and Production Technologies** Advanced Welding Computer Integrated Manufacturing Human Factors Engineering Joining and Fastening Technologies Measurement Techniques Structural Dynamics
Information Technologies Animation and Full Motion Video Application Software Artificial Intelligence Computer Modeling and Simulation Data Representation Date Retrieval and Update Expert Systems Graphics Hardware and Software Handwriting and Speech Recognition High-Level Software Languages Natural Language Neural Networks Operating Systems Optical Character Recognition Processor Architecture Semantic Modeling and Interpretation Software Engineering Transmitters and Receivers	**Electronic Components** Logic Chips Sensors Submicron Technology **Information Technologies** Broadband Switching Digital Infrastructure Digital Signal Processing Fiber Optic Systems Hardware Integration Multiplexing Spectrum Technologies
Powertrain and Propulsion Airbreathing Propulsion Low Emission Engines Rocket Propulsion	**Powertrain and Propulsion** Alternative Fuel Engines Electrical Storage Technologies Electric Motors and Drives

Table 2.1. US Competitive Position in Critical Technologies (continued).

Technologies in which the United States is Strong	Technologies in which the United States is Competitive
Materials and Associated Processing Technologies Advanced Metals Membranes Precision Coating **Engineering and Production Technologies** Design for Manufacturing Design of Manufacturing Processes Flexible Manufacturing High Speed Machining Integration of Research, Design and Manufacturing Leading-Edge Scientific Instruments Precision Bearings Precision Machining and Forming Total Quality Management **Electronic Components** Actuators Electro Photography Electrostatics Laser Devices Photonics **Powertrain and Propulsion** High Fuel Economy/ Power Density Engines	**Materials and Associated Processing Technologies** Display Material Electronic Ceramics Electronic Packaging Materials Gallium Arsenide Silicon Structural Ceramics **Engineering and Production Technologies** Integrated Circuit Fabrication and Test Equipment Robotics and Automated Equipment **Electronic Components** Electoluminescent Displays Liquid Crystal Displays Memory Chips Multichip Packaging Systems Optical Information Storage Plasma and Vacuum Flourescent Displays Printed Circuit Board Technology

Source: Council on Competitiveness, *Gaining New Ground: Technology Priorities for America's Future*, pp. 31-34.

Table 2.2. US Department of Commerce Estimate of Relative Trends for 13 Emerging Technologies.

	US vs. Japan	US vs. Europe
Losing Badly	Advanced Materials Biotechnology Digital Imaging Technology Superconductors	Digital Imaging Technology Flexible Computer- Integrated Manufacturing
Losing	Advanced Semiconductor Devices High-Density Data Storage High-Performance Computing Medical Devices and Diagnostics Optoelectronics Sensor Technology	Medical Devices and Diagnostics
Holding	Artifical Intelligence Flexible Computer- Integrated Manufac- turing	Advanced Material Advanced Semiconductor Devices High Density Data Storage Optoelectronics Sensor Technology Superconductors
Gaining		Artificial Intelligence Biotechnolgy High-Performance Computing

Source: US Department of Commerce, *Emerging Technologies: A Survey of Technical and Economic Opportunities* (Washington, DC : NTIS, 1990), xiii.

In contrast to the aggregate trends in productivity rates, and, to a lesser extent, developments in US industrial R&D spending, the sectorial studies produced by various government agencies and outside think tanks painted a far bleaker picture of the US competitive position. The difficulties faced by America's high technology industries were readily attested to by corporate executives facing stiff foreign competition. Despite their narrow focus, these reports had a tremendous influence on the national debate over US technology policy and economic policy in general. Indeed, they helped stir fundamental doubts about whether the United States was definitively, and irreversibly, in decline.

A Nation in Decline?

Unmistakably, the developments detailed above point to the conclusion that, despite significant improvements in its economic performance over the past decade, the United States has entered a period of sustained decline relative to its economic rivals in Europe and Japan. The economic hegemony enjoyed by the United States following World War II has largely been offset by rapid economic growth abroad. While the United States continues to enjoy a substantial lead in overall productivity levels, other industrialized nations are steadily closing the gap, eroding America's edge and challenging the country's title as the global technological leader.

Evidence of the relative decline of the United States, however, does not support the conclusion that the country has entered a period of absolute decline. More importantly, straight-line projections of the economic trends of the past four decades into the future are likely wide off the mark. The economic recovery and growth of America's trading partners in Europe and Japan was inevitable, particularly given the US policy of building up those economies to serve as bulwarks against Soviet expansionism. With US technical assistance and transfers of capital, and with four decades of hard work, these countries have been able to regain their former positions in the industrialized world. If anything, the persistence of US advantages in productivity levels suggests the tremendous strength of the US economic system.

The issue, therefore, is not of decline, relative or absolute, but of the move toward greater equality—technological and economic—among the nations of the industrialized world. While there are certainly significant problems with the US economy, the remedying of these problems offers an opportunity for building on an already strong technological and economic foundation and should not be seen as a critical requirement to prevent a slide into the economic abyss.

If trends in productivity rates and per capita income expose America's economic decline as more myth than reality, the question arises as to why the perception of decline has become so pervasive. There are several possible explanations. The rapid increase in foreign competition, and particularly the Japanese penetration of the US automobile and electronics markets, were likely to be disturbing for many Americans simply because they challenged US technological leadership in highly visible sectors. One can speculate that the Japanese penetration of the US automobile market was especially troubling because of the importance of the automobile in American culture and mythology. More generally, technology holds a unique place in American culture, perhaps more so than in any other country. For a nation inspired by the accomplishments of Edison and Ford, the rise of foreign competence in high-technology manufacturing undoubtedly raised a degree of self-doubt.

More concretely, it was inevitable that the effects of foreign competition would be unevenly distributed. For companies and industries rocked by foreign imports, the new equality among the industrialized world spelled nothing short of disaster. Moreover, the discontented (e.g., the automobile industry, textile workers, semiconductor manufacturers, etc.) were organized and vocal in their complaints about the destruction wrought by foreign corporations. In contrast, the chief beneficiaries of foreign competition—American consumers—can seldom compete for the country's attention. The natural tendency to blame one's troubles on someone else, while claiming full credit for one's successes, ensured that Washington and the public at large heard relatively little about those industries that were prospering in the new global economy.

Even allowing for such atmospherics, however, it is clear that the past decade was a period of substantial structural change in the US economy, both in terms of its composition and the distribution of its rewards. By any measure, the 1980s were a period of tremendous growth, with 19 million jobs created and real per capita income rising by 18 percent.[37]

For many, however, the patterns of economic life were upset during the 1980s. Large corporations, which had come to dominate America's industrial landscape during the 1950s and 1960s, stumbled badly in the early 1980s and never fully recovered. After several decades of steady expansion, the *Fortune 500* companies in 1979 produced 58 percent of the nation's wealth and employed 16.2 million workers. However, the recessions of the early 1980s took a severe toll from which the *Fortune 500* have yet to rebound. By 1989, these companies were producing just 42 percent of the nation's income. More importantly, employment had fallen to around 12.5 million, even as job growth overall had *increased* by 19 million.[38] Moreover, the membership in this corporate elite became more volatile than ever before, with an annual turnover

---

37. George Bush, *Economic Report of the President* (Washington, D.C.: US Government Printing Office, February 1992), 305, 334.
38. John Case, *From the Ground Up* (New York: Simon & Schuster, 1992), 32.

of 28 companies during the 1980s compared to ten companies per year in the 1960s.[39]

The loss of stability by America's corporate giants probably took with it a large measure of the security of the American workforce. The rapid growth and assured profitability of large corporations during the 1950s and 1960s allowed them to offer many workers guaranteed lifetime employment at steadily rising wages. These guarantees were largely lost during the 1980s as corporate "rightsizing," restructurings, and divestitures shook any sense of job security for many Americans, and contributed to the pervasive belief that something had gone terribly wrong with the American economy.[40]

Compounding this sense of dislocation were the changing requirements for success in the American economy that emerged in the 1980s. The rapid diffusion of technology and capital around the world made it far simpler to establish production facilities abroad. As a result, it became increasingly difficult for low-skilled workers in the United States to command significantly higher wages than low-skilled workers abroad. Although manufacturing jobs fell only marginally during the decade, opportunities for secure, long-term employment with large US manufacturing companies declined markedly. Whereas workers with only high school diplomas might have previously obtained secure, high-wage positions in the economy of the 1950s and 1960s, the 1980s demanded higher skill levels and greater flexibility. Moreover, the job growth of the 1980s was primarily generated by smaller, often newly established firms that offered fewer guarantees of long-term job security.

Finally, increasing social inequality during the 1980s contributed to the widespread sense of economic decline. In theory, the economic growth of the past decade should have resulted in real improvement in living standards throughout the economy. However, several studies indicate that the economic rewards of the 1980s were skewed severely toward the wealthiest portion of the population. According to the Congressional Budget Office,

---

39. For a discussion of the changing structure of the US economy and the implications for American competitiveness and social equality, see Michael Prose, "Is America in Decline?" *Harvard Business Review* Vol. 70, No. 4 (July-August 1992): 34-45.
40. The fact that few are suggesting that the federal government should step in now to prop up either IBM or General Motors suggests that many analysts recognize the dynamism in the structure of today's economy. Peter Passell, "Is G.M.'s Fate Still Crucial to the US?" *The New York Times*, November 6, 1992, D-1.

between 1977 and 1989 the wealthiest one percent of families in the United States accounted for 70 percent of the overall increase in average family incomes (44 percent if adjusted for changes in family size). The top twenty percent of families accounted for over 100 percent of the increase in incomes. In contrast, the family incomes for the bottom 40 percent actually declined over the decade, despite real increases in per capita income over the decade.[41]

Federal reserve figures confirm this trend toward greater inequality, showing that the share of the total net worth of all families grew from 31 percent in 1983 to 37 percent in 1989. In contrast, the share held by the bottom 90 percent fell from 33 to 32 percent over the same period. A study by the Economic Policy Institute showed a similar trend, estimating that the top one-half of one percent of American families received 55 percent of the total real increase in wealth between 1983 and 1989.[42] At the same time, the wealth of the country's lower-middle and bottom classes declined in real terms. In fact, disparities in the growth of wealth were even more severe than the trend toward greater inequality in income distribution. Other factors, including declining real estate prices, have probably also served to undermine the confidence of many Americans in the long-term health of the economy.

Consequently, much of the challenge of the next decade will be to design appropriate public policy responses to facilitate these changes in the US economy and to redress the social problems of rising inequality and greater instability in the American job market. In developing these policies, the focus should be on how to develop mechanisms that speed, rather than impede, structural changes in the economy. This will require significant changes in the US health, training, unemployment compensation, and pension systems. Sustained economic growth through the development and application of new technologies will be only one part of a larger solution.

41. US Congressional Budget Office, "Measuring the Distribution of Income Gains," CBO Staff Memorandum, March 1992.
42. Edward Wolff, "The Rich Get Increasingly Richer: Latest Data on Household Wealth During the 1980s," Economic Policy Institute, October 1992.

3
American Enterprise and the Global Technology Environment

The economic transformations underway in the world economy are forcing American businesses to rethink how they will operate and survive in a more competitive business environment. Although the United States continues to enjoy considerable economic and technological advantages, it will find itself increasingly challenged by foreign competitors. Moreover, as businesses have sought to do business within this changed environment, they have increasingly integrated their operations across national borders, blurring the boundary between the US and world economy.

This chapter summarizes the most oft-cited weaknesses in the development and application of new technologies by American corporations. Actions to correct these defects could yield important improvements in the nation's well-being, and better prepare US companies to compete in tomorrow's economy. The chapter also focuses on the broader developments in the US and world economies that have served to transform the ways in which technologies are brought to market. These developments are changing the manner in which business is conducted and greatly complicate efforts to design national technology policies in an increasingly integrated world economy.

Technological Weaknesses in US Industry

Despite their considerable strengths, there are indications that US companies are at a disadvantage in several important respects relative to their overseas rivals. While the evidence may not support the more extreme claims that the US industry faces technological ruin, a decade of study by researchers intent on identifying the causes of America's economic difficulties has yielded a number of important insights into the weaknesses of the American technical enterprise. These specific problems could, if left unaddressed, undermine the long-term prospects of American high-technology industries.

The reported symptoms of American industry's technological problems are manifold, including failures in general management practices, destructive financial pressures from outside investors, failure to keep pace with a rapidly changing global technological environment, feeble internal management of technology development, and an ineffective, and, at times, counter-productive, federal technology policy. While there are no doubt many specific causes for these various problems, competitiveness assessments of the past decade have tended to focus on three primary areas: (i) short time horizons of US managers and shareholders, leading to less than optimal R&D investment levels and priorities; (ii) failure to commercialize technologies in a timely manner, often leading to the erosion of American companies' initial technological advantages; and (iii) consistent underinvestment in process technologies that prevents US industry from competing in high volume, high-technology markets. Each of these areas will be examined briefly below.

Short Time Horizons of Managers and Investors

One particularly popular explanation for America's technological problems has been the perceived short time horizons of US management and investors.[1] The ability of managers to plan and invest for the long-term growth of their companies is perceived as crucial to future competitiveness. By making sustained investment in product and process research and development over a number of years, companies can open up new markets sooner than their competitors. Moreover, by pressing this initial technological advantage in emerging markets despite sometimes minimal returns on their investment, these companies can establish dominant positions that allow them to recover their earlier investments.

Unfortunately, managers and investors in the United States appear less willing than their counterparts overseas to continue investing in promising technologies when the near-term returns appear meager. Although US companies are often pioneers in high-technology fields, many suggest that there is a widespread inability in the United States to convert these early leads into long-term advantages due to this unwillingness to undertake long-term investments in refining and commercializing technologies. Japanese managers, and, to a lesser extent, European executives, are generally credited with having a longer-term

---

1. See, for example, Michael Dertouzos, et al., *Made in America: Regaining the Productive Edge* (Cambridge, Mass.: The MIT Press, 1989) 53-66.

perspective. For example, the longer time horizons of Japanese managers supposedly allowed them to turn an American invention (the videocassette recorder) into a tremendously successful consumer product. Although the US firm Ampex developed the first commercial VCR, Japanese companies spent two decades perfecting the device and the production techniques required to mass market it. This dedication, despite the years of poor economic returns from their work, appears to be an important contributor to the success of Japanese industry in many high-technology fields. Many observers believe that few American firms are willing to make a similar commitment.

The longer time horizons and long-term strategic planning of many Japanese firms have also been demonstrated by their tendency to enter the low-end of new markets where profit margins are least attractive. By entering these low margin, low-technology sectors and enduring years of poor profits, Japanese companies often acquired valuable experience and technological insights which allowed them to compete more successfully later on. In many instances, US firms withdrew from these markets only to find that Japanese firms move "up scale," successively challenging established firms until their product lines covered the entire spectrum of goods. The history of the Japanese penetration of the US auto industry is a prime example of such behavior.

In a similar vein, the portfolios of R&D projects among German and Japanese firms also tend to have a greater number of long-term projects, again illustrating the relatively longer time frames used to evaluate their management decisions. These longer-term projects place these companies in a much better position than US firms when it comes to developing or adapting new generations of advanced technologies.

The reasons for the short-term focus of American managers are complex, but most revolve around differences in the real or perceived cost of capital. Until recently, it was convenient to blame the higher cost of capital in the United States for the short time horizons of US managers. Higher capital costs increase the "hurdle rates" by which R&D projects are evaluated, forcing managers to apply a higher discount rates to calculations of the future returns from research and development. Given differences in capital costs in the United States and Japan, the argument went, a Japanese manager might be able to wait twelve years for a project to begin yielding returns, whereas his American counterpart, looking at the same project, would only be able to afford an eight year delay. This effectively diminishes the number of attractive investment options for US companies and severely limits the number of long-term projects any firm is willing to undertake.

Although the argument is sound, recent empirical studies cast doubt on the notion that a sustained differential between US and Japanese capital costs exists. Recent studies suggest that, in fact, there has been no significant difference in capital costs for manufacturing firms operating in the United States and those operating in Japan.[2] Instead, as will be discussed in chapter seven, the myopia of American managers derives more from the structure of US capital markets and of US capital budgeting procedures, leading to the *perception* that capital costs are higher in the United States. While the effect on firm behavior is the same, the appropriate policy responses are quite different given this distinction.

There are a number of additional factors that are believed to contribute to the short-term perspective of US managers. Macroeconomic instability over the past decade, with its shifting interest rates, fluctuations in inflation, and large movements in exchange rates have forced executives to assign higher risk premiums to long-term R&D projects than would their overseas competitors.[3] Similarly, frequent and substantial changes in US tax policies, including the tax deductions for research and development expenses, help to compound the uncertainties surrounding any long term investment.

Failures to Commercialize New Technologies

Related to the problem of short time horizons is the widely held perception that US companies are less able to commercialize the results of their R&D efforts rapidly. Although the United States remains the world's leading producer of scientific and technological breakthroughs, it seems to have difficulty translating these advantages into successful products in the marketplace. As the evolution of the videocassette demonstrates, US firms often seem to fail to translate laboratory successes into sustained commercial advantages. As the MIT Commission on Industrial Productivity noted in its 1989 study of US manufacturing,

---

2. W. Carl Kester and Timothy A. Luehrman, "The Myth of Japan's Low-Cost Capital," *Harvard Business Review* (May-June 1992): 130-138.
3. Competitiveness Policy Council, *First Annual Report to the President and Congress: Building a Competitive America*, March 1, 1992, 11.

Investment in basic scientific and engineering research *is* essential for long-term economic growth. Defense research *can* bear commercial fruit. But the nation's technological strength depends on far more than the health of its research laboratories, important as that is. Prowess in research does not lead automatically to commercial success. New ideas must be converted into products that customers want, when they want them, and before competitors can provide them, and the products must be made efficiently and well.[4]

Part of the problem with commercialization in the United States stems from the degree of organizational separation often maintained at US facilities. Traditionally, product designers have worked in isolation from manufacturing engineers, often designing products that are difficult and costly to produce. Designs were then "thrown over the wall" to engineering, which then has to develop the necessary process technologies to manufacture the items cost-effectively. These organizational barriers have been roundly criticized as a major cause of increased costs and slowed product introductions that plague many parts of US industry.

Of course, many US companies have responded to these criticisms by redesigning their product development teams and restructuring their corporate research and development efforts. Chrysler's new centralized product development center, with its emphasis on bringing all aspects of new product development under one roof, is an attempt to overcome these problems. By forming development teams comprised of representatives from product design, engineering, manufacturing, marketing, and finance, companies are better able to anticipate production and marketing difficulties before finalizing product designs. Given that the majority of the costs of any manufactured item are set during the initial design phase, this approach promises significant reductions in product cost and development time. Such multifunctional teams are common in Japan, and are gaining favor among some US companies.

While US companies have often been slow to introduce new products and processes, there is some evidence that Japanese companies may have focused too heavily on these objectives at the expense of corporate profitability. Tougher economic conditions in Japan have forced a slowdown in the rate of new product introductions by Japanese companies. Nissan, for example, is moving to shift its product cycle from four years to five.[5] Also, in

---

4. Michael L. Dertouzos, *Made In America*, 66.
5. Andrew Pollack, "Japan Eases 57 Varieties Marketing," *The New York Times*, October 15, 1992, D1, D19.

an effort to boost profits, cut costs, and rationalize product lines, a number of Japanese companies are paring the number of variations offered to customers and stretching product cycles. Even with these changes, however, Japanese producers still often enjoy considerably shorter product development cycles than do US and European manufacturers, where new car introductions, for example, can take up to ten years.

Failure to Invest in Process Technologies

A third oft-noted problem with the American technology development process is the failure of US companies to invest in process, as opposed to product, technologies. The success of Japanese companies in cutting costs, improving product quality, and speeding product introductions is largely attributed to their heavy emphasis on optimizing manufacturing processes rather than on introducing new products. The differences between US and Japanese practices in this area are particularly striking. According to Edwin Mansfield,

> The American firms...devote about two-thirds of their R&D expenditures to improved product technology (new products and product changes) and about one-third to improved process technology (new process and process changes). Among the Japanese firms...the proportions are reversed, two-thirds going for improved process technology and one-third going for improved product technology.[6]

Moreover, Japanese companies typically concentrate on the continuous incremental improvement of existing products and processes rather than revolutionary development of entirely new goods and manufacturing techniques. As Table 3.1 shows, Mansfield found that half of all US R&D spending is devoted to developing entirely new products and processes, whereas only one-third of Japanese R&D spending is devoted to such development. Instead, the remaining two-thirds of Japanese investment is devoted to incremental improvements in existing technologies.

The Japanese emphasis on product and process improvements is reflected in their allocation of scientific and technical resources as well. Typically, Japanese companies employ a greater percentage of their technical work force at actual production facilities. In contrast, US companies have tended to concentrate their R&D resources within centralized corporate laboratories.

---

6. Edwin Mansfield, "Industrial R&D in Japan and the United States: A Comparative Study," *American Economic Review*, Vol. 78, No. 2 (May 1988).

Table 3.1. Composition of US and Japanese R&D
Expenditures, 1985

R &D expenditures devoted to:	Japan (percent)	United States (percent)
Basic Research	10	8
Applied Research	27	23
Products (rather than process)	36	68
Entirely new products and processes	32	47

Note: These percentages are based on a survey of 100 firms in four industries in Japan and the United States. The categories are not mutually exclusive; therefore, percentages sum to more than 100.

Source: Edwin Mansfield, "Industrial R&D in Japan and the United States: A Comparative Study," *American Economic Review*, Vol. No. 78, 2 (May 1988).

While most of the problems in this area are blamed on US companies themselves, some of the blame for the relative lack of attention to process improvement has been laid at the federal government's doorstep. The federal government has concentrated primarily on funding basic research and development for new product technologies. In the defense field, in particular, improvements in manufacturing technologies were given far less weight in funding decisions than incremental improvements in system performance. This trade-off was justified by the urgency of the cold war, which made military planners and policymakers willing to pay the necessary price for even minimal improvements in performance.

Recently, however, policymakers have placed greater emphasis on financing developments in manufacturing technologies, in part to lower the cost of military systems and in part to promote US commercial competitiveness. These efforts, such as the military's Manufacturing Technology (MANTECH) program, the government-supported semiconductor manufacturing consortium, Sematech, and various flexible manufacturing initiatives, have provided modest amounts of funding to develop new manufacturing techniques and encourage defense firms to improve their process technologies. While these efforts will likely have some beneficial results in changing the behavior of defense firms, changes in DOD acquisition policies to emphasize producability and overall procurement value can be expected to yield more substantial results.

Even when advanced process technologies have been developed and are widely available, US companies have been slow to incorporate them into their operations. Indeed, surveys of small manufacturers (which employ approximately 35 percent of all manufacturing workers) suggest that the problems with US industry stem not from a failure to develop advanced process technologies but from a delinquency in investing in *proven* technologies to improve their manufacturing operations.[7] A substantial number of these firms still employ technologies and production strategies that were developed in the 1950s. A Census Bureau survey of over 10,000 small manufacturers, for example, revealed that less than 40 percent of these firms used numerically controlled machines, while even fewer employed computer-aided design (36.3%), factory networks (14.2%), or simple pick-and-place robots (5.5%).

Therefore, at least for small and medium-sized manufacturing firms, the challenge is not one of developing new process technologies but of applying existing technologies to their operations. Consequently, efforts to develop and transfer advanced, often unproven manufacturing techniques and technologies to such firms ignore the actual problems faced by small manufacturing enterprises. Indeed, observers have estimated that new technologies being developed in the government's Automated Manufacturing Research Facility, for example, are of interest to no more than three to five percent of all manufacturers. In fact, some contend that there is already more technology currently available than these companies could use in the next ten years.

The problems of small- and medium-size manufacturers in process engineering have been compounded by the widespread reluctance of American companies to cooperate with their suppliers and customers in order to bring about improvements in production operations and product quality. In Japan, such cooperation is widespread, constituting the majority of the cooperative relationships existing between separate companies. (Cooperation among directly competing firms, on the other hand, is rare.) The Japanese practice of cross-ownership of equity between suppliers and their customers is often a means of cementing this cooperative relationship, helping to establish a long-term, mutually beneficial commitment between companies.

---

7. US General Accounting Office, *Technology Transfer: Federal Efforts to Enhance the Competitiveness of Small Manufacturers* (Washington, D.C.: US General Accounting Office, November 1991).

In contrast, US firms have more often than not treated their suppliers and customers as adversaries, using price quotes as the primary determinant of buying decisions and eschewing long-term relationships in favor of unconstrained flexibility. While this approach might be entirely reasonable in a narrowly defined financial sense, it often forestalls opportunities for productive collaboration on technology improvement. To some extent, the introduction of Total Quality Management (TQM) practices and Just-In-Time (JIT) inventory systems by many major US companies has helped to ameliorate these problems, forcing firms to abandon their reluctance to cooperate with suppliers in order to improve the efficiency of their manufacturing operations. However, on average, US companies remain less willing to cooperate with upstream and downstream companies than their counterparts in Japan, eliminating an important avenue for transferring process technologies between leader and follower firms.

Other Technological Shortcomings

In addition to these major themes, the debate over technological competitiveness has identified a number of contributing factors that negatively impact US technological competitiveness. For example, the tendency for large US technology firms to be headed by nontechnical management personnel is often blamed for the failure of these companies to integrate adequately their technology and business strategies. Similarly, the shortage of technically competent workers is widely perceived as a barrier to the rapid introduction of new technologies, particularly process technologies. In this respect, the problems of the American educational system are usually compounded by the unwillingness of US companies to invest significant resources in training any but their most senior employees.

Finally, numerous problems have been identified in the process used by the federal government to regulate and invest in the development and diffusion of new technologies. These shortcomings will be addressed more fully in the second half of this book, but they include such practices as overemphasis on defense technology, institutional barriers to technology transfer between government laboratories and private industry, artificial separation of the defense and civil production and technology bases, product liability regulations that slow new product introductions, inappropriate tax policies that discourage investment in R&D and employee training, and inefficient or ineffective implementation of governmental responsibilities.

A View from Industry

Although these factors all serve to reduce the ability of US companies to compete in the global economy, it is difficult to determine from the public debate which deserve the greatest amount of attention. A survey of its members conducted by the Industrial Research Institute (IRI) for the National Science Board's Committee on Industrial Support for R&D provides some insight on business's perspective on the reasons for America's competitive problems and their relative importance.[8]

Asked to rank the primary sources of the nation's perceived difficulties, survey respondents overwhelmingly listed failures in general management practices as the leading cause of the nation's competitive problems. Chief among the management failures listed were short time horizons, an overemphasis on quantitative measures of performance rather than a strategic vision, and a failure by companies to integrate technology into their business strategy. External financial pressures were also blamed for many companies' difficulties, with the rise of institutional investors and their demand for short-term returns on investments seen as the most damaging. In contrast, high capital costs, government regulations, labor costs and the debt burdens imposed by the merger and acquisition boom of the 1980s were viewed as far less significant.[9]

IRI members listed the changing global technological environment as the third most important factor contributing to the erosion of US competitive position. However, there was far less agreement on the importance of these changes, with significant variations among different industrial segments. For example, in the transportation and instruments sectors, changes in the global environment were considered the single most important factor affecting their businesses. In communication services, rubber production, research and development services, and the metal product fabrication field, changes in the global technical enterprise were ranked last in terms of their importance, suggesting

---

8. National Science Board Committee on Industrial Support for R&D, *The Competitive Strength of US Industrial Science and Technology: Strategy Issues*, Appendix B, "IRI Survey: Questionnaire and Results" (Washington, D.C.: G.P.O., August 1992).

9. As is discussed in chapter seven, the management failures identified in the survey and the negative impact of institutional investors are largely attributable to the capital allocation system which has evolved in the United States.

that even in high technology sectors the impact of foreign competition varies significantly across industries.

Those firms that believed the changing world technology environment was having a fundamental effect on their business prospects cited the "growing difficulty of controlling enough technological competitive advantage to sustain an entry barrier" as an important problem. They also reported that the "declining lead times and faster product turn-over cycles" of many international markets have transformed the business environments within which these firms operate. Both of these developments reflect the increasing competitiveness of foreign high-technology industries. Clearly, this erosion of American technological hegemony has made it more difficult for US companies to preserve their competitive position on the basis of technology alone. As the respondents noted, the growing number of skilled workers overseas made foreign companies increasingly able to challenge the US competitive position.

The IRI executives ranked poor technology management practices as the fourth most important factor affecting US competitiveness. In particular, respondents cited the slow rate at which products are developed and commercialized in the United States, and the reluctance of companies to invest in new, enabling technologies, as major problems.

Finally, survey respondents ranked failures of federal technology policy as the least important cause of America's economic problems. In fact, federal technology policy ranked high (second) in importance only among representatives of the communications services sector and research and development services communities. That these two groups felt that technology policy was especially important to their competitiveness is hardly surprising; federal research grants represent a significant portion of the R&D services industry's revenues, while federal regulations (particularly the Modified Final Judgement on Bell operating companies) are critical in shaping the telecommunications services sector. Among those firms whose futures are less directly tied to federal policy, however, government technology policy was perceived as far less important to their competitive future.

In general, the results of the IRI survey lend credence to the diagnoses of America's technological problems outlined earlier. The competitive environment facing American companies has changed significantly in recent years, with foreign competition, in particular, exposing a number of important flaws in the manner in which the United States develops and applies commercial technology. Beyond simply rearranging the competitive environ-

ment, however, increasing foreign technical capabilities and the
emergence of truly global competition promise to change more
fundamentally how high-technology companies operate.

Changes in the Global
Technology Environment

At their root, many of the arguments for direct federal support
for the technology efforts of US companies implicitly assume that
a US technology base exists, distinct in some meaningful way
from the technology bases of other nations. As discussed in
chapter two, this perspective is increasingly out of touch with
evolving realities. The globalization of technology is a dominant
force shaping today's world economy. Indeed, calls for a more
activist federal technology policy stem in large part from the
recognition of this shift in the geographic distribution of the
world's technological capabilities. What is not typically noted,
however, is that the very process of globalization calls into question the notion that technologies, industries, or even corporations
have distinctive nationalities.

The globalization of technology raises serious challenges for
any single nation seeking to improve its relative economic position by promoting technological advancement. Pursued in isolation, government strategies to develop cutting edge technologies
risk degenerating into neomercantilist ventures that run counter
to global technological and economic trends and threaten the
country's long term economic well-being. Alternatively, such
measures might succeed in enhancing the technological capabilities of US-based corporations, only to find that the benefits do not
flow exclusively, or even preferentially, to American society at
large. In order to avoid either of these pitfalls, policies must be
formulated that are both compatible with ongoing global technological trends and consistent with the overall goal of improving
the economic well-being of the United States.

The rise of European and Japanese competition in high-technology markets once dominated by US-based firms provides
ample evidence of the proliferation of technical capabilities. This
process of globalization is two pronged. First, new reservoirs of
scientific accomplishments and technological competence have
emerged in Europe and Japan that rival those of the United
States. This represents a profound change in the global technological landscape that has characterized the postwar world. As
the industrial powerhouses of Europe and Asia have rebuilt their

economies and invested heavily in improving their technological capabilities, the US position as the world's technological leader has gradually eroded. These new centers of excellence have challenged the notion that the United States can automatically rely on the persistence of its technological superiority to ensure its long-term prosperity.

Second, these reservoirs of technical accomplishment are becoming increasingly integrated, spilling across national borders and washing away the lines between the American technology base and those of its trading partners. In many ways, this process of integration predates the rise of foreign technological capabilities. For much of the postwar period, foreign companies relied on the United States for the latest technical and managerial innovations. Through acceptance of US direct investment, licensing agreements, and coproduction arrangements, the nations of Europe and East Asia were able to build up their domestic technology base. Indeed, a primary focus of Japanese R&D efforts for much of the postwar period has been to search out, apply, and improve foreign (mainly US) innovations. Throughout the 1950s and 1960s, while the United States dominated virtually the entire technological horizon, this flow was primarily unidirectional, with US technologies being transferred to foreign companies or to US subsidiaries abroad.

Gradually over the past two decades, however, as foreign industry has become more capable, the flow of technology has become more bidirectional, with the United States steadily increasing its consumption of foreign technologies and engineering know-how through imports, license agreements, and foreign direct investment. US-based corporations have come to rely increasingly on Japanese and European technologies in certain high-technology sectors. This reliance, often characterized negatively as foreign dependence, has nevertheless permitted companies based in the United States to provide products and services that otherwise would have been beyond America's technological reach. The largest US-based firms, with operations around the world, have taken this process of integration even further, conducting business on a global scale and seeking out new technologies and opportunities wherever they may be, irrespective of borders. Through overseas expansion, strategic partnerships, and a host of other arrangements, the most successful US corporations help ensure that new technologies move around the world at heretofore unprecedented speeds. As a result, technology, often in the form of pure information, has become increasingly difficult to contain within a nation's frontiers.

All these developments make the formulation of a *national* technology policy exceedingly difficult. By blurring national boundaries and encouraging firms to think and act globally, the dissemination of technical resources has diminished the ability of any single country to define coherent national policies in isolation. Unfortunately, the unique experience of the United States over the past forty years has not prepared most American policymakers or company executives for the global challenges that lie ahead.

Global Integration of National Technology Bases

The steady increase in foreign technical capabilities would be troublesome enough for the formulation of US technology policy if such talents were strictly confined within national borders—if the challenge consisted simply of matching the technological strength of our economic rivals on a national basis. However, the rise of these new centers of technical expertise has also coincided with an unrelenting shift toward greater integration of the world's (or, more accurately, the industrialized world's) technology base. This process of integration is longstanding, if incomplete. Through it, firms in the United States, Japan, and Europe have gradually become ever more dependent on technical resources spread around the globe. What most distinguishes the current period from the past, however, is the fact that the United States has begun to be a major consumer, as well as the largest producer, of technical know-how.

The flow of technology across national borders takes a number of forms. In its most basic form, technology—embodied in products and services—has spread from country to country through international trade. Global sourcing of electronic components, advanced materials, and digital machine tools contributes to the integration of the world's technology base. An IBM personal computer, for example, may feature a power supply produced in Japan, a monitor built in Hong Kong, and a microprocessor designed by Intel of the United States but manufactured by Hitachi in an East Asian manufacturing facility. In turn, these countries rely on US-developed software and microprocessors for their own computer manufacturing operations. This trend toward global sourcing and increased trade in high-technology components suggests the emergence of "global webs" of innovation, where multinational corporations draw human, physical, and technical resources from around the world.[10] Even major US-based exporters such as Boeing have to some degree become primarily assemblers for components manufactured elsewhere. For its part, Boeing concentrates on the highly sophisticated design, engineering, and systems integration work involved in producing large commercial transport aircraft.

Technology is also traded directly through the sale or licensing of patents, technical knowledge, copyrights, and other forms of intellectual property. Throughout the postwar period, the United States has been a net exporter of technology to the rest of the world. Figure 3.1 shows US exports and imports of technology in terms of royalties received and US payments for foreign technologies since 1960. As the figure indicates, despite a significant rise in US payments for foreign technologies in recent years, the US net balance continued to rise throughout the 1980s. In 1988 alone, US earnings from such trade were over twice its payments to foreigners.

The vast majority of this trade, however, was between US corporations and affiliated corporations or subsidiaries abroad. These affiliates (in which US companies own at least a 10 percent share), paid roughly $32.6 billion in 1988 for technologies developed in the United States, approximately 93 percent of total US receipts. Interestingly, foreign affiliates also represented the primary source of technologies from abroad, accounting for 95 percent of all US payments in the same year. These statistics are confirmed by evidence from some of America's largest high technology companies. IBM and Hewlett-Packard, for example, conduct an estimated 30 percent of their research and development work in affiliates located overseas.[11] Such technology transfers are a primary mechanism for moving new technologies around the world.

In contrast, technology sales to unaffiliated foreign firms amounted to just $2.4 billion in 1988, with payments totaling only slightly more than $1 billion for the same year. In this category, Japanese firms were by far the largest importers of US technolo-

---

10. For a discussion of such global webs and their implications for American workers, see Robert B. Reich, *The Work of Nations: Preparing Ourselves for 21st-Century Capitalism* (New York, New York: Alfred A. Knopf, 1991).
11. National Academy of Engineering, Committee on Engineering as an International Enterprise, *National Interests in an Age of Global Technology*, Thomas H. Lee and Proctor P. Reid, eds. (Washington, D.C.: National Academy Press, 1991), 40-41.

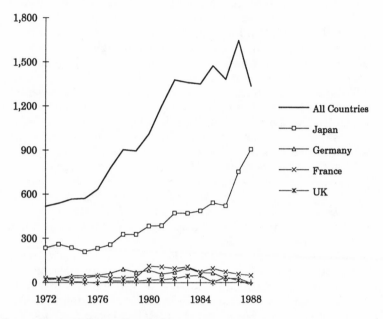

Source: National Science Foundation.

Figure 3.1. US Net Balance of Technology Royalties and Fees Associated with Unaffiliated Foreign Residents.

gies as measured in royalties, accounting for roughly 42 percent of the US total. Other major consumers of US technologies include companies from the United Kingdom and Germany. In turn, Canada and the United Kingdom were the largest unaffiliated exporters of technologies to the United States, with 1988 US payments to these countries equalling $224 million and $143 million, respectively.[12]

For its part, Japan remains a large consumer of US technologies both through affiliate firms and unaffiliated technology transfers. As suggested above, the licensing of foreign technologies has been a key component of Japan's bid to increase its own technological capabilities. For much of the postwar period, the Japanese economy played a game of "catch-up," dictating a strategy of emulating the success of technology leaders (i.e., US corporations). In

---

12. National Science Foundation, *International Science and Technology Data Update: 1991* (NSF 91-309) (Washington, D.C.: National Science Foundation, 1991), 114-117.

line with this approach, a primary focus of the Japanese government's science and technology policy has been monitoring foreign technical developments, and negotiating license agreements on behalf of Japanese corporations. This kept the cost of foreign technologies down, while ensuring that they were shared broadly among domestic industries.[13] In fact, Japan remains the largest consumer of US technologies, despite its much improved technological performance. In 1989, for example, license fees from Japan totaled $2.6 billion. At the same time, however, payments by the United States to Japan reached $490 million, making Japan America's second largest technology supplier overall.[14]

As foreign companies have improved their technical and scientific capabilities, their ability to absorb and apply new technologies rapidly has also increased. Previously, the overwhelming US lead in advanced technologies made it difficult for foreign firms to adopt US innovations simply because they lacked the "receiving" mechanisms necessary to understand and use the existing technology. As these skills have developed, the rate of international technology transfer has increased. As one report observed, the "diffusion of technologies is increasingly disconnected from the trade in products which embody the technologies."[15] For those nations capable of developing technological infrastructures advanced enough to take advantage of these increased technology flows, the future holds the possibility of even more rapid technological progress and change.

The high level of trade in intellectual property between US firms and affiliated foreign firms reflects the important role played by foreign direct investment in the process of weaving the world's technology base together. For much of the postwar period, large US corporations were the dominant force in the expansion of foreign direct investment. During the 1950s and 1960s, much of this investment followed the pattern outlined by product cycle theory, with innovative activities and initial high-wage, high-technology manufacturing taking place within the United States.[16] These products were then sold domestically and

---

13. David C. Mowery and Nathan Rosenberg, *Technology and the Pursuit of Economic Growth* (New York: Cambridge University Press, 1989), 221-223.

14. US General Accounting Office, *High Technology Competitiveness: Trends in US and Foreign Performance* (GAO/NSIAD-92-236) (Washington, D.C.: US General Accounting Office, September 1992), 33-34.

15. Organization for Economic Cooperation and Development, *The Newly Industrializing Countries: Challenge and Opportunity for OECD Industries* (Paris: OECD, 1988), 8.

exported to the rest of the world. As products matured, and cost competition became critical, US corporations often moved production overseas to take advantage of lower labor costs and less costly business environments. These new foreign plants would then begin to export products back to the United States. Meanwhile, US corporations would move on to the next generation of technology, starting the entire cycle over again.

While such product-cycle investment kept most of the highly sophisticated activities within the United States, it nevertheless transferred considerable amounts of technology—in the form of product and process know-how—overseas. This inevitably allowed foreign economies to improve their technical capabilities faster than otherwise would have been possible, making them ever more able to compete with US-based manufacturers.

In the 1970s and 1980s, this model of trade and foreign direct investment patterns changed considerably. First, European and Japanese corporations significantly increased their own outward direct investment levels. Between 1980 and 1989, the European share of the world's total stock of outward direct investment rose from 44.9 percent to 50.2 percent, and Japan's increased from 3.8 percent to 11.5 percent. Meanwhile, the US share of the world total declined from 42.5 percent to 28.3 percent.[17] Over the past fifteen years, in particular, foreign direct investment in the United States has grown substantially. Between 1973 and 1989, the ratio of the US investment stock abroad to foreign investments in the United States fell from around 5:1 to parity, representing a radical transformation of the investment patterns established during the 1950s and 1960s.[18]

Moreover, the motives underlying direct investment abroad are considerably changed from what they were three decades ago. Today, firms are likely to pursue overseas investments in order to leapfrog protectionist barriers and improve market access, to track the activities of foreign competitors, or to acquire foreign technologies and gain access to foreign technical talents. This last motive is particularly important to the growing integration of the world's technology base. Whereas previously product-cycle

16. Raymond Vernon, "International Investment and International Trade in the Product Cycle," *Quarterly Journal of Economics 80* (May 1966): 190-207.
17. John Rutter, *Trends in International Direct Investment*, Staff Paper No. 91-5 (Washington, D.C.: US Department of Commerce, International Trade Administration, July 1991), appendix table 1.
18. John Rutter, *International Direct Investment*, app. tables 1 and 6.

investment helped to globalize production operations while keeping high-value research and development activities largely confined to the originating country, foreign direct investment today is leading to the globalization of the entire range of firms' activities. US corporations are relying increasingly on research laboratories abroad for new technologies. IBM's breakthrough in high-temperature superconducting materials, for example, was widely perceived as a major accomplishment of American technology. In fact, however, the work was carried out in an IBM-owned Swiss industrial laboratory by Swiss and German scientists. Other examples, such as Texas Instruments' software lab in Madras, India, and Toyota's Southern California design studios serve to demonstrate the increasing complexity of the global technological infrastructure.[19]

Foreign direct investment in the United States follows a similar pattern, despite concerns that US-based foreign manufacturing subsidiaries might only perform routine, unskilled assembly work. Those concerned about a "headquarters effect" fear that foreign-owned companies will keep high-value added, high-skilled jobs at home, creating only low-wage positions in their US subsidiaries. While this would tend to be consistent with product-cycle-type direct investment, it does not appear to be characteristic of foreign direct investment in the United States over the past two decades. Indeed, the most recently available figures generally indicate that foreign subsidiaries spend approximately the same amount on highly skilled research and development activities as do domestic firms. While research has shown that this pattern does not hold true for firms that have only recently expanded overseas (e.g., Japanese automobile manufacturers), it does hold for the majority of mature multinationals that operate on a truly global scale.[20]

19. David C. Mowery and Nathan Rosenberg, "New Developments in US Technology Policy: Implications for Competitiveness and International Trade Policy," CEPR Publication No. 166 (Stanford, California: Center for Economic Policy Research, July 1989), 8.

20. Edward M. Graham and Paul R. Krugman, *Foreign Direct Investment in the United States* (Washington, D.C.: Institute for International Economics, 1989), 58-59. For example, on the behavior of Japanese auto industry in America, see Martin Kenney and Richard Florida, "How Japanese Industry is Rebuilding the Rust Belt," *Technology Review* (February-March 1991): 25-33; and US General Accounting Office, *Japanese-Affiliated Automakers: Management Practices Related to Purchasing Parts*, GAO/T-NSIAD-92-5, (Washington, D.C.: US General Accounting Office, November 14, 1991).

The integrative effects of direct investment extend beyond the creation or acquisition of foreign subsidiaries. Inevitably, given their prominence in the US technical effort, research universities have become a key focus for foreign corporations and citizens seeking to gain access to American technical know-how.[21] In order to monitor ongoing university-based research and development efforts, foreign companies and their US subsidiaries have become major contributors to university research projects and have established centers near some of the nation's preeminent institutions. Moreover, foreigners comprise an ever increasing portion of the nation's student population, particularly at the graduate level. These students offer a major injection of bright and innovative talent into the US research effort, while at the same time serving as another mechanism for transferring US research results back to their home countries.[22]

Finally, in recent years, strategic alliances between large, global corporations have furthered the process of integration. These international collaborative ventures, ranging from marketing agreements to narrowly defined joint ventures to broad "risk-sharing partnerships," offer corporations access to foreign capital, skills, and technologies. Alliances have formed across a broad range of industries, including steel, automobiles, electronics, and biotechnology. In automobiles alone, joint ventures exist between General Motors and Toyota, Ford and Mazda, and Chrysler and Mitsubishi. The reasons for the creation of such alliances are complex. Most obviously, collaborative ventures offer yet another method for sharing risks, costs, and technologies. In addition, they also offer a means to leapfrog restrictive national trade policies and open up tightly controlled government markets. The growth of collaborative ventures in the defense industry, long considered the most "national" enterprises of all, illustrates the importance of such transnational alliances for companies hoping to compete in foreign markets.[23]

---

21. See Evan Herbert, "Japanese R&D in the United States," *Research and Technology Management* (November-December 1989): 11-20. For a more alarmist analysis, see Gina Kolata, "Japanese Labs in US Luring America's Computer Experts," *The New York Times*, November 11, 1990, A-1, 24.
22. For statistics on foreign students in the United States, see National Science Foundation, *International Science and Technology Data Update*, 60-84.
23. On the globalization of the aerospace industry, see Aerospace Industries Association, *The US Aerospace Industry in the 1990s: A Global Perspective* (Washington, D.C.: AIA, September 1991). See also Lt. Col.

To a growing extent, these alliances are now being undertaken in order to gain access to foreign technologies and know-how. The 1992 announcement of a collaborative venture between Texas Instruments and several Japanese electronics manufacturers to develop chip sets for high definition televisions is but one example of such technology sharing arrangements. The high cost of developing sophisticated products forces firms to seek out partners who will share the risks and who can minimize technological obstacles by supplying much needed expertise. The motives of the participating partners need not be symmetrical, however. In the case of US and Japanese auto makers, US firms have generally sought to acquire Japanese design, manufacturing, and managerial know-how, while the chief benefit for Japanese companies may be the development of a method to overcome US voluntary export restraints on Japanese automobile imports. Whatever their motivation, partners in these alliances help stimulate even more rapid diffusion of advanced technologies and increased interdependence across the industrialized world's technology base.

Adjusting to the New Realities

Although the trends toward technological parity and global integration are clear, it would be premature to abandon the notion that most firms based in the United States continue to share a common and unique national identity. Despite the fact that up to 70 percent of US manufactured goods now face international competition, the "internationalization" of US industry is mainly restricted to the largest US-owned companies. Many manufacturers continue to operate primarily in the isolation of the domestic market and most make little effort to export their products. Nor is there evidence that most US-based firms attempt to exploit foreign technologies to any significant degree, aside from simple purchases of foreign-produced components.

Nevertheless, any technology policy must be compatible with the accelerating pace of technology diffusion, rising foreign capabilities, and the growing network of transnational connections.

Willie Cole, Lt. Col. Richard Hochberg, and Commander Alfred Therrien, *Europe 1992: Catalyst for Change in Defense Acquisition* (Defense Systems Management College, September 1992), Chapter 3 and Appendix C. On high-technology partnerships with Japanese firms, see Peter Fuchs, "Strategic Alliances: How US Start-Ups are Tapping into Japanese Capital, Markets and Technologies," *Business Tokyo*, April 1991.

Trends in the US and world economies point toward four key issues.

The Transience of US Hegemony The US position after World War II was an historical anomaly, largely brought about as a result of the destruction of the world's other leading industrialized nations. This situation represented nothing less than a windfall for US corporations and the US economy. However, in the years since the war, the economic preeminence enjoyed by the United States came to be seen as a birthright. To the extent that this perception influences policy today, the results of any initiative are likely to prove disappointing.

The United States will never regain the position it held in the 1950s, nor should it necessarily try. An enormous postwar head start and heavy government investment was unable to alter the fact that our trading partners have been able to make up much of the ground they lost during the war. Despite the calls by many politicians and interest groups for the US to strive to dominate every technology deemed vital to the world's economic future, it is unreasonable to expect US-based firms to achieve such a goal when they are surrounded by equally able competitors. Creativity, intelligence, and inventiveness are not unique American traits that can guarantee our economic well-being. Instead, technology policy must seek outcomes which are sustainable over the long-term and proportional to the overall size and scope of the American economy.

The Rise of Alternative Sources The natural inverse of the relative decline in the US position is the rise in foreign technical capabilities. Although often portrayed as the source of America's current economic woes, the new sources of technical and scientific expertise offer tremendous opportunities for strengthening the American economy. Instead of having to rely solely on US research and development efforts to develop new product and process technologies, US-based companies are able increasingly to draw on a much broader international base of technical knowledge. As Japanese and European firms advance to the point that they are operating on the cutting edge of technology, the *world's* supply of new innovations has exploded.

Unfortunately, US-based firms are relatively ill-equipped to take advantage of these new opportunities. The nineteenth-century American talent for scanning and adopting technologies originating abroad has been lost. In the words of the MIT Commission on Industrial Productivity,

Parochialism has...blinded Americans to the growing strength of scientific and technological innovation abroad, and hence to the possibility of adapting the discoveries for use in the United States. The dominance of American science and technology in the early postwar decades was so great that companies could operate as if American laboratories were the only ones generating useful knowledge. American firms therefore failed to build up the networks of contacts abroad that underpin systematic attempts at technological scanning.[24]

In contrast, the past forty years taught European and Japanese companies the opposite lesson. Particularly in Japan, the monitoring of foreign technologies and their immediate application became the essential challenge for research and development establishments. Japan's current dilemma, unsurprisingly, is to develop the necessary research structures to sustain work at the forefront of science and technology.

The Free Flow of Technology Both of these trends point to an even freer flow of new technologies and scientific discoveries across international borders. As a result, it will become even more difficult for the United States to reserve for itself the returns from innovative research, even if that research is conducted by Americans working for US-owned companies in facilities located within America's borders. This is particularly true in the case of the large global firms which are in the best position to seek out and apply new inventions anywhere in the world.

The case of Sematech is illustrative. Despite its avowed goal of improving US semiconductor production skills, several of the 14 original participants in the effort have formed separate strategic alliances with Japanese firms in a wide range of related product segments. Texas Instruments, IBM, NCR, Motorola, and Intel all have agreements with foreign companies to work on new semiconductor design and development. Given the fluidity of information, complex and restrictive regulations on how and where these firms can use the knowledge they gain from collaborative research promise to be futile.

Ambiguous Corporate Nationalities This leads inevitably to the question of the nationality of any particular firm or its products. In the past, a firm's owners, its employees, and its suppliers shared a common nationality. This made it simple for government policy to treat corporations owned by US citizens as

---

24. Dertouzos, *Made in America*, 51.

American and those owned by foreigners as foreign. Likewise, products assembled in the United States were made from American materials and components, making them readily identifiable. This simple picture has grown immensely more complex over the past two decades, and the definition of what is, and what is not, an American company or product has become blurred.[25] Nationalities of owners and employees may no longer coincide, and the interests of US-based corporations need not be identical to those of the nation. Attempts simply to assist US-owned companies may benefit shareholders, but may do nothing to promote the economic well-being of the United States. Likewise, discriminatory measures aimed at foreign-owned companies may actually hurt US workers. For example, though Zenith may be the only US-based manufacturer of color televisions still in business, the fact that it manufactures most of its televisions in Mexico is surely cause to be wary of directing federal support to it for high definition television research solely on the basis of the location of the company's headquarters.

These broad trends underway in the global economy and the world's technology markets dictate a careful review of any proposed solution to the technology challenges facing the US economy. At the very least, they raise serious doubts about the wisdom of pursuing any government-funded effort to develop and commercialize new technologies when there is no guarantee that the benefits of such investment would flow preferentially to US citizens. A more practical approach to technology policy might balance any development effort with an attempt to improve the United States' ability to host the most advanced technologies and industries, whatever their country of origin.

---

25. See Robert B. Reich, "Does Corporate Nationality Matter?" *Issues in Science and Technology*, Vol. 7 (Winter 1990-91): 40-44 and "Who is Them?" *Harvard Business Review*, Vol. 69 (March-April 1991): 77-88. For a rebuttal of Reich's arguments, see Ethan B. Kapstein, "We are Us: The Myth of the Multinational," *National Interest*, Vol. 26 (Winter 1991-92): 55-62 and Laura D'Andrea Tyson, "They are Not Us: Why American Ownership Still Matters," *American Prospect*, No. 4 (Winter 1991): 37-38, 40-53.

4

American Precedents and the Politics of Technology

In his January 1991 federal budget submission to the Congress, President Bush unveiled a major new technology initiative designed to revolutionize the nation's data networks and inspire a new generation of unimaginably fast supercomputers. Heralded in lofty terms, the High Performance Computing and Communications (HPCC) initiative was to bring together eight federal agencies to develop the next generation of computers and computer networks capable of solving scientific problems that require computational power far beyond the abilities of today's models. In the process, the program would also yield substantial commercial benefits for the United States, both by allowing US computer companies to leap ahead of their foreign competition and by giving other companies access to high-speed computers to support their own research and development efforts. Given the Bush administration's strong opposition to anything resembling a federal industrial policy, the HPCC initiative represented a major step toward a more aggressive, focused strategy to assist America's high-technology industries.

The HPCC initiative received a warm welcome on Capitol Hill, in large part because a nearly identical measure had been introduced earlier by then-Senator Albert Gore, Jr. (D-TN), chairman of the Science and Technology subcommittee of the Commerce, Science and Technology Committee. In fact, the health of America's high performance computer industry had been a point of concern for congressional observers since the mid-1980s. As a result, the Congress steadily increased funding for research on advanced computing over the course of the decade despite often intense budgetary pressures. At the same time, it urged the administration to prepare a comprehensive plan to govern US supercomputing research.

In particular, Senator Gore had pushed for a number of years for a strategy on high performance computing, nearly identical to that offered by President Bush. In May 1989, he introduced the "National High Performance Computing Act of 1989" (S. 1067). That bill would have authorized a total of $1.75 billion over five years to support expanded federal research, development, and application of advanced computing technologies. In particular, it targeted research on scalable, massively parallel computer systems and the construction of a National Research and Education Network (NREN) to link far-flung researchers with supercomputers around the country. For Gore, this new data network would be the modern equivalent of the federal highway construction effort of the 1950s, a program in which his father—also a senator from Tennessee—had played an instrumental role.

Despite broad support for the initiative, S. 1067 fell victim to bureaucratic wrangling in the Congress over which agency—and therefore which congressional committee—would exercise leadership and control over the program. Because Gore's initiative depended on higher research spending by the Departments of Defense and Energy, the Senate committees which oversee R&D activities within these two departments—Armed Services and Energy—both had to introduce legislation to increase spending on computing research and development. For its part, the Armed Services subcommittee on Industry and Technology, under the chairmanship of Senator Jeff Bingaman (D-NM), readily agreed to Gore's plan. Bingaman had been a strong advocate of increased spending on technologies in order to improve US economic competitiveness. Gore's supercomputing project was in keeping with this vision, and the Senate Armed Services Committee (SASC) gladly authorized $30 million in additional spending on computer research for fiscal 1990.

The Senate Energy Committee was less cooperative, however, balking at the supporting role allotted to the Energy Department in the project. Instead, the committee chairman, Senator J. Bennett Johnston (D-LA), introduced his own version of the high performance computing bill which called for DOE to play a far larger role than that envisioned by the Gore bill. The Energy Department, most notably DOE's Sandia, Los Alamos, and Lawrence Livermore National Laboratories, had long been among the federal government's most intensive users of supercomputers in the design and development of the nation's nuclear arsenal. To the committee, therefore, it was entirely appropriate for DOE to play a major role in defining the requirements for the next generation of computers. Moreover, under Johnston's bill, DOE would assume control of the NREN, reflecting DOE's previous experience with data networks.

In addition to these substantive arguments, Senator Johnston's committee was concerned about its own ability to oversee and direct the new technology initiative. With many Americans anxious over the US ability to compete in the global economy, the political benefits of being recognized as a champion of America's high-technology industries have increased substantially. In essence, DOE's role in the program would dictate the extent of influence the Senate Energy Committee could exercise over the effort. If, as Gore proposed, the National Science Foundation served as the program's leader, then Gore's Science and Technology subcommittee would take the lead—and the credit.

The struggle between the two committees continued throughout the session, finally agreeing to disagree in October 1990. The Energy committee accepted much of Gore's language, but the two committees left the issue of who would direct the program and control the NREN up to the Bush administration.

While the House did not face quite the same jurisdictional problems confronted by the Senate, and support for the bill was strong, the bill failed to pass by the end of the session. The long delay in the Senate, the ideological opposition of the ranking minority committee member, Senator Robert Walker (R-PA), and a last minute budget crunch in the final days of the session doomed the legislation. Nevertheless, despite the Congress' failure to pass the bill, it still approved an increase of almost 10 percent for funding high performance computing activities throughout the government for fiscal 1991, and passage of Gore's legislation seemed assured during the next session of Congress.

Reading the writing on the wall, and responding to the energetic leadership of the President's Science Advisor, Alan Bromley, the administration preempted the Congress and launched its own high performance computing initiative in early 1991. The program, which was nearly identical to the 1989 Gore legislation and the previously released Office of Science and Technology Policy (OSTP) plan, promised to spend $638 million on high performance computing in fiscal 1992, a net increase of roughly $149 million over the fiscal 1991 budget.[1] Given the strong congressional support expressed during the previous session, and the desire of most in Congress to appear supportive of efforts to improve America's technological competitiveness, the president's proposal sailed through Congress with only minor modifications.

Since its initiation, however, the HPCC program has run into a number of challenges. Most notably, many in industry have

---

1. Office of Science and Technology Policy, *Grand Challenges: Higher Performance Computing and Communications, The FY 1992 US Research and Development Program* (Washington, D.C.: National Science Foundation, 1991), 24.

charged that the Defense Advanced Research Projects Agency (DARPA), given responsibility for directing hardware research, had been biased in its support of new computing technologies, unfairly favoring the designs of two manufacturers at the expense of the rest of the industry. Long a supporter of both parallel processing and data networking research, DARPA had gradually focused its computing research on two companies, California's Intel Corporation and Thinking Machines of Massachusetts. This more focused approach drew fire from competing supercomputer designers who had been excluded from the new DARPA research team and saw their future market prospects dying on the vine. The US computer manufacturer nCube was most vocal in its opposition, charging that the DARPA bias toward Intel and Thinking Machines was distorting an immature market and would drive innovative companies promoting other designs out of the market. Indeed, an early beneficiary of DARPA's support, Bolt, Beranek and Newman, closed its advanced computing operations entirely when it was unable to secure funding for a follow-on generation of parallel processing machines that were to pursue a technological path different from that being developed by Intel and Thinking Machines.

Smaller companies also complained about DARPA's perceived bias. In 1992, the Dallas Small Business Innovative Research organization filed a formal complaint on behalf of its members alleging that they were being injured by DARPA's preference for larger companies. According to reports, the group's members filed the complaint anonymously out of fear that if they complained directly and openly to DARPA, they would be penalized when bidding on future DARPA contracts.[2] Despite its strong support for the HPCC program, members of Congress were not oblivious to these complaints from industry.

In its consideration of the fiscal 1992 defense authorization bill, SASC, in particular, noted that several manufacturers had been concerned about DARPA's practice of using an option in existing research contracts to purchase significant numbers of computers originally developed through DARPA's computing research program. These computers were then resold to federal agencies on favorable terms. While the stated goal of this practice was to get new systems into users' hands quickly and to promote development of advanced systems, the agency's practice also had the effect of putting non-DARPA sponsored supercomputers at a severe

---

2. Lucy Reilly, "HPCC Under House Panel Scrutiny," *Washington Technology*, July 9, 1992, 25.

cost disadvantage. SASC wrote that "early markets for such advanced computers are so limited that DARPA's practices have created the appearance that it is distorting the sale of computers in these markets."[3]

The Committee therefore directed DARPA, as part of its work under the HPCC program, to refine its procedures to use full and open competition when buying prototype systems. Furthermore, SASC directed that such contracts should be of limited duration and cover only the number of systems needed for "concept validation and critical feedback for supporting research."[4] Moreover, the Committee stressed that DARPA should not make "vender-specific requirements in order to ensure that [it] and others involved in government-sponsored research have the freedom to choose from an increasing number of sources" of advanced computers. In addition, the committee recommended that DARPA develop a policy of recovering R&D costs by charging a fee for each DARPA-developed high performance computer sold for use in government-sponsored research. The Committee believed that this would (1) provide a revolving fund for further research and (2) serve to eliminate "distortion in this market caused by DARPA's support" of particular computer technologies.

In the end, Congress inserted specific language in the fiscal 1992 defense bills directing the Defense Department to conduct a thorough review of DARPA's award procedures for both procurement and R&D contracts for new supercomputers. It also instructed the director of DARPA to review and refine the agency's acquisition procedures for high performance computing to ensure that proper procedures are followed. Finally, reflecting the complaints of nCube and others, Congress noted that supercomputer modernization "can be accomplished through a number of different means, and therefore [the approach] should fit the mission, needs, and existing capabilities of the particular laboratory."

Despite these recommendations, complaints about the program's implementation continued. The following year, during deliberations on the fiscal 1993 defense budget authorization bill, the House Armed Services Committee (HASC) became so annoyed with DARPA's failure to open its contract award procedures up to outside review and criticism that it recommended withholding all

---

3. Committee on Armed Services, United States Senate, *National Defense Authorization Act for Fiscal Years 1992 and 1993* (Report 102-113), 145.
4. Senate Armed Services Committee, *National Defense Authorization*, 146.

funds for the program until an adequate review mechanism could be established. The committee also directed the General Accounting Office, the investigatory arm of the Congress, to begin a review of DARPA's high performance computing program to determine if it was being carried out effectively and in compliance with applicable federal regulations.

Fearing a permanent cutoff of funding, representatives of the supercomputing industry quickly weighed in, expressing alarm at the House action. The High Performance Computing Coalition, an advocacy group of computer industry representatives, complained sharply that the House move would slow down progress in cutting edge technologies and do injury to the competitiveness of the US supercomputing industry. While it is doubtful that HASC ever intended a cutoff in funding, in the end, the committee's pressure tactics had their intended effect, forcing DARPA to restructure its management of the HPCC program to the Congress' satisfaction.

Whatever the program's eventual accomplishments, the initiative on high performance computing and networking is perhaps typical of the American approach to commercial technology development. A large-scale, high-profile effort designed to capture the public's imagination with "grand challenges" and "information highways," the program was designed as much to stifle complaints about the Bush administration's reticence on technology policy issues as to promote US economic competitiveness. Because the federal government had no bureaucratic home for such a program, policymakers relied on existing structures, particularly within the Department of Defense, to support the effort. Although popular in Congress, the measure nevertheless became mired in concerns over its management and the role of government bureaucrats in "picking winners and losers." The size of the program—over half-a-billion dollars per year—facilitated the formation of a number of constituency groups with a direct interest in the continuation and expansion of the effort. The size of the effort also stirred considerable grumbling from those left out of the program, who saw their exclusion as deadly to their future business prospects. Despite the criticisms by those who would not benefit from the government's largesse, computer industry groups have nevertheless called for the program's expansion, calls that were partially answered by the technology proposals of the Clinton administration.[5] Finally, constituent

5. Computer Systems Policy Project, *Perspectives on US Technology and Trade Policy: The CSPP Agenda for the 103rd Congress*, October 1,

complaints and concerns over the program's accountability inspired direct intervention by Congress in the management and direction of the program. This intervention reached beyond mere complaints about the administrative structures in use, instead raising questions about the very appropriateness of the technological choices being made by federal program management officials.

Technology Policies in America

These developments suggest the difficulty of formulating and carrying out a consistent policy on commercial technology development in the United States. Of course, technology policy is not new to the United States. Indeed, for much of its long history, the government has recognized the importance of technological advancement and has undertaken programs designed to stimulate the development and application of new technologies. For example, the Constitution's provisions protecting the rights of inventors and policies establishing standard weights and measures helped to establish a well-ordered environment for innovation in America. To help develop the telegraph, Congress awarded Samuel Morse a $30,000 grant to build a telegraph line from Washington to Baltimore. Army officials also encouraged standardized manufacturing practices in the small arms industry. Government investment in new canals and railroads also stimulated economic and technological advances. Most significantly, beginning with the Morill Act of 1862, the federal government launched a coordinated program of basic and applied agricultural research that helped make American farmers the most productive in the world.[6]

Aside from these notable exceptions, however, government support for commercial technology development prior to World War II was limited. In general, federal programs were limited to research efforts designed to meet accepted government mission requirements, and were undertaken by the responsible agency (e.g., Agriculture, War) rather than by a centralized science organization. Moreover, what research the government did conduct was most often conducted in-house by scientists and engineers employed directly by the government. In turn, the United

1992, 8.
6. Bruce L. R. Smith, *American Science Policy Since World War II* (Washington, D.C.: The Brookings Institution, 1990).

States relied primarily on private inventors and entrepreneurial corporations to develop new technologies for the commercial marketplace. The government also left the responsibility for the funding of basic scientific research to the private sector, an arrangement preferred by most scientific organizations that feared government support would bring with it government interference.

These attitudes changed sharply during and immediately after World War II, reflecting a number of changes in the government's perception of the role of science and technology. Most obviously, the contribution of scientists and engineers to the war effort firmly established a close link between technology and national defense. The massive Manhattan Project, as well as the development of radar and other military technologies, convinced government decision-makers of the need to invest heavily in research and development in order to strengthen the nation's military capabilities. Consequently, with the dawning of the cold war, America's peacetime defense spending soared to unprecedented levels, as did the government's investment in the development of military technologies.

Aside from increased support for defense R&D, the other major change in US government policy toward science and technology following the war was the emergence of a broad consensus supporting government investment in basic scientific research. Vannevar Bush's 1945 report, Science—The Endless Frontier, laid out the essential framework justifying sustained federal support in science for the postwar era. By investing in research on the frontiers of science, the report argued, the United States would contribute to its defense, its economic strength, and its sense of national purpose:

> Progress in the war against disease depends upon a flow of new products, new scientific knowledge. New products, new industries, and more jobs require continuous additions to knowledge of the laws of nature, and the application of that knowledge to practical purposes. Similarly, our defense against aggression demands new knowledge so that we can develop new and improved weapons...[because] without scientific progress no amount of achievement in other directions can insure our health, prosperity, and security as a nation in the modern world.[7]

Vigorous federal support for basic scientific research was also seen as essential to maintaining the competitiveness of the US

---

7. As quoted in Bruce Smith, *American Science Policy, 43.*

economy. Whereas America had been able to depend on Europe as an important source of scientific and technological advances during the nineteenth century, America's industrial expansion at the beginning of the twentieth century and the destruction wrought by World War II rendered this approach obsolete. The tremendous growth and increasing sophistication of the US economy during the first quarter of the century firmly established America's industrial giants as leading innovators in the world economy. Meanwhile, the destruction of Europe and its scientific infrastructure meant that the United States could no longer rely on others to blaze the scientific trail.

The consensus that emerged after World War II on federal support for research and development therefore comprised three main elements. First, the federal government would take on primary responsibility for funding basic scientific research, to be conducted by private universities, corporations, and government laboratories. Second, the Department of Defense would invest heavily in both basic research and technology development in order to provide the nation with the weapons and military technologies necessary to confront the Soviet threat. Finally, in most cases, responsibility for commercial technology development would be left to the private sector. Private sector efforts would be assisted by the solid foundation of basic scientific research conducted at the government's expense, and, occasionally, by spin-offs from defense research and development efforts. However, commercial technology spending levels and research agendas were to be set by the private sector through market mechanisms.

Despite this third element, this new consensus provided a basis for a substantial increase in federal support for research and development spending (see Figure 4.1). Between 1953 and 1961, federal R&D spending grew annually in real terms by 14 percent. The escalation of the cold war and the Soviet launch of Sputnik in 1957, in particular, helped to fuel increased federal research spending throughout the 1950s and early 1960s. After this initial run up, spending growth slowed during the late 1960s as the war in Vietnam intensified and in the 1970s as the US economy slumped. However, the reintensified cold war of the late 1970s and early 1980s helped again to push up federal research and development spending. In fact, most of the increase during the early 1980s was spurred by the substantial growth in defense R&D spending that accompanied the Reagan military build-up.

For most of this period, the basic consensus on the proper federal role in promoting technology held firm. This consensus helped build a comprehensive and capable scientific estab-

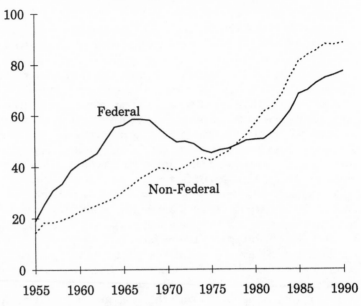

Source: National Science Foundation.

Figure 4.1. US Research and Development Spending, 1955-1990 (Billions of Constant 1992 Dollars).

lishment in the United States, and fostered development of the most sophisticated armed forces in the world. In addition, rapid economic progress during the 1950s and 1960s seemed to vindicate the government's decision not to intervene directly in commercial markets.

Consequently, although federal R&D investments have grown enormously, they have remained relatively limited in their scope. Government intervention in the technology development process has been the exception rather than the rule. Congress, the White House, and the public have generally accepted the appropriateness of federal funding for research and development of technologies only when it was necessary for such socially desirable activities as national defense, energy, and space exploration. While these programs may have had significant commercial spinoffs, they were generally not rationalized on the basis of their contribution to the nation's economic well-being.

Occasionally, however, the federal government deviated from this general path and directly supported the development of commercial technologies. Heavy federal assistance for the development of agricultural technologies continued at its prewar pace throughout the postwar period. In addition, the federal government undertook a number of large technology demonstration projects designed to foster the development of new commercial products and industries. Among others, these civilian efforts included government programs to develop a supersonic transport aircraft, commercial satellite technologies, breeder reactors, synthetic fuels, and photovoltaic technologies. A 1991 review of previous government efforts to promote these civilian technologies found nearly all succumbed to serious political or budgetary problems, however. In the words of the study's authors,

> The history of federal R&D commercialization programs...is hardly a success story. On the basis of retrospective benefit-cost analysis, only one program—NASA's activities in developing communications satellites—achieved its objectives and can be regarded as worth the effort. But that program was killed because it came into conflict with more important political forces than the advancement of commercial technology. The photovoltaics program made significant progress, but it was dramatically scaled back for political reasons....The remaining four programs [supersonic transport, Clinch River Breeder Reactor, space shuttle, and synthetic fuels program] were almost unqualified failures.[8]

Nevertheless, although these programs consumed billions of dollars over their life spans, they represent only relatively minor diversions from the basic course of American science and technology policy of the postwar period. For most of this period, commercial research received at best only indirect federal support.

Spin-Offs from Military Technology

Although few, if any, military projects have been justified primarily for their potential to contribute to the nation's economic competitiveness, most agree that US military research has yielded important commercial benefits and has served in some ways as a de facto commercial technology support program. The examples of such spin-offs from military technology are numerous. The early development of the computer industry in the United States was driven in large part by military investment in computer research and development during the 1940s and 1950s. Likewise, the commercial jet aircraft industry benefitted greatly from military research. The Boeing 707 commercial airliner, for

---

8. Linda R. Cohen and Roger G. Noll, *The Technology Pork Barrel* (Washington, D.C.: The Brookings Institution, 1991), 365.

example, was based closely on the design of the KC-135 military tanker, and a major share of the 707's development costs were borne by its military sibling.[9] In fact, the commercial benefits from America's large investment in defense technologies was sometimes viewed with alarm by US allies abroad, who believed that the United States would only extend the economic and technological advantages it enjoyed after the war through its heavy spending on developing high-technology weaponry.

The spin-off of military technologies to the commercial sector has been largely unintentional, however, more the product of private efforts to apply technologies originally developed for defense applications rather than of some concerted federal effort. In fact, critics contend that the serendipitous nature of the process and the relatively meager returns from such a large investment in military R&D raise doubts about the efficacy of spin-off entirely. In only a handful of cases has a military technology been converted directly into a successful commercial product. Raytheon's development of the microwave oven based on its work on military radars is a prominent example. In most cases, the relationship between the military and commercial markets is more complex. At times, as in the case of supercomputers, substantial and early defense purchases of an emerging technology helps pave the way for the accelerated commercialization of a new technology. Alternatively, as in the case of jet aircraft engines, simultaneous developments in military and commercial sectors were mutually reinforcing.[10]

The ability to transfer technologies between military and commercial laboratories thus depend on a variety of factors, from the suitability of the technology itself to the receiving mechanisms available in the private sector. For most of the postwar era, government interest in commercial spin-offs from its military research was of secondary interest. In fact, only recently has the government specifically undertaken efforts to rationalize the process of transferring government-developed technologies to the private sector.

---

9. David C. Mowery and Nathan Rosenberg, *Technology and the Pursuit of Economic Growth* (Cambridge, UK: Cambridge University Press, 1989), 185.
10. John Alic, et al., *Beyond Spinoff: Military and Commercial Technologies in a Changing World* (Boston, Massachusetts: Harvard Business School Press, 1992), 64-75.

The End of Consensus and the Rise of a New American Technology Policy

As economic growth slowed in the 1970s and foreign products began to penetrate the US market en masse during the 1980s, many began to question the efficacy of the government's hands-off policy on commercial technology and called for more active federal support for commercial technology development. The growing technical competence in America's overseas rivals prompted increasing concern among congressional leaders, executive branch officials, academics, business leaders, and policy analysts about the state of America's technological competitiveness, its implications for the nation's long-term economic health, and the government's possible role in fostering a more competitive economy. As a result, many now seek to expand the government's efforts to improve the long-term prospects of the economy through regulatory changes and widespread federal investment in commercial technologies. Although similar, if more ambitious proposals for a comprehensive federal "industrial policy" failed to gain widespread support in the past, the troubles of America's manufacturing sector and the economic slowdown of the early 1990s stimulated interest in a growing number of initiatives to improve the technological strength of selected commercial industries.

The roots of recent proposals to provide incentives for greater investment in technology reach back to 1980 and the passage of the Stevenson-Wydler Technology Innovation Act. That legislation specifically directed federal agencies to improve private sector access to federal research. Other measures, including the enactment of the research and development tax credit in 1981, the passage of the 1984 Cooperative Research Act to relax antitrust laws for research projects, the revision of the National Science Foundation's charter in 1985 to expand its role in support of engineering, the 1986 passage of the Technology Transfer Act, and continuing US efforts to negotiate stronger worldwide protection of intellectual property rights continued this trend. These early efforts focused primarily on general measures designed to facilitate private investment in research and development, as well as to stimulate the transfer of government-funded technologies to the private sector. Politically, they have proven to be the least problematic because they leave the key decision of where to allocate research and development funds largely in the hands of the private sector, raise few distributional issues, and involve little in the way of direct expenditures (although some measures did reduce federal tax revenues).

With the establishment of Sematech in 1987, however, the United States took a major step toward the development of a far more ambitious technology policy. Although government involvement was rationalized on national security grounds and the initiative's $100 million annual stipend has come from the Defense Department, the program nevertheless represented a marked departure from previous years' practices in that the government became directly involved in funding specific technologies intended for the commercial marketplace. Indeed, Sematech explicitly refrained from designing defense-specific semiconductor manufacturing technologies out of a concern that such a focus could render the effort irrelevant to the ongoing race in the commercial market. This trend toward more focused initiatives concentrating on specific technologies continued with the 1988 Omnibus Trade Act, which established the Advanced Technology Program within the Commerce Department's National Institute on Standards and Technology, the announcement of the High Performance Computer and Communications program in 1991, and congressional funding of numerous "dual-use" technology development efforts within the Department of Defense.

Given these legislative successes, other proposals to allocate federal funds to what were labeled "critical" or "enabling" technologies have gained momentum. Congressionally mandated critical technologies reports prepared by the Defense and Commerce Departments, as well as by a commission reporting to the Office of Science and Technology Policy, gave legislators, business leaders, and policy analysts who favor a more activist federal policy specific guidelines as to where to funnel federal dollars. Moreover, numerous reports highlighting the need for a more coherent federal technology policy have been published by various industry organizations and private think tanks over the past several years.

In addition, support for an enhanced federal role in commercial technology development has been spurred on by the end of the cold war. As lawmakers struggle to define new missions for America's vast defense technology infrastructure and to help the nation's defense industries convert to civilian production, the possibility of promoting greater commercial competitiveness by redirecting federal R&D funding has become increasingly politically salient. The obvious success of American military technology and, by extension, of the huge government-funded industrial complex that stood behind it, seemed to demonstrate the efficacy of direct government intervention in support of important technologies. It could be argued that if similar critical technologies were identified in the commercial world, the federal government might achieve comparable successes.

These efforts to directly subsidize the development of certain commercial technologies proved far more controversial than the more general incentives enacted earlier, however. In particular, the Bush administration vehemently opposed any proposal that it construed as a form of industrial policy. Its dismissal of Dr. Craig Fields, former head of the Defense Advanced Research Projects Agency (DARPA) for his support of High Definition Television research, the distancing of the White House from the National Critical Technologies report, and long-delayed and grudging agreement to establish the congressionally mandated Critical Technologies Institute were symbols of the Bush administration's reluctance to start picking winners.

Nevertheless, on September 26th, 1990, the Executive Office of the President submitted a 13-page report to the Congress entitled "US Technology Policy." Prepared by the Office of Science and Technology Policy, in coordination with various federal departments and agencies, the report outlined the elements and objectives of a wide range of federal policies on technology development and diffusion. Specifically, the report noted that the federal government was responsible for (1) encouraging technology investments through monetary and fiscal policies; (2) providing a legal environment that eliminates unnecessary obstacles to innovation; (3) eliminating regulatory barriers to integration of government and commercial production; (4) easing technical data rights requirements to facilitate the commercialization of government-funded technologies; (5) providing a stable regulatory environment; (6) negotiating comparable regulatory guarantees with America's trading partners; (7) promoting international standardization efforts; and (8) enforcing intellectual property rights at home and abroad. Most significantly, the report explicitly acknowledged, for the first time, the federal government's responsibility for participating "with the private sector in precompetitive research on generic, enabling technologies that have the potential to contribute to a broad range of government and commercial applications."[11]

To some, the mere existence of such a document represented a watershed in federal policy toward technology. For the Bush

11. Office of Science and Technology Policy, *US Technology Policy*, September 26, 1990, 5.

administration, which had previously rejected a federal role in commercial technology development so stridently, the report constituted a recognition that an explicit policy on technology promotion had fast become a political necessity.

The Path Not Taken: Industrial Policy in Japan

The debate over whether the United States should embark on a new strategy for promoting commercial technology has been heavily influenced by various interpretations of how effective the industrial policies of other nations have been. Given its tremendous economic successes of the 1980s, particularly in penetrating the US market and sharply competing in a number of high-technology manufacturing sectors, Japan has become the most often cited example of the tremendous returns from a well-conceived government industrial strategy. For the past four decades, the Japanese bureaucracy, led by the Ministry of International Trade and Industry (MITI), has used a wide range of instruments to move the Japanese economy toward higher-value industries and away from industries dependent on low wage rates or natural resources.

Despite more than a decade of Western study, however, the degree to which Japan's postwar industrial policy has succeeded is still open to controversy. Clearly, some of the sectors targeted by Japan's industrial policies, such as semiconductors, have grown into world-class industries. However, the contribution of industrial policy to the success of Japanese automobile manufacturers or consumer electronics producers was minimal, at best. Moreover, in other areas, the Japanese bureaucracy has pursued policies that have had a serious, negative impact on the country's overall productivity levels and standards of living (e.g., in agriculture and retailing). Whether these failed policies are products of some systemic problem with industrial policy as pursued in Japan, or instead reflect the effects of other forces in Japanese society, is open to question. What is clear, however, is the fact that the greater willingness of the Japanese bureaucracy to intervene in commercial markets entails as many risks as it does opportunities.

It is also impossible to draw a direct link between government support for particular Japanese manufacturing sectors and the improved welfare of the Japanese people. While some observers proclaim Japan's industrial targeting policies and the structure of Japanese business as the primary reason for the country's postwar success, others cite more mundane characteristics—high savings and investment rates, a strong educational system and work ethic, intense domestic competition, and the country's openness to foreign technologies—as better explanations of the country's good fortunes. At most, Japanese government policies probably had a modest, positive effect on the development of a select number of industries.[12]

In any event, Japanese postwar industrial policy was premised on a long tradition of government intervention and direction of the economy, beginning with the Meji government in the 1870s and its policies to catch up economically and technologically with the West.[13]

More than a century of experience with a strong centralized bureaucracy and close coordination between government and industry has given the Japanese a very different conception of the proper role of government than the one that prevails in the United States. In Japan, direct government intervention in the economy is generally regarded as entirely legitimate and, indeed, absolutely necessary. Moreover, the government bureaucracy enjoys a measure of respect that is virtually unthinkable in the United States. Powerful government ministries operate with a minimum of interference from the country's weak Diet and profit from the stable rule of the centrist Liberal Democratic Party. Moreover, government officials maintain very close ties with industry executives, leading to coordinated policies which greatly benefit Japanese industry, and, on occasion, erupt into major political scandals. Finally, and in contrast to the situation in the

---

12. A recent notable failure of the Japanese approach was the "Fifth Generation' computing program launched in 1982 and recently brought to a close with disappointing results. MITI's commitment to its original vision of the next generation of computers eventually proved to be a liability in the highly volatile computer industry. See Andrew Pollack, "'Fifth Generation" Becomes Japan's Lost Generation," *New York Times*, June 5, 1992, D1, 3. Similarly, the government-supported 20 year effort to develop high definition television technology has produced a system based on obsolete technology. "Do Not Adjust Your Set," *The Economist*, February 27, 1993, 65-66.

13. For an overview of Japanese industrial policies, see Daniel I. Okimoto, *Between MITI and the Market: Japanese Industrial Policy for High Technology* (Stanford, California: Stanford University Press, 1989); and Office of Technology Assessment, *Competing Economies: America, Europe, and the Pacific Rim* (Washington, D.C.: OTA, October 1991), 239-291.

United States, consumers are not well represented in the Japanese bureaucracy, and their rights are often sacrificed to the interests of Japan's major producers.

Shaping Technology Policy in the American Political Context

While some elements of the Japanese technology development model may be appropriable by others, the political culture in the United States promises to make it extremely difficult to sustain such a policy over the long term. Clearly, the current political climate offers an opportunity for positive federal action to strengthen the technological foundations of the US economy. The widespread interest within government and industry in promoting productivity through technological advancement represents a positive development, whatever form it ultimately takes.

The challenge, of course, is to ensure that this political momentum is harnessed and translated into real economic improvement. This requires policies that both accommodate US values and channel the inevitable constituent calls for special treatment toward higher purposes. During much of the postwar period, American trade policy accomplished just such a feat. To open the US market to foreign trade (and thereby improve US economic welfare), policymakers answered calls for protectionism by promising to open foreign markets. For the most part, this growth-oriented strategy succeeded, although its particular formulation is probably responsible for the current tendency to respond to closed foreign markets with threats of protectionist measures. The challenge for a successful technology policy will be to accomplish a similar balancing act.

A large part of the problem in making decisions on technology policy is the widespread hostility provoked by any attempt by the US government to become more involved in the day-to-day operations of the private economy. The American tendency toward laissez-faire economic policy is not simply a passing fancy or Republican ideological fixation, but rather reflects a basic preference for individual decision over governmental action. This preference is embodied in the Constitution, which closely circumscribes the federal government's power in the economic realm. Moreover, few Americans share their Japanese or European counterparts' faith in the ability of government ministries and bureaucracies to choose the best course for the economy, except in the broadest of terms. Such a lack of trust in centralized authority is pervasive and applies to large institutions, public and private, and often makes decisions by major corporations as suspect as those of governmental bureaucracies. While the Reagan and Bush administrations' faith in laissez-faire capitalism was probably overzealous, the free market economic philosophy does provide a useful rationale for decentralizing authority over the economic sphere and ensuring the maximum latitude for individual initiative. At least in theory, leaving the entire range of detailed economic decisions to millions of individuals will yield optimal outcomes in all but a narrow set of circumstances.

By establishing a basic prejudice against government involvement in the economy, moreover, laissez-faire ideology tends to help forestall attempts by powerful special interests to manipulate the political system to favor their particular interests. A general American faith in free markets does not, of course, translate into enduring abnegation on the part of established industries and their workers, particularly when facing tough economic times. Such groups represent powerful political forces and can be expected to look to the federal government for relief in times of trouble. Because mature industries tend to have developed broad and deep constituencies, their influence on the political process can be disproportionate relative to their continuing economic significance. In contrast, emerging sectors that may dominate tomorrow's economy sometimes have relatively little power in terms of money or interested constituents.

Once the federal government does decide to intervene selectively in the commercial technology development process, however, the demands on policymakers mount rapidly. Most obviously, there is the substantial risk that private interest groups will divert technology policies to serve their parochial interests at the expense of the national well-being. As US science and engineering budgets have grown, so too has the number of interest groups seeking to obtain the benefits of public largesse. As the president of the National Academy of Engineering, Robert M. White, has observed,

"Pork-barrel" science and engineering has become a reality and entered the lexicon. The total of such pork-barrel grants and contracts for FY 1990 alone was $130 million. Between 1980 and 1989, more than $900 million was earmarked for 300 academic research and facilities projects. Coalitions, lobbying groups, and industry associations have mushroomed in the past quarter century. Professional societies are in Washington in force. In just the past two decades, the number of nonprofit science and technology associations in the United States has grown by 138 percent—educational associations by almost 90 percent.[14]

Among these groups, the Council on Research and Technology (CORETECH), the Council on Competitiveness, the Aerospace Industries Association, Function 250 Coalition, the Advanced Technology Coalition, the Semiconductor Industries Association, the Computer Systems Policy Project, the Association for Manufacturing Technology, and the Electronics Industries Association are but a few of the most active in trying to influence federal policy. In fact, the OSTP and DOD list the Electronics Industries Association, Council on Competitiveness, Aerospace Industries Association, and Computer Systems Policy Project as major contributors to their critical technology reports, giving some indication of both their positive contributions to, and potential abuse of, the technology policy formulation process.

The growth and activism of these lobbying groups reflects the simple fact that well-organized, well-funded constituencies can have a disproportionate impact on public policy. In relatively noncontroversial areas such as R&D funding, small, knowledgeable, and dedicated groups can wield significant influence. They have the capital and expertise to produce the analyses and reports bolstering their particular arguments.

Moreover, since a targeted technology policy would disburse benefits selectively in the economy, recipients will inevitably have a great interest in protecting that flow of public funds. In contrast, the interests of the larger number of nonrecipients are more diffuse, making it difficult to prevent special interests from exercising undue control. Once funds begin to flow to a particular group, strong constituencies are formed that will fight to keep the dollars coming. Without some sort of counterbalance, it is likely that funding will continue to be channeled in the same direction, regardless of whether the once-favored industry or technology is still economically relevant. The case of Sematech is instructive. Despite the fact that its original charter called for government funding to end in 1992 after five years of support, the semiconductor consortium shows every sign of becoming a permanent caller at the federal door, with Congress and industry succeeding in pressuring the Bush administration to maintain support for

---

14. Robert M. White, "Science, Engineering, and the Sorcerer's Apprentice," *Science and Technology Yearbook: 1991* (Washington, D.C.: Association for the Advancement of Science, 1991), 160-161.

the program, and the Clinton White House vowing continued financial support.

Likewise, government officials have ample reason to seek out advice from these groups. Policymakers and program officers inevitably have little direct access to firsthand market data, making them highly dependent on outside sources for financial and technical information. Naturally, ready and willing advisors with well-organized information and knowledgeable spokespersons represent tremendous resources. At the same time, program managers dedicated to promoting commercial technologies want to cultivate strong relationships with the major players in industry to ensure both that new technologies are adopted and that their programs are actively supported by industry during the budget process—to say nothing of their interest in future employment opportunities. The enthusiasm with which many in the national laboratory system are embracing increased cooperation with industry derives as much from their narrow interest in continuing to receive funding from the federal government as from their commitment to improving the nation's economic competitiveness.

In contrast to these specific groups, the interests of the rest of the nation are far less focused. In addition, smaller or newer companies, with little capital to spare for lobbying efforts in Washington, inevitably find it more difficult to obtain a hearing during the technology selection process. Likewise, those firms that generally do not do business with the government are unlikely to have the specialized knowledge necessary to inject their views into the policymaking process. Corporations already possessing experience with government contracting will possess a distinct advantage. Defense contractors, in particular, are well aware of how the political process can influence resource allocations. More generally, traditionally defined high-technology industries have been the primary beneficiaries of public R&D spending, making them better adept at manipulating the public policy process to serve their parochial interests.[15]

15. Only 12.3 percent of the R&D conducted by low-technology industries (textiles, food, wood products, etc.) was funded by the federal government in 1984. In medium-technology industries (electrical equipment, chemicals, machinery, etc.), the figure was 17.2 percent. In contrast, 41.5 percent of all R&D conducted by high technology industries (medicines, computers, electronic components, aircraft, etc.) was paid for by the government. Congressional Budget Office, *Using Federal R&D to Promote Commercial Innovation* (Washington, D.C.: Congressional Budget

Nor has the behavior of Congress given politically aware private firms any reason to suspect that these practices will not continue. Members have not shied from using the budget process to direct funds to their favored research projects, institutions, or scientists. Although it was unable to distinguish among the motivations behind Congress' actions, OSTP calculated that the fiscal 1991 budget included 492 earmarked R&D projects costing $810 million.[16] Twenty-five of these earmarks called for the establishment of new centers, institutions, or other organizations, while 111 provided $428 million for designated R&D facilities across the country. Added to this are the many cases where legislators take their constituents' cases directly to program officials, through letters, phone calls, or requests for information and explanations, thereby subtly influencing the direction of government programs.

In addition, each political party has its own institutional biases that tend to push policy toward the special interest goals of their core constituencies.[17] Even as Republican opposition to increased government intervention diminished, party leaders remain hesitant to engage in designing any systematic policy on technology and industrial competitiveness. Even in the area of infrastructure investment, the Bush administration resisted any major increases in government spending. At the same time, however, Republicans have been willing to offer special treatment for the US financial community, reflecting its traditional bias toward the owners of capital. The Savings and Loan bailout and the heavy emphasis on financial instruments (capital gains tax cuts, investment incentives, etc.) to stimulate economic growth serve as manifestations of this tendency.

In contrast, the Democratic Party, with its traditional union constituencies, is inclined toward solutions favoring the rights of labor even when job preservation runs counter to the requirements of international competitiveness. Labor unions are particularly interested in the preservation of the manufacturing sector since these industries represent the core of their membership. Moreover, Democratic solutions are more likely to be shaped by the needs and desires of the Congress, where political fiefdoms

---

Office, April 1988), 42.

16. Office of Management and Budget, *The Budget of the United States*, Fiscal 1992, 63-64.

17. For a discussion of this issue, see Kevin P. Phillips, "US Industrial Policy: Inevitable and Ineffective," *Harvard Business Review* (July-August 1992): 104-112.

are long established and the influence of key members on particular issues is strongly felt.

Conclusions

Critics of federal support for technology recognize these bureaucratic and political realities of government decision-making in the United States. They fear that once the barrier to selective involvement is surmounted, a flood of demands on the public purse will ensue. Even while these critics may accept that targeted support theoretically is justified in some areas, they are concerned that restricting support to those cases may prove politically impossible. Without a firm and widely accepted methodology for choosing one technology over another for support, reasonable people can easily disagree over funding priorities, leading to justifications of almost any subsidy program. Moreover, given constituent pressures to obtain their "fair share" from public coffers, members of Congress are understandably anxious to lobby for particular projects. Such projects could divert resources to economically questionable endeavors under the guise of improving America's technological competence. Indeed, it is relatively easy to argue that almost any industry is critical to the economic future of the nation. In such circumstances, the net economic effect of even the most carefully crafted technology support program might prove negative.

It is also important to recall that the success of any technology program can only be measured in the long-term. Annual movements of productivity growth rates will mean little if they are not sustained for an extended period of time. Consequently, designing politically robust programs is essential. For example, small, low-profile technology support programs offer one method for promoting commercial technologies without courting political disaster and the premature death of a particular program, should something go wrong. However, such programs might be unable to generate the necessary political constituencies to compete effectively in the annual budget process. The relative budgetary success of such "big science" projects as the human genome project, space station Freedom, and the superconducting supercollider at the expense of lower profile and less expensive efforts would seem to bode ill for less grandiose technology policy alternatives. However, although larger programs generate the necessary level of political interest, they also run much higher risks of catastrophic failure. Moreover, to the extent that they begin to be viewed as "pork barrel" programs rather than legitimate efforts to stimulate technology development, they are likely to become targets of a critical public.

Calls for so-called "pragmatic" approaches that dispense with rigorous analyses of the potential costs and benefits of any particular program in favor of "strategic vision" may fit the current political climate. However, such policies may quickly lose their appeal as circumstances change. What some might consider close government-industry cooperation today may very well be construed as collusion tomorrow. This is particularly true if the needs and desires of other interest groups (e.g., consumers, labor) are left unmet.

More dangerous still is the rising tide of "economic nationalism" that infects much of the debate over US competitiveness. While politicians and constituency groups both have strong political interests in capitalizing on such sentiments, the results for the nation's well-being could be disastrous. At the very least, narrowly focused US policies to support specific domestic industries would seriously undermine American arguments against foreign subsidy practices. US complaints about European Airbus subsidies or unfair Japanese industrial policy programs will ring hollow if Washington begins providing direct subsidies itself. Such an approach only promises to set off a round of subsidy wars for which the United States is ill-prepared and in which all sides eventually lose. Similarly, US efforts to restrict the flow of federally funded technology to foreign firms would almost certainly result in foreign retaliation, cutting off access to important sources of new technology at precisely the moment when the United States can most benefit from the know-how of its trading partners.

In the end, however, as US-based corporations become increasingly transnational, policymakers may be less likely to continue to equate these companies' interests with those of the nation. As technologies developed in the United States with public funds are transferred overseas (as is inevitable), the calls for some explanation (and someone to blame) could serve as a counterweight to the Washington influence of large high-technology companies. While this might be a positive development, there remain numerous political obstacles to the formulation of a successful technology policy. Were these obstacles to prevent any real progress in this area, however, what would be lost is not simply a particular set of policies, but a unique opportunity to fundamentally improve how the United States supports the technological underpinnings of its economy.

While many have called for the creation of institutional structures to carry out an aggressive technology strategy that would be immune from political influence, the prospects for accomplishing such a feat are not promising. As the size of a federal commercial technology program increases and the distributional effects become clear, there seems little chance that the Congress will refrain from attempting to exercise detailed influence over the program's direction. What is required is to design programs that accept the inevitability of political intervention, yet are robust enough to offer some hope of achieving some public benefit.

Part Two

National Objectives and Policy Alternatives

5

Technology Policy and the
Nation's Security

A major impetus behind the current push to adopt a more aggressive federal commercial technology policy is the evident success of US efforts to develop advanced military technologies. The overwhelming capabilities of the US military demonstrated during Operation Desert Storm testified to the government's ability to foster the development of extraordinarily advanced technologies. Declining military budgets, however, threaten to sap the strength of the military R&D establishment. Meanwhile, the rise of foreign economic competition has prompted many to suggest that the nation's defense R&D effort should be restructured to promote US military and economic security.

Regardless of the decisions taken on commercial technology policy, the development and application of defense technologies present their own unique set of challenges that must be addressed separately. Changes in the global distribution of technological resources and longstanding trends in the relationship between defense and civilian technologies promise to alter fundamentally the environment within which the United States develops and produces military equipment.

For much of the postwar period, mutually reinforcing political, economic, and security conditions within the United States supported rapid and dramatic advances in military technology. The experience of World War II established the importance of technology to the nation's security, while the outbreak of the cold war fostered a clear national imperative for sustained American efforts to maintain the most sophisticated military forces in the world. The United States emerged from World War II as the technological and economic leader of the world. Relatively prosperous and confronted with no serious overseas economic challengers, the United States was able to expand its defense industrial complex rapidly with little concern for the economic consequences of such policies.

At the same time, the military threat posed by the Soviet Union served as a useful stimulus for the US defense research structure, creating a highly competitive climate and providing tangible incentives for the US research community to accelerate their efforts. The effects of the first Soviet atomic bomb test on US hydrogen bomb research and of Sputnik on American space and missile programs highlight the importance of a competitive environment for the achievement of rapid technological advances. Only the Soviet Union had the will and ability to compete militarily and technologically with the United States. That fact, and the ever persistent threat of "next generation" Soviet weapon systems, helped drive American research and development efforts forward.

The American military's preference for technological sophistication over numerical superiority—quality over quantity—further fueled the defense technology race. In large measure, the performance of individual systems, as opposed to the effectiveness of total forces, became the central criterion for evaluating military equipment. While this sometimes led to cases where fractional improvements in performance were achieved at extraordinary costs, it also created a tremendous impetus to exploit any and all technological opportunities, stimulating additional technological achievements.

Finally, the sheer size of US defense procurement and R&D budgets, with their promise to contractors of substantial financial rewards, helped attract the country's best scientific and technical talent to the defense effort. By 1990, 342,000 engineers, or 18 percent of all US engineers, were employed in defense or defense-related work. Twenty-six percent of all US electrical and electronics engineers worked on military projects, while 43 percent of all aerospace engineers were engaged in defense.[1] For these individuals, the opportunities and challenges presented by defense research, not to mention the relatively high wages, helped attract them to the defense sector.

Within this environment, military technology progressed more rapidly than commercial technology during the years following the war. Huge government investments pushed the limits of defense research far beyond what was taking place in the commercial sector, establishing it as the standard-bearer of the national technical effort. Throughout the 1950s, defense R&D alone accounted for approximately half of all R&D activity undertaken within the United States. With the acceleration of the space program in the 1960s, the combined space and military R&D total

---

1. US Congress, Office of Technology Assessment, *After the Cold War: Living with Lower Defense Spending*, OTA-ITE-524 (Washington, D.C.: US Government Printing Office, February 1992), 103-104.

constituted the lion's share of R&D conducted in the United States. In 1964, for example, the federal government was spending 65 percent more on defense and space research than was spent by nonfederal sources for all other types of research and development.[2] In many instances, technologies developed initially for the military eventually flowed into the commercial sector, yielding economic as well as military benefits. Research on military tanker and transport aircraft, for example, found its way into new designs for commercial airliners. Research on digital military computing served as the foundation for the commercial computer market. To a large extent, this transfer of technology was in one direction; military systems typically incorporated few advanced technologies developed outside of the defense R&D structure. Even when they did, as in the case of the first semiconductors, such privately funded technologies were often pursued with the large and sophisticated military market clearly in mind. As a result of this diffusion of military technologies, the funneling of public funds to the development of high-technology weaponry was sometimes portrayed as a means of promoting American economic, as well as military, objectives.

The Defense Revolution

With the end of the cold war, the shift in economic and technological weight among the leading industrialized nations, and the growing technological importance of the commercial sector, there has been a dramatic revolution in these patterns of defense technology development. This transformation is political, economic and technological. Fundamental changes in the security environment, as well as the increased economic power of Europe and East Asia, have shifted the focus of policy away from military concerns. As the emphasis on defense declines, so too has the priority assigned to developing and deploying new defense technologies. Development and production plans for numerous other "cold war" weapons have already been scaled back or canceled. Army plans for a new high-technology tank to counter a future Soviet armored threat, for example, became hopelessly irrelevant once it became obvious that a next-generation Soviet tank was

---

2. National Science Foundation, *National Patterns of R&D Resources: 1990* (NSF 90-316) (Washington, D.C.: National Science Foundation, May 1990), 55.

not likely to materialize any time soon. Similarly, European governments participating in the European Fighter Aircraft (EFA) program have simplified their requirements and scaled back their technological objectives in light of the vastly changed security environment in Europe. In fact, the end of the cold war has spurred cutbacks in military spending not only in the United States and Europe, but around the world as well, reducing demand for high-technology military hardware. This is in sharp contrast to the situation a decade ago. Throughout the early- and mid-1980s, worldwide spending on military equipment rose substantially, fueled by President Reagan's defense build-up in the United States, continued growth in Soviet military budgets, increased defense spending in Europe, and the massive purchases by the belligerents in the eight-year Iran-Iraq war. By 1988, global defense spending had reached a peak of $1.2 trillion (in 1993 dollars).[3] This rapid expansion prompted a substantial increase in the number and size of the world's major defense manufacturers. Defense sector employment in the United States alone increased roughly 66 percent between 1980 and 1988. By the end of the decade, the US defense spending boom of the early 1980s had given the United States the most advanced, most capable defense technology and production base in the world.

But, with the disappearance of the Soviet Union and the concomitant reductions in US and European defense spending, worldwide defense spending is now set to decline steadily over the current decade, and is projected conservatively to fall to about $800 billion (in 1993 dollars) by 1997. Even relatively optimistic forecasts of US military spending foresee annual real reductions averaging over four percent through the year 2000. Similarly, European defense spending is also declining as domestic needs in key countries (France, Germany, Britain) displace issues of national security at the top of these countries' political agendas. At the same time, the end of superpower competition around the globe has also reduced the overall level of defense trade substantially. Only the nations of East Asia and the Middle East are expected to increase defense spending over the 1990s. As a result, these shrinking international markets will be characterized by intense competition as Western suppliers confront a host of old

---

3. Barry M. Blechman, *Worldwide Defense Electronics Market: Outlook 1992–1993* (Washington, D.C.: International Defense Technology, Inc., 1992), 39.

and new supplier nations, including China, North and South Korea, and the nations of the former Soviet Union. The implications of these trends for American defense manufacturers are clear. Neither domestic sales nor exports to developing nations will be sufficient to sustain the industry at its current size and structure. Already burdened by overcapacity, the West's defense sector will undergo a difficult adjustment process over the next five years.[4] Lower defense spending levels have already forced some firms to exit the business, while others are attempting to consolidate their positions and concentrate on core businesses where they have a chance at being a market leader.

Absent the financial incentives offered by earlier defense budgets, US contractors can also be expected to decrease their investment in new product and process technologies. According to a recent survey, capital expenditures by the largest US-owned defense companies have fallen dramatically in recent years, reducing the production capabilities available to the United States in times of crisis. Overall, these firms cut capital spending by 36 percent between 1987 and 1991, from around 4 percent of sales to less than 3 percent. As a result, net plant (capital investment minus depreciation) actually began to decline in 1990, with new depreciation exceeding new investment by over 20 percent in 1991. Further investment in new plants, equipment, and advanced manufacturing technologies is expected to decline even more in the years ahead.[5]

Even as the defense sector embarks on this difficult adjustment process, the relevance of military technologies to the commercial sector seems increasingly tenuous, undermining the argument that funding defense R&D creates spin-offs that benefit the economy as a whole. As defense researchers tackle arcane challenges involving stringent, defense-specific performance requirements, their ability to contribute to the nation's economic prosperity declines. Moreover, the unique institutional structures and procedures that characterize the defense sector hinder, rather than promote, integration of civilian and military technol-

---

4. On the consolidation of the US defense industry, see Jerrold T. Lundquist, "Shrinking Fast and Smart in the Defense Industry," *Harvard Business Review* (November-December 1992): 74-85 and Martin J. Bollinger and John R. Harbison, *Consolidation in Aerospace/Defense: What's Next?* (Bethesda, MD: Booz•Allen & Hamilton, Inc., 1992).
5. David M. Koonce, "Current Trends in the Defense Industry: A Financial Overview," unpublished report, Martin Marietta Corporation, May 1992.

ogy markets, making the transfer of defense technologies to the commercial sector even more difficult. Meanwhile, commercial technologies have become ever more sophisticated. Technologies that were once the sole preserve of the military—automated information processing systems, mobile communications, and advanced miniaturized electronics—are now dominated by the requirements of the commercial market. Through the process of market competition, moreover, research efforts in these fields are advancing faster than corresponding efforts in defense laboratories. As this trend continues, military systems seem likely to become ever more dependent on technologies that are driven primarily by the demands of the commercial marketplace.

The Internationalization of the US Defense Industrial Base

Given the increased interpenetration of global commercial technology markets, a natural byproduct of the military's expanded use of commercial technologies has been the growing US dependence on foreign technologies and components in its military systems. In fact, the globalization of the industrialized world's defense industries is one of the most prominent features of the evolving post-cold war defense industrial base. According to a study of the aerospace industry,

> The "internationalization" of aerospace is the increasing trend toward business relationships that cross national borders. It encompasses the growing trade in aerospace systems and components. It includes direct investment, coproduction and licensing arrangements, and more and more frequently, joint ventures and collaborative arrangements in the design, production and marketing of aerospace products and systems. Internationalization is occurring in both the civil and military sectors of aerospace, spurred by the increasing competition in aerospace production as a large number of countries acquire sophisticated technological capabilities.[6]

Globalization, in the form of foreign component and subsystem sourcing, international sales, marketing agreements, cooperative development and production programs, strategic alliances, joint ventures, mergers, and acquisitions, has been an important trend in the industrialized world's defense sectors for the past five

---

6. Aerospace Industries Association, *The US Aerospace Industry and the Trend Toward Internationalization* (Washington, D.C.: AIA, March 1988), 6.

years. Defense companies have sought foreign partners in order to remain internationally competitive, using such alliances and acquisitions as a means of broadening potential markets, pooling technical expertise, sharing risks and development costs, and achieving economies of scale.

In many respects, the forces driving the globalization of Western defense industries parallel developments in the commercial aerospace and advanced electronics sectors, with high product development costs, globally dispersed technological resources, and the need to achieve economies of scale pushing firms to expand on a worldwide basis. The defense sector, however, has also been characterized by shrinking demand, making international consolidation, in one form or another, more common than expansion. Moreover, whereas internationalization in the commercial sector has involved both European and Japanese firms, Tokyo's strict restrictions on defense exports has sharply limited that country's participation in the ongoing process of defense sector globalization.

In the past, transatlantic arms cooperation was largely the product of American and European partnership in defending against the Soviet military threat. Following World War II, the United States encouraged its European allies to rebuild their armament industries in order to counter the huge armed forces retained by the USSR. Between 1947 and 1980, twenty-eight US missile and aircraft designs were manufactured by foreign companies in twenty allied nations. Through these coproduction and licensed-production arrangements, the United States helped its allies regain their positions as leading military powers.

In the process, however, the United States and Europe also fostered expensive overcapacity in the West's defense production base. Recognizing this fact, and the need to ensure that allied forces could fight effectively together, NATO launched an effort to eliminate redundant and incompatible systems under the umbrella of a policy called RSI (rationalization, standardization, and interoperability). Driven primarily by military considerations, US and allied efforts to promote arms collaboration continued throughout the 1970s and 1980s, albeit with only modest success. To a degree, these efforts were hampered by conflicts between national security objectives and economic forces. Defense companies in both Europe and the United States had little interest in cooperation, while policymakers tended to view the excess costs of maintaining independent defense production capabilities as tolerable requirements for maintaining the trappings of national sovereignty. To the extent that cooperation proceeded, it did so because of the threat posed by the Soviet Union and the desire in the West to increase cohesion within the alliance. With the end of the cold war, many policymakers in Europe and the United States apparently concluded that the political-military rationales for arms cooperation had disappeared, resulting in the collapse of many of these government-inspired collaborative efforts.

The experience of the Persian Gulf War demonstrated, however, that defense collaboration and the interoperability of defense systems are more important than ever. Whereas the nuclear stalemate between NATO and the Warsaw Pact had fortunately avoided any real test of the effectiveness of the alliance's armed forces to fight together, the messy international situation that emerged following the dismantlement of the USSR could be characterized by more, rather than less, frequent military engagements. As in the Gulf, large scale US military operations are likely to be collaborative ventures undertaken with America's closest European allies. Given the need to deploy forces rapidly, the increased speed and deadliness of military operations, and the growing importance of fully interoperable information systems, common weapons, procedures, and standards will likely become more important in the future.

In addition, the need for greater integration of defense industries within the Atlantic Alliance is now accentuated by two dominant economic and technological trends in defense markets. First, defense spending is declining substantially worldwide in response to the vastly changed geopolitical climate and will no longer support the previous levels of defense production. Second, the costs of developing advanced weaponry are continuing to increase, while the sources of relevant technologies are becoming increasingly dispersed among the advanced industrialized nations. These two factors are unlikely to be reversed, and they will push companies to consolidate their positions while seeking increased access to foreign markets and technologies.

Declining defense spending makes it more difficult to procure sufficient numbers of modern weapons to reach economically efficient rates of production. Slower production rates and limited domestic markets in turn drive up the unit costs of new weapons, further reducing the number of systems that can be purchased. This economic fact has long influenced European defense programs, forcing European countries at various times to emphasize arms exports, transnational codevelopment and coproduction, mergers, and, in many cases, less than optimal performance characteristics for new weapons in order to hold down technology development and procurement costs.

As the United States reduces its own military spending, American defense companies are beginning to face many of these same pressures, pushing them toward greater emphasis on national and international cooperation and consolidation. Teaming arrangements for such programs as the F-22 Superstar fighter, the RAH-66 Comanche helicopter, and the space-based Follow-on Early Warning System demonstrate the growing trend toward technology-pooling and risk-sharing in sophisticated military programs. Moveover, the involvement of a number of European defense manufacturers in important US defense development efforts, such as the Theater High-Altitude Air Defense (THAAD) missile, the Terminally-Guided Warhead for the Multiple-Launch Rocket System, and the Mobile Subscriber Equipment (MSE) communications system, demonstrates the willingness of American manufacturers to seek out foreign technical expertise.[7]

This latter phenomenon reflects the fact that the sources of advanced military technologies have become more diffuse. The United States is no longer the only producer of militarily significant high-technology equipment and technologies. As a result of substantial R&D spending, European defense companies in many cases have joined US manufacturers on the technological front lines. Similarly, heavy Japanese investment in civilian research and development has yielded important dual-use technologies with many applications in advanced military weapon systems. While the United States will likely retain its overall technological leadership given its much larger defense budgets, Japan and Europe have emerged as leaders in specific technical fields. Applying their expertise to defense could yield substantial military benefits for both Europeans and Americans.

Led by cross-border cooperative agreements and mergers in Europe, the West's defense industries are becoming increasingly integrated into a single defense industrial base. Because of its much smaller domestic defense market—one-third that of the United States—Europe's major defense companies consolidated earlier than those of the United States. Much of this restructuring has taken place at the national level; between 1985 and 1990, European defense and aerospace firms were involved in roughly 220 mergers and acquisitions with other national firms.[8] Figures

---

7. For example, Hughes Aircraft has placed increased emphasis on international cooperation. Carol Reed, "Hughes: No Longer Business As Usual," *Janes Defense Weekly*, August 1, 1992, 27, 30.
8. Aerospace Industries Association, *The US Aerospace Industry in the 1990s: A Global Perspective* (Washington, D.C.: AIA, Sept. 1991), 49-50.

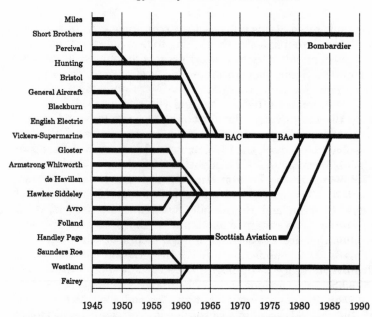

Figure 5.1. Consolidation of UK Military Aircraft Manufacturers.

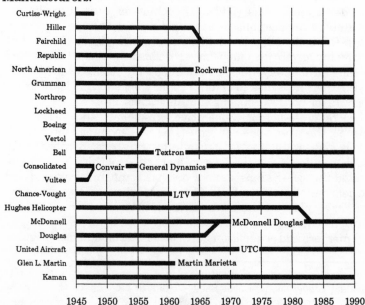

Figure 5.2. Consolidation of US Military Aircraft Manufacturers.

5.1 and 5.2 illustrate the differing rates at which consolidation has taken place among British and US military aircraft producers. Britain had moved from having 19 producers of military aircraft following World War II to just two in 1990—British Aerospace for fixed-wing aircraft and Westland for helicopters. In contrast, by 1992 the United States still supported 10 military aircraft producers, half as many as existed in 1945.[9]

In addition to consolidation at the national level, European defense firms have moved to merge operations across borders. During the period 1985 to 1990, roughly 40 transnational mergers and acquisitions took place involving defense companies from different European nations. More recently, several major mergers have taken place, such as the merger of the helicopter operations of France's Aerospatiale and Germany's Messerschmitt-Bölkow-Blohm, and the takeover of the UK's Plessy by Britain's General Electric Corporation (GEC) and Siemens of Germany.

European nations have also moved to collaborate on the development of major weapon systems. The European Fighter Aircraft program, the EUCLID research effort, the Future Surface-to-Air Family of missiles (FSAF) development program, and the recently announced Anglo-French plan to design a new naval frigate highlight the ongoing trend toward integration of European defense industries across national boundaries. These multinational development projects feature extensive collaboration between companies, either through strategic alliances or cross-border subcontracting arrangements. Despite the inherent difficulties involved in such efforts, rising R&D costs and declining markets have dictated the expansion of these transnational efforts.

Finally, European firms have invested in US defense firms either as majority owners or minority stakeholders. Indeed, European investment in America's defense industrial base has a long history—Aerospatiale's purchase of Vought Helicopters in 1974, Schlumberger's buyout of Fairchild-Weston in 1979, GEC's acquisition of Cincinnati Electronics in 1987, Matra's purchase of Fairchild Space and Defense and CAE's acquisition of Link Flight Simulation in 1988, British Aerospace's investment in Reflectone in 1989, and Siemens' buyout of Cardion Electronics in 1990.[10] On other occasions, European firms have taken minority positions in joint ventures with US defense companies, such as the

9. Martin J. Bollinger, *Consolidation in Aerospace/Defense*, 4.
10. "Thomson-CSF and City of Dallas Plan to Fight Back on LTV Buyout," *Defense Marketing News*, May 29, 1992, 3.

forty-nine percent stake taken by Aerospatiale, Alenia, and Alcatel in Space Systems/Loral.

Of course, the strong negative US reaction to Thomson-CSF's unsuccessful bid for the missile division of the LTV Corporation in 1992 placed a chill on European direct investment in major US defense companies. In fact, the Byrd amendment to the 1993 Defense Authorization Bill, named for West Virginia Senator Robert Byrd (D-WV), expressly forbade the sale of any US defense contractor that had received $500 million or more in DOD or DOE contracts.[11] While the negative congressional response to the Thomson-CSF bid will seriously constrain the form by which future transatlantic consolidation takes place, the impetus for further cutbacks in Western defense overcapacity will remain strong so long as defense budgets to fall and defense R&D costs continue their steady rise.

Despite American outrage at the Thomson-CSF case, US defense companies have by no means been passive as these relations have formed in Europe. Although generally cautious about direct investment in Europe because of the still-fragmented nature of its defense industry, many US aerospace and defense firms have nevertheless begun to establish European subsidiaries and purchase overseas allies. For example, between 1985 and 1990, US companies were merged with, or took over, 84 European aerospace companies.[12] Table 5.1 lists a select number of US aerospace/defense company subsidiaries and partly owned affiliates in Europe.

For the most part, however, US defense companies have relied on transatlantic alliances with European firms as the primary vehicle for gaining market access and sharing new technologies. According to former Deputy Secretary of Defense Atwood, "These alliances enable us to share research and development costs with our allies, and in so doing, free up vital national resources for other pressing problems. We need to stimulate more cooperation, not less."[13] Prompted in part by the prospect of a united Euro-

---

11. US Congress, 102d Congress, 2d Session, *National Defense Authorization Act for Fiscal Year 1993: Conference Report* (Report 102-966) (Washington, D.C.: US Government Printing Office, October 1, 1992), 153-154.
12. Aerospace Industries Association, *The US Aerospace Industry in the 1990s*, 49-50.
13. Donald Atwood, Deputy Secretary of Defense, "Speech to the National Security Industry Associations," July 17, 1989, cited in Paul R. Sullivan, "Strategies for Global Aerospace Companies," mimeograph, Global Partners, Boston, Mass., November 20, 1990, 12.

Table 5.1. European Subsidiaries and Affiliates of Selected US Defense Companies.

	European Subsidiaries	**Partly Owned Affiliates**
Allied Signal	United Kingdom (1), Germany (5), France (1), Spain (1), Switzerland (1), Ireland (2)	
General Dynamics	Turkey (1)	Turkey (1)
General Electric	Germany (1), France (1)	Germany (1), France (1)
GM Hughes	United Kingdon (2), Germany (2), Spain (1)	Germany (2)
Honeywell	United Kingdon (1), Germany (6)	
Litton	Germany (1), France (1), Italy (1)	
Lockheed	United Kingdom (1)	United Kingdom (1)
Raytheon	United Kingdom (1)	
Rockwell	United Kindom (1), Germany (2), France (2)	
Textron	United Kingdom (1), Germany (1)	
United Technologies	Germany (1), Italy (1), Netherlands (1)	

Source: Barry Miller, "Global Links in the Aerospace Industry, *Interavia Aerospace Review*, June 1991, p.15.

pean arms market, as well as by specific technological opportunities offered through collaboration with West European defense companies, these agreements have proliferated to the point where virtually every major US prime contractor has established a network of subsidiaries, joint ventures, marketing arrangements, and strategic alliances with their European counterparts.

Table 5.2 highlights the extent of transatlantic alliances involving high-technology defense manufacturers. For example, Lockheed and Aerospatiale, as well as General Dynamics and British Aerospace, have penned agreements to cooperate on a broad range of future projects. France's Matra is working with McDonnell Douglas and Lockheed to market missile products in the United States and around the world. Lockheed is also working with Thorn EMI on Air Force bomb fuses, Thomson-Sintra on the AN/AQS-934 acoustic signal processor, and Aermacchi in a bid for the Joint Primary Aircraft Training System. MBB is working with Rockwell International on the X-31 experimental fighter aircraft, and with Boeing/Sikorsky on the RAH-66

Table 5.2. Selected US-European Defense Industrial
Cooperative Arrangements, 1985-1991.

US Firm	Foreign Participant	Product
1989		
Bell-Boeing	British Aerospace (UK), Dornier (FRG), Aeritalia (It)	Possible marketing of V-22 tilt-rotor aircraft
Boeing	Thomson (Fr)	SDI free electron laser
DARPA	DGA (Fr)	Research on reactive armor
Ensign Bickford	British Aerospace/Royal Ordnance (UK)	Explosive products
General Electric	Ferranti (UK)	High-altitude reconnaissance system
General Electric	GEC Ruston (UK)	T-700 engines (Blackhawk)
Hercules Aerospace	BAT (It)	Composite structures
Hewlett-Packard	Dassault (Fr)	Antenna test equipment
Hughes-E-Systems	MBB (FRG)	Arms verification technology
Hughes-Lockheed	Aermacchi (It)	PATS bid
Hughes-Raytheon	MBB (FRG)	AMRAAM production
IBM	Siemens (FRG)	64 megabit chip
ITT	TRT (Fr)	US Air Force radio altimeter bid
Lockheed	Aerospatiale (Fr)	Euroflag
Lockheed	Aerospatiale (Fr)	Long-term MOU (commercial)
LTV	Phillips, HSA (Nd)	FAADS bid
LTV	SEP (Fr), AEG (FRG)	ERINT missile
Martin Marietta	Dowty (UK)	ALFS dipping sonar
McDonnell Douglas	Matra (Fr)	Missile/munitions marketing
McDonnell Douglas	Westland (UK)	Apache AH-64 attack helicopter
McDonnell Douglas	Sogitec (Fr)	Mission planning system
Motorola	Thomson (Fr)	88000/RISC technology exchange
Nasco	Ficantier (Sp)	Shipbuilding and design
Pratt & Whitney	Aeritalia (It)	Engines
Pratt & Whitney	Airmotive Ireland (Ir)	Test engine cases
Pratt & Whitney	Nordam (UK)	JT8/Boeing 737
Raytheon	Thomas Sintra (Fr)	SQQ-32 sonar

Table 5.2. Selected US-European Defense Industrial
Cooperative Arrangements (continued).

US Firm	Foreign Participant	Product
Raytheon-Martin Marietta	MBB (FRG), ERIA (Sp), Bristol (UK), Fokker (Nd), Plessey (UK)	NAAWS bid
Sundstrand	Labinal (FR)	Auxiliary power system
Teledyne	Fokker (Nd)	F-50 aircraft
Thiokol	British Aerospace (UK)	Rocket propellant
Texas Instrument	Thomson (Fr)	Obstacle evasion system (ROMEO)
Unisys	Westland (UK), Agusta (It)	EH101 sales (pending)
Westinghouse	Dassault (Fr)	Microprocessor coproduction
1990		
Beech Aircraft	Pilatus (Sz)	PC-9 trainer for JPATS program
Brunswick Corp.	Aarding BV (Nd)	Composite aerospace products
Chrysler Technologies Corp's Airborne Systems (CTAS)	Aeritalia (It)	G222 turboprop for C-27A
GE Aerospace	GIA (Fr)	Helicopter turreted gun systems
GE Aerospace	Thomson (Fr), Thorn EMI (UK), Siemens	Advanced counter-battery radar
GE Astro-Space	Deutsche Aerospace (FRG)	ASTRA-1C satellite
General Electric	SNECMA (Fr)	CFM56 series turbofan
General Electric	SNECMA (Fr)	CF6-80E1 engine
General Electric Aerospace	GIAT (Fr)	MOU helicopter gun turret
General Electric	SNECMA (Fr)	GE90 commercial turbofan
E-Systems	Elekluft, Burkhart Grob Luft und Raumfahrt, Compangy KG, MBB (FRG)	Support for Egrett aircraft
Evans & Sutherland Simulation Division	Telefunken (FRG)	ESIG-1000 simulators
General Dynamics	British Aerospace (UK)	M1A2 turret and M119 light howitzer
Lockheed	Thorn EMI Electronics (UK)	BLU109B bomb fuses

Table 5.2. Selected US-European Defense Industrial
Cooperative Arrangements (continued).

US Firm	Foreign Participant	Product
Westinghouse Electric	Pilatus Britten-Norman (UK)	Fit Turbine Islander aircraft with APG-66 radar and WF-360 electro-optical system
Rockwell	MBB (FRG)	JPATS
1991		
ARINC Research Corp.	Alenia (It)	Vessel traffic system
Boeing	Thomson (Fr)	MOU defense and space technologies
Hughes Network Systems	Swedish Telecom (Sw), PTT Telecom Netherlands (Nd)	Satellite hub and remote earth stations
IBM	Westland (UK)	EH-1-101 Merlin helicopter
Lockheed Sanders	Matra (Fr)	MOU to produce air defense systems
Lockheed	Marshall of Cambridge (UK)	MOU to develop L-1011 TriStar freighter
LTV-IBM-LHTEC	Aerospatiale (Fr)	Panther 800 helicopter
McDonnell Douglas	British Aerospace (UK)	T-45 Goshawk
Raytheon	Thomson-CSF (Fr)	TSM 2022 Sonar for export to Egypt
Alliant Techsystems	Ferranti (UK)	Land mines
Alliant Techsystems	Giat (Fr)	MOU for ammunition and precision weapons
Alliant Techsystems	Honeywell Europe (Bel)	Marketing support agreement
Alliant Techsystems	Raufoss (Nor)	Air-to-air and air-to-ground ammo
Boeing	Thomson (Fr)	MOU for defense and aerospace marketing
Control Data	Thomson (Fr)	MOU for joint marketing
E-Systems-Hughes	Deutsche Aerospace, Elefkluf, Grob (FRG)	Egret II high-altitude platform
GE Astro Space Division	Marconi Space Systems (UK)	Satellites for INMARSAT Council
Lockheed Sanders	Matra (Fr)	MOU for Mistral and P-STAR
Martin Marietta	Computing Devices Ltd. (UK)	Airborne reconnaissance equipment

Table 5.2. Selected US-European Defense Industrial Cooperative Arrangements (continued).

US Firms	Foreign Participant	Product
Raytheon	Deutsche Aerospace (FRG)	Patriot, Hawk, and other missiles
Titan	Ericsson (Sw)	GBS, Giraffe
TRW	Thomson (Fr)	Advanced IFF for F-16 upgrade proposal
Westinghouse	Alcatel (Fr), Reseux (Fr), Elektronik-System (FRG), Italtel (It), Logica (UK), Racal (UK)	Air-Space Management Systems, part of NATO's ACCS

Source: *Defense News, Janes Defense Week, Aviation Week and Space Technology, Aerospace Daily, Defense Daily,* Office of Technology Assessment, *Global Arms Trade* (Washington, D.C.: OTA, 1991), 14-15.

Comanche attack helicopter. Over the past several years, Martin Marietta has joined with any number of foreign firms, including Thomson-CSF on the MLRS terminally guided warhead, Dowty of the UK for the ALFS dipping sonar, and MBB, AEG Telefunken, and Siemens on an advanced version of the Patriot surface-to-air missile.

These agreements vary considerably in terms of their scope and duration. Some, such as the Lockheed/Matra arrangement, are slightly more than marketing agreements, involving little in the way of direct transfers of technology. Other relationships are more elaborate, involving considerable technology sharing, codevelopment and coproduction. All major subcontracting commitments, such as LTV's development of the VT-1 for Thomson-CSF, codevelopment programs, such as the MLRS terminally guided warhead, and strategic alliances, such as that between Lockheed and Aerospatiale, carry with them the potential for extensive technology sharing. In fact, according to a recent North Atlantic Council group examining Alliance defense trade, "It is clear that the flow of technology is the dominant factor in industry-to-industry collaboration."[14] Technology sharing between the United States and its European allies is taking on a regular and increasing pace. In fact, the NATO Council of National Armament Directors' (CNAD) "code-of-conduct" statements covering the treatment

14. North Atlantic Council, "Conference of National Armaments Directors Group on NATO Defence Trade: Key Areas Affecting Defence Trade Among the Allies," mimeograph, January 17, 1992, 2.

of allied defense industries stresses the need to increase technology sharing so as to improve the West's military capabilities and better rationalize defense production.

The Context for Military R&D Policy

Declining defense spending, the shifting relationship between military and civilian technologies, and the globalization of Western defense industries all have significant implications for the future of defense research in the United States. Moreover, none of these trends is likely to be reversed within the foreseeable future. Specific threats to America's security and its interests will no doubt persist. However, the chance that a new threat will emerge comparable to the one once posed by the Soviet Union is remote. Nor should the United States expect to restore the ahistorical economic and technological dominance over other industrialized nations that it enjoyed after World War II. The accelerating pace of commercial technological change and the important contribution now made by foreign firms to that change ensures that US military technology will never again assume the preeminent role it once did. Clearly, while military research may make occasional contributions to the broader economy, it will be much less important to the nation's welfare than it once was.

The task for military planners and policymakers is to manage these challenges rather than try to reverse them. The United States must learn to balance military requirements against concerns about cost, vulnerability to foreign dependencies, and national independence. Despite continued insistence by many that the United States must maintain a technological edge over all potential rivals, the pace of military innovation will most likely slow as US defense budgets decline and the urgency of the cold war wanes. Trends in technology will continue to offer opportunities to increase the effectiveness of US forces, but to exploit these opportunities the US military will have to confront new problems stemming from the increasing globalization of the world's technical resources. Moreover, rapid commercial advances across a wide spectrum of technologies portend the decline of the DOD as a driving force behind technological progress.

Trends in Technology

Three major trends define the technological challenges confronting the US defense community: (1) the widening divergence of military and commercial technologies; (2) the growing importance of commercial technologies in military systems; and (3) the increasing dependence of US weapon systems on foreign technologies and components.

Divergence of Military and Civilian Technologies

Defense research has been viewed as an engine of economic growth in the United States during much of the postwar period. Heavy defense R&D spending during the 1940s and 1950s yielded significant spin-offs to the commercial economy. This funding allowed the United States to develop industries that would go on to dominate the global market. IBM, Wang, Digital Equipment, Control Data, and Cray Research all received significant boosts from military research on digital computing during the 1950s. In fact, during those years, between 75 to 80 percent of all US R&D on computing was supplied by the military.[15] Defense R&D played a significant role in the development of a number of other commercial technologies as well, including fiber optics, jet aircraft, nuclear power, and satellite communications.

In contrast, more recent defense research efforts seem to have yielded fewer commercial rewards. In part, the reduced importance of defense R&D to the commercial economy may be simply a product of its relative decline vis-à-vis private R&D spending. In 1960, half of all R&D in the United States was funded by the Pentagon. By 1990, the defense share had fallen to one-third. Over the same period, DOD's share of worldwide R&D funding fell from one-third to one-sixth.[16]

The declining relative size of the US defense research investment has been compounded by two additional developments. First, a growing portion of military research is focused on meeting requirements so uniquely military that their applicability to commercial products is negligible. Second, administrative and regulatory procedures imposed on defense contractors and military laboratories has discouraged the transfer of research results to the commercial marketplace. Combined, these two conditions have tended to isolate military research activities—as well as the companies, government agencies, scientists and engineers so involved—from the larger commercial market.

Inevitably, military research addresses many problems that bear little relevance to the commercial marketplace. The chance

15. Kenneth Flamm, *Creating the Computer* (Washington, D.C.: The Brookings Institution, 1988), 29-79.
16. National Science Foundation, *National Patterns of R&D Resources: 1990*, 55.

that investments in signature-reduction ("stealth") technologies, for example, or electronic countermeasures, or radiation-hardening technologies will result in significant commercial spin-offs is remote. Since World War II, commercial spin-offs of military research have declined as the generic similarity of military and civilian systems has diminished. Postwar investments in jet aircraft and strategic bombers had greater relevance to the civilian aircraft industry than do the technologies embodied in the airframes of advanced tactical fighters. Similarly, today's military satellite communications requirements bear little resemblance to those for commercial satellites. As the DOD moves to develop increasingly unique weapons platforms and components, the connection between defense and civil research agendas becomes more tenuous.

Even when DOD pursues "dual-use" technologies, it may do so in a manner that diminishes the usefulness of the research to the private sector. The ten-year Very High Speed Integrated Circuit program was initiated with the expectation that it would yield considerable commercial benefits. However, the declining importance of the military market to the commercial microelectronics industry, the slow military development process, and DOD's emphasis on applied research and development undermined potential commercial spin-offs from the effort.[17] In pursuing a particular line of research, military program managers may make trade-offs between cost and performance to achieve certain characteristics, such as ruggedness and resistance to countermeasures, that bear little relevance to the commercial market. Moreover, the military's traditional focus on performance over cost often discourages research on cost-reduction strategies and innovations in manufacturing processes necessary for commercial market success. Finally, the regulatory environment surrounding all of DOD's work discourages firms from integrating their military and civilian research operations. This administrative and organization separation consequently reduces opportunities to share technological breakthroughs across corporate lines.

As will be discussed later, there are opportunities to increase the commercial returns from defense R&D by addressing the unnecessary administrative burdens placed on military research. However, the declining relative significance of military R&D

---

17. David C. Mowery and Nathan Rosenberg, *Technology and the Pursuit of Economic Growth* (New York: Cambridge University Press, 1989), 147-150.

spending and its highly specialized focus will place unavoidable limits on future commercial spin-offs from defense research. Despite this, research on defense-specific technologies will continue to be necessary so long as they contribute to the nation's security. In fact, given smaller US defense budgets, it is critical that DOD focus its energies on those defense technologies that offer the greatest military payoffs.

Defense Dependence on Commercial Technologies

While DOD acquisition regulations discourage the easy transfer of defense technologies to civilian applications, they also forestall the application of advanced commercial technologies to military projects. As a result, the costs of maintaining the barriers between the defense and commercial technology sectors promise to increase substantially in the years ahead as commercial research spending outstrips DOD's efforts.

Defense R&D spending will likely remain stagnant at a time when worldwide private research and development investment will continue to grow substantially. Already, private R&D spending in the United States has grown faster and more consistently than that of the federal government for several decades. Moreover, private R&D expenditures overseas have also increased significantly. In Japan, for example, annual private R&D spending exceeds the country's *entire* defense budget; in absolute terms, privately funded nondefense R&D in Japan in 1988 was 88 percent of *total* US defense R&D spending.

Even if one assumes that current trends in defense spending will be reversed at some point, defense R&D will continue to be overshadowed by heavy private investment in commercial R&D around the world. For example, for the five years between 1987 and 1991, DOD spent approximately two billion dollars on research on semiconductors and microelectronics. Meanwhile, in 1989 alone, the top five US and top five Japanese merchant semiconductor manufacturers spent roughly $4 billion on R&D.[18]

While much of this private investment is directed toward technologies that may have little relevance for military forces, the overlap between commercial and military technologies is growing. Already, military systems are dependent on advanced micro-

---

18. Department of Defense, *Critical Technologies Report* (Washington, D.C.: US Department of Defense, May 1, 1991), 1-10; National Advisory Committee on Semiconductors, *Toward a National Semiconductor Strategy* (Arlington, VA: National Advisory Committee on Semiconductors, February 1991), 9.

electronics and display technologies whose primary customers are in the private market. Whereas military R&D pioneered technology development in these fields, today it plays a relatively minor role. Moreover, despite huge DOD purchases, the commercial market will be the prime technology mover for future technical developments. For example, in 1965, the US military consumed roughly 72 percent of all integrated circuits produced in the United States. By 1990, military consumption accounted for just eight percent of the US total.[19] With its more intense competition, larger production volumes, and higher investment levels, the commercial microelectronics market is destined to advance more rapidly than can DOD's own electronics programs.

As a result, the Defense Department is increasingly trying to integrate existing commercial products and technologies into its military systems. The services have already turned to commercial computers to satisfy many of their computing needs. For example, the incorporation of readily available laptop personal computers into existing data processing, logistics, and command and control networks has yielded substantial military returns. Even the most complex military systems are now derived from commercial technologies. For example, the Army's Mobile Subscriber Equipment tactical communications network was adapted from commercial cellular telephone technologies. Indeed, the Army's 30-year plan for information systems specifically emphasizes greater use of commercial, off-the-shelf equipment by "militarizing" the container rather than the computer itself.[20]

The trend toward more rapid technological progress in commercial markets is likely to accelerate over the coming decade. Consequently, the military will become increasingly dependent on commercial markets to provide the technologies it believes are crucial to tomorrow's military forces. Of the 21 technologies listed in the 1991 DOD Critical Technologies plan, 15 were identified as having significant commercial applications, including high performance computing, composite materials, biotechnology, and software engineering, among others. Exploiting commercial market developments will require that DOD become adept at purchasing commercial products and increase its emphasis on designing

---

19. John Alic, et al., *Beyond Spinoff: Military and Commercial Technologies in a Changing World* (Boston, Mass.: Harvard Business School Press, 1992), 260.
20. "Army Information Systems Plan Targets Off-the-Shelf Hardware," *Defense Electronics*, May 1991, 8.

its systems around commercially available technologies and processes.

Global Sourcing and Foreign Dependence

In recent years, the national security consequences of increased DOD use of foreign-supplied components has received considerable attention.[21] In particular, observers fear that dependence on foreign suppliers could result in disruption or threats of disruption of critical defense technologies during crises or wartime, thereby preventing the US military from obtaining necessary military equipment and constraining the US military's freedom of action. Such vulnerability to interruptions in supply could, theoretically, place the United States at the mercy of foreign governments or companies, or make it vulnerable to foreign political disturbances, thereby undermining American military capabilities and national security.

DOD and its contractors purchase foreign products and subcomponents for a variety of reasons. In the past, foreign participation in US defense programs and American cooperation on joint weapon development efforts have been undertaken for political, military, and economic reasons.[22] The Nunn Amendment programs, as well as the Foreign Comparative Testing Program, are specifically geared to increase defense cooperation, interoperability, and cost-effectiveness by encouraging US purchases of foreign military hardware. In these cases, foreign sourcing is accepted as a cost for achieving other objectives. For their part, defense companies and their subcontractors also make use of foreign defense technologies to meet performance and cost goals that cannot be satisfied by US-owned or US-based companies. Occasionally, defense contractors also purchase foreign components to fulfill offset agreements made in connection with foreign military sales.

US imports of complete weapon systems and defense-specific components have been relatively limited, however. Of greater

---

21. On this issue, see Defense Science Board, *Report of the Task Force on Defense Semiconductor Dependency* (Washington, D.C.: US Department of Defense, December 1986); Theodore Moran, "The Globalization of American Defense Industries," *International Security* (Summer 1990): 57-99; Ethen B. Kapstein, "Losing Control—National Security and the Global Economy," *The National Interest* (Winter 1989-90), 85-90.
22. See US Congress, Office of Technology Assessment, *Arming Our Allies: Cooperation and Competition in Defense Technology* (Washington, D.C.: US Government Printing Office, 1990).

concern for many is the US dependence on foreign sources for an increasing range of commercial or "dual-use" technologies. However, despite persistent reports of US foreign dependence, the Department of Defense has developed no consistent means to measure the phenomena.[23] In its 1991 report on the US defense industrial base, the Defense Department acknowledged both the importance of foreign sourcing and its inability to thoroughly track its reliance on foreign producers:

> DOD purchases thousands of materials, parts, components and finished goods from foreign manufacturers, just as other governments purchase such items from the United States. Since these purchases involve numerous weapon systems, thousands of contractors and subcontractors, and millions of parts and components, comprehensive information on foreign sourced items is not routinely available to DOD....By the time the product is embedded in a DOD weapon system, it has become very cumbersome and costly to monitor all of the original sources of the technology and product.[24]

In general, restrictive legislation (e.g., "Buy American" provisions) has prevented significant foreign purchases at the prime contractor or major system level. However, as one moves down through the ranks of the sub-tier suppliers, these regulations have less and less effect. In these cases, the final product may be produced by a US-based company, but many of the components may be supplied from or assembled overseas. For example, a Department of Commerce study of three US Navy systems identified 14,000 participating contractors and estimated that from 12 to 20 percent of all components were foreign sourced. Other studies have cited Dynamic Random Access Memory (DRAM) semiconductors, flat-panel displays, precision optics, ball bearings, and advanced machine tools as examples of DOD's dependence on foreign suppliers.[25] As of yet, however, no comprehensive

---

23. See US Congress, General Accounting Office, *Industrial Base: Significance of DOD's Foreign Dependence* (Washington, D.C.: US General Accounting Office, January 1991).

24. Undersecretary of Defense (Acquisition) and Assistant Secretary of Defense (Production and Logistics), *Report to the Congress on the Defense Industrial Base* (Washington, D.C.: US Department of Defense, November 1991), 4-3.

25. See, for example, Defense Science Board, *Report of the Task Force on Defense Semiconductor Dependency*; The Analytic Sciences Corporation, *Foreign Vulnerability of Critical Industries* (Arlington, Virginia: The Analytic Sciences Corporation, March 1, 1990); Ethan B. Kapstein, "Losing Control," *National Interest*; and Theodore H. Moran, "The

database has been developed to track this information, and DOD officials have tended to discount the potential threat posed by foreign sourcing.[26]

At the same time, attempts to counteract foreign sourcing create their own dilemmas. For example, legislative requirements that components be purchased domestically run counter to the dominant trends in many high-technology industries. In order to prosper in a global economy, American high-technology manufacturers must diversify their own technical resources in order to better incorporate foreign technologies into their own products. Insisting that US computer manufacturers certify that their products are domestically produced would not only impose substantial administrative costs, but would also virtually guarantee that no commercially competitive firms would contract with DOD. Indeed, even establishing requirements to identify the ultimate sources for a product's component parts in order to systematically track DOD's use of foreign equipment would constitute a significant disincentive for non defense firms to sell to the government.

Whatever the extent, foreign sourcing carries potential risks and benefits for the United States. The economic benefits—access to new technologies, lower costs, better performance—are obvious. These economic benefits in turn can produce military payoffs—foreign sourcing permits the United States to purchase more capable systems in greater numbers than would be possible under autarkic conditions. Even when such foreign purchases take place in the most administratively burdensome context—as part of formal international collaborative programs—the economic rewards can be substantial. According to a 1992 Defense Inspector General report, the United States saved an estimated $141 million through its participation in 20 cooperative programs. This represented about 11 percent of the total cost of these development efforts.[27]

In contrast, evaluating the risks of foreign sourcing is a more subjective undertaking, depending critically on a variety of assumptions about future technological, political, and military developments. Even in cases of complete foreign dependence, the

---

Globalization of American Defense Industries."

26. According to DOD, "Although foreign vulnerabilities are potentially of great concern to DOD, they represent an exceedingly small proportion that are foreign sourced today." Undersecretary of Defense (Acquisition), *The Defense Industrial Base*, 4-4.

27. "DOD Inspector General Estimates International Collaboration Savings," *Aerospace Daily*, November 20, 1992, 280.

potential for harm to US national security interests is uncertain. Should foreign suppliers cooperate fully with the United States, then dependence poses little problem. On the other hand, if foreign producers are uncooperative and alternative sources for key components are unavailable, the consequences could be severe.

DOD divides these levels of dependency into three broad categories: (1) foreign sourcing; (2) foreign dependency; and (3) foreign vulnerability. According to DOD, "Foreign sourcing is a fact of life" and involves the purchase of foreign components to meet cost, performance, availability, or quality requirements which existing domestic suppliers cannot satisfy.[28] Foreign dependency refers to purchases of foreign components that are not available from US- or Canada-based producers. Such cases are of greater concern, and the risks of foreign dependency are assessed on the basis of the importance of the item, the likelihood of disruptions in supply, the availability of alternatives, and the time it would take to develop domestic production capability. Finally, foreign vulnerability refers to cases where "the loss of access to a single foreign source supplier would impair the nation's capability to field a critical weapon system or otherwise endanger national security."[29]

These three situations in turn involve a range of risks that fall into two broad categories: surge/mobilization risks and technology base and reconstitution considerations.[30] Surge and mobilization vulnerabilities are relatively short-term, in that they may constrain American freedom of action for a period of a few months to a few years. Foreign cutoffs or restrictions of supply could occur for a variety of political, economic, or logistical reasons. At the extreme, the United States could be engaged in a direct conflict with the supplying nation, or the supplying nation could be captured by America's adversary, making trade impossible. Less severely, foreign governments might disagree with US policy, restricting exports to the United States either as a means of protest or in an attempt to influence the US position. Even if foreign governments support US policies, foreign domestic political conditions and foreign policy considerations could still disrupt

---

28. Undersecretary of Defense (Acquisition), *The Defense Industrial Base*, 4-3.
29. Undersecretary of Defense, *The Defense Industrial Base*, 4-4.
30. National Defense University Report, as cited in US General Accounting Office, *Industrial Base: Significance of DOD's Foreign Dependence*, 12-13.

supplies during a crisis. Japanese pacifism, or civil unrest in South Korea, might make exports to the United States politically or even physically impossible. Likewise, European dependence on oil from the Arab states may make it diplomatically impossible for some governments to support US policy toward Israel during a crisis.

Finally, even barring such political conflicts, foreign suppliers can be less reliable than US-based manufacturers. Foreign firms may be far less willing to grant the American military priority over its other customers, regardless of whether foreign governments support US policy. Whereas the Defense Production Act of 1950 authorizes the president to compel domestic firms to supply necessary defense goods during a national emergency, the United States has no such influence over suppliers abroad.[31]

In the event of a crisis, a disruption in supply of critical foreign-sourced components could affect the ability of the United States to replace or repair its military equipment. While small military confrontations could likely be fought with existing US stockpiles of weapons even after substantial cuts in military inventories, maintaining US combat capabilities during larger contingencies could require surge production to replace critical spare parts and expendable systems.[32] Under such circumstances, foreign supply disruptions could raise costs and diminish US capabilities.

At a minimum, a cutoff might force the United States to undertake a costly search for alternative sources, either domestically or abroad. Aside from locating new producers, other responses might include cannibalizing military and civilian equipment or redesigning weapon systems to allow the use of close substitutes. If alternatives could not be found, the United States might even decide to establish or convert domestic produc-

---

31. These problems could affect both foreign firms and US-owned subsidiaries abroad equally. Indeed, some US-based multinationals may pursue their own interests during a crisis. As one Fortune 500 executive commented, "The United States does not have an automatic call on our resources. There is no mindset that puts this country first." Louis Uchitelle, "US Businesses Loosen Link to Mother Country," *The New York Times*, May 21, 1989, A-1.

32. Additional purchases and production of specific items is likely in any conflict. Prior to the Gulf War, for example, the United States purchased a large number of commercial GPS receivers and accelerated production of a range of defense items from desert boots to electron tubes to measurement devices. See Aerospace Education Foundation, *Lifeline Adrift: The Defense Industrial Base in the 1990s* (Washington, D.C.: Air Force Association, September 1991), 13-15.

tion capacity should a particular item be deemed important enough to warrant the expense. In all cases, the critical dimension is time: How long would it take for the United States to establish new suppliers for the needed component? If this lead time exceeds the time necessary for the production of other components, then the foreign-supplied defense component becomes the weakest link in the chain. If, however, other components take longer to fabricate, then they serve to constrain surge production more than the foreign-sourced goods.

If alternative suppliers are impossible to locate before existing stockpiles are exhausted, US military capabilities could be affected. In theory, the consequences could range from the merely annoying to the catastrophic. US military forces might be able to reorient their tactics, employing other weapon systems and equipment to accomplish the same mission. However, more nightmarish and implausible scenarios might entail higher levels of US casualties, or even defeat, as the ultimate outcome of foreign supply disruptions.

In the aftermath of the cold war, however, the task of preparing for likely contingencies while ensuring that the US military has access to foreign technologies is relatively modest. Few obvious security threats remain that would severely tax the ability of the armed forces to respond with existing weapon stocks. Even as US forces decline in number, their ability to engage in small-scale operations would not appear to be vulnerable to foreign cutoffs of key technologies or components. Moreover, as the war against Iraq demonstrated, future large-scale US military interventions are likely to be undertaken in cooperation with the rest of the industrialized world (i.e., Europe and Japan), helping to ensure that the United States has access to critical supplies from these nations.

However, at some point in the future, the United States may be faced with new security threats which demand that it reconstitute large military forces. The perceived decline of heavy US manufacturing and certain high-technology industries raises obvious concerns that the United States could one day find that it no longer has the defense technology base necessary to support its national security strategy. The contraction of US defense industries, combined with foreign penetration of important dual-use markets, could theoretically complicate efforts to purchase requisite weapon systems and components. Moreover, declining military procurement spending will result in a loss of defense manufacturing and R&D capacity. Absent costly programs to sustain this capacity through low-rate production or direct subsidies, any future military build-up will likely rely even more extensively on harnessing the production capabilities of the commercial market. To the extent that foreign firms continue their penetration of the US market, the United States could find itself even more dependent on foreign producers. If foreign producers are unwilling to sell to the US military, or limit DOD's access to the latest technologies, this dependence might prevent the United States from obtaining the components and materials deemed necessary for fielding a technologically superior force.

While such developments are possible, there are strong reasons to suggest that the United States would find the necessary resources to overcome such obstacles should they arise. Most importantly, the rise of a security threat sufficient to require the United States to reconstitute its military forces would take a considerable amount of time, thereby offering sufficient warning to allow the country to reconstruct military production facilities as necessary. Moreover, a complete cutoff from all or even most advanced foreign technologies is highly unlikely. In effect, this would require a sharp break with both Europe and Japan, our closest allies, and closest rivals for technological leadership.

Public Policy Questions

Although these developments are all closely related, they prompt three distinct questions: (1) Should DOD pursue strictly military technologies, or should it expand its focus to include research in important dual-use areas?; (2) How should DOD respond to its dependency on foreign technologies?; and (3) What are the technological challenges likely to be faced by US forces?

The Defense Research Agenda

Many proposals have been put forward to shift the defense research agenda toward greater support for dual-use technologies that might offer both military and economic returns.[33]

---

33. Indeed, given the military payoffs from a number of advanced, commercially viable technologies, these proposals argue that it is only appropriate that DOD participate in their development. The Bush Administration and the Pentagon generally rejected such an approach, arguing instead that as defense budgets decline, it is even more important for DOD to focus its efforts squarely on defense-specific technologies which promise significant military benefits. Funneling scarce defense dollars into dual-use technologies that would likely be developed without DOD's assistance anyway only ensures that critical, defense-specific tech-

However, President Clinton has shown much greater willingness to shift defense R&D into more commercially promising areas. Following the lead of such "dual-use" proponents as Senator Jeff Bingaman (D-NM), the President vowed to expand DOD's research agenda to promote both commercial and military competitiveness, increase the share of the federal R&D budget devoted to commercial research, and promote greater cooperation between the national laboratories and private industry.[34]

Although such a strategy may be attractive, particularly in an era of reduced international tensions, strong arguments can be made for keeping the defense R&D agenda focused on military requirements. At the very least, few would dispute the need to continue to fund research on defense-specific technologies deemed critical to the nation's security. Despite the limited commercial potential of such work, the high military returns fully justify such investments. In such cases, the relevant decision for DOD, therefore, is to weigh the costs of such research (which, as the only consumer, it will bear entirely) against its expected military payoff broadly defined (e.g. insurance against surprise, potential combat applications, etc.). This is a task with which DOD is well acquainted, even if its judgment over the years has at times appeared questionable.[35]

DOD support for dual-use technologies—technologies with both commercial and defense applications—poses a more vexing set of questions. Given the rising salience of economic objectives, many argue that DOD should invest in dual-use research such that both economic and military objectives can be met.[36]

---

nologies are underfunded.

34. William J. Clinton, "Technology for America's Economic Growth: A New Direction to Build Economic Strength," February 22, 1993. Indeed, the president signaled his intention to broaden the research agenda of DOD's vanguard research agency, the Defense Advanced Research Projects Agency (DARPA) by dropping the word "Defense" from its name.

35. Indeed, even when DOD has focused exclusively on developing military technologies, it has often encountered tremendous difficulties producing and fielding new systems. Its spotted record suggests that, given a broader mission encompassing commercial technology development, DOD would likely suffer even more setbacks. See Comptroller General of the United States, *Weapons Acquisition: A Rare Opportunity for Lasting Change* (GAO/NSIAD-93-15) (Washington, D.C.: US General Accounting Office, December 1992).

36. See, for example, Carnegie Commission on Science, Technology, and Government, *Technology and Economic Performance* (New York, NY: Carnegie Commission, September 1991), 39-41.

Arguments for and against DOD support for R&D in dual-use technologies are various, but they all address a set of key issues. The strongest argument against DOD investment in dual-use technologies is that this R&D would be conducted by private industry regardless of DOD efforts. In such cases, DOD would be spending scarce funds for technologies that it could eventually purchase from private developers, as one consumer among many. In fact, the greatest promise of expanded DOD use of commercial products is precisely its ability to reap the economic and technological benefits already enjoyed by private sector consumers. If the government spends R&D monies to promote such commercially viable technologies, it would simply substitute public funds for private, thereby transferring resources to industry without increasing the amount of militarily useful research conducted.

Even in such cases, however, early government investment could speed the development of dual-use technologies, allowing US military systems to incorporate such technologies sooner. By providing money early in the development process, some maintain that DOD could complement market investments and thereby obtain the military advantages earlier than would otherwise be possible. In such cases, DOD planners must decide whether the military advantages of faster technology development warrant government investment. The expected benefits of the technology itself should not be the criterion for making such time-driven investments, but rather the military benefits arising from more rapid introduction of a technology.

In turn, these benefits must be balanced against the risks posed by government intervention. Direct DOD involvement might actually derail a promising technology by emphasizing technical or performance considerations that are not relevant to the commercial market (as with the VHSIC project). This may hasten the pace of innovation, but result in the creation of a defense-dependent industry that is unable to exploit the benefits of commercialization. If this were the case, DOD would not only have to cover most of the development costs, but would also be forced to pay higher procurement costs than if the commercial market had developed the particular technology without government assistance. In such cases, the calculation of costs and benefits becomes one of balancing anticipated military benefits of early introduction against the risk-adjusted cost estimate of developing the technology. At the very least, this argues for minimal DOD involvement in directing or managing research on dual-use technologies in order to avoid imposing DOD requirements on what is essentially a private-sector industry.

Policies designed to speed the introduction of new technologies beg the question of whether the US military procurement system is prepared to benefit from the accelerated introduction of dual-use technologies. Given that development times for weapon systems are extraordinarily long, resulting often in the incorporation of obsolete technologies in fielded weapon systems, a more direct method of speeding the introduction of new technologies may involve revisions to the development process itself, rather than attempts to speed the introduction of dual-use technologies. While some have stressed the importance of latent technological capabilities, military technological superiority derives ultimately from the sophistication of the forces in the field, not from the technologies in the laboratories. For example, by the time the defense procurement system is able to insert Sematech-inspired sub-0.35 micron semiconductors in enough military systems to provide some measurable increase in capabilities, the commercial market would likely have long since developed more sophisticated semiconductors.

In fact, the inability of DOD to adapt new technologies rapidly may have a negative effect on US commercial competitiveness. Numerous analysts have observed that demand conditions are critical to innovation. Technically sophisticated early buyers of new products offer markets and market feedback to companies, which in turn helps them increase volume, improve quality, lower costs, and recover their initial investment more quickly. With its national security mission, DOD is theoretically in the position to justify the risks of such early demand. However, its slow acquisition process and its historical aversion to incorporating commercial, off-the-shelf products limits its effectiveness in performing such a role.

There is also the contention that some dual-use technologies might never be developed without DOD support. Private markets may simply be unable to overcome the initial barriers (e.g. need for basic research, high costs) to make such investments profitable without government support. In such cases, DOD research could open up new technological fields which could then be exploited commercially by private firms. While the promise of commercial returns would seem to reduce the anticipated costs of such research to the nation at large, basing DOD funding decisions on such expectations is problematic. As suggested previously, predicting the direction of commercial markets is inherently difficult. For government officials to make these choices is even more demanding, given their lack of contact with the market process. Predicted commercial benefits may never materialize, or never live up to original expectations. On the other hand, confronted with an insurmountable technical obstacle, market participants may search for less daunting but equally effective alternative solutions. In such cases, the original DOD investment calculation would be rendered meaningless. If DOD balances the military payoffs against costs minus anticipated commercial returns, and these returns are never fully realized, then it would have misallocated its investment.

This is no trivial matter. The central mission of the Defense Department is to develop and maintain the armed forces necessary to defend the nation and its interests militarily. Given that the nation's resources are limited, all R&D investments must be judged by their relative contribution to the fulfillment of this mission. Consequently, "potential" commercial returns should not be considered by the military when making its R&D funding decisions. If the private sector is not currently pushing toward a particular technology, there is no guarantee that it ever will. DOD decisions should be made strictly on the basis of what will yield the highest military returns for the money.

Some consider this perspective too narrow. Given the Department's drain on the nation's scientific and technical talent, and its extensive use of the results of the country's investment in basic scientific research, it is only reasonable that DOD be expected to "pay something back to the system," they argue. This approach, however, is misguided. DOD has no mission responsibility for funding basic research; there are separate government agencies specifically assigned that task (e.g., National Science Foundation, National Institute of Health). Certainly, DOD should be expected to lobby for large budgets for these agencies, but it should not be asked to replace them. Moreover, the assumption that DOD is unfairly draining the nation's pool of technical talent ignores the fact that heavy defense R&D spending creates substantial incremental demand for trained scientific and technical personnel. This demand also raises the wages that scientists and engineers can demand across the board, creating incentives for more people to go into these fields than perhaps otherwise would.

The push to have the Defense Department assume responsibility for programs in civilian technologies is based more on politics than on any special "moral responsibility" of DOD. Defense has historically commanded greater funding than other agencies because of its national security mission. As a result, funding for basic research was more readily obtainable for DOD than for other government institutions (e.g., the National Science Foundation). As defense budgets decline, however, DOD's willingness to continue to invest in basic research will also diminish. Historically, the services have cut basic research categories first when defense budgets have diminished.

Finally, some have argued that DOD at a minimum should increase its emphasis on promoting manufacturing technologies. Improvements in machine tools and related equipment could potentially yield significant benefits for the military in terms of improved productivity, lower costs, enhanced efficiency, and greater quality and output. Greater investments in process technologies consequently would seem to be one area in which Defense R&D in dual-use technologies could directly yield financial returns to the government.

While the goal of improving the emphasis on productivity and efficiency within the defense industry are laudable, the emphasis on technology development is misplaced. In the commercial economy, process technology improvements are implemented because the incentive system encourages such investments. By increasing productivity and efficiency, private companies stand to lower prices, improve quality, attract more customers, and, ultimately, improve their financial performance. Technologies are introduced when they offer real financial returns.

In contrast, for much of the past forty years, defense companies have operated under a completely different incentive system. In military procurement, the emphasis has historically been on performance, with cost being far less important. Through "cost-plus" contracts and bidding criteria that give greater weight to performance objectives, defense contractors have learned that improvements in the manufacturing process are much less important. Greater defense research on new process technologies would do nothing to change this incentive system and would thus provide little reward for the military. Although defense research in this area might benefit the commercial sector with its inherent incentive to implement such improvements, such investments would contribute little to US military capabilities.

To a degree, DOD acquisition reforms since the mid-1980s have begun to eliminate this historical bias in defense contracting in favor of performance versus cost. As a result of the Packard Commission's recommendations and others, DOD has taken steps to emphasize value over performance in its weapons purchases. These trends are likely to be amplified by declining defense spending that will make defense officials even more sensitive to cost considerations when designing and developing new weapon systems. While many defense manufacturers no doubt remain tied to the tenets of the old system, some have begun to upgrade their production facilities to become more competitive.

While these developments are encouraging, progress within the defense sector has been slow, and serious disincentives to investment in manufacturing technologies remain.[37] As is the case with companies in the commercial sector, defense companies need to pay greater attention to the application of proven manufacturing. New investment in state-of-the-art process technology research is required only by the most sophisticated producers. In fact, defense-sponsored research on manufacturing technologies could potentially lead to innovations that further separate the defense and civilian markets. To the extent that these technologies are narrowly focused on the needs of defense, their potential contribution to commercial market productivity gains will likely be limited.

The real promise of civil-military defense integration lies in the use of common products and processes to improve DOD's access to the latest technologies, and to expand the domestic production capabilities available for emergency defense production. Future weapon systems should therefore be designed with civilian production technologies in mind, rather than a reliance on highly pecialized defense production methods. In contrast, DOD funding of manufacturing R&D may lead to new methods for improving the productivity of these specialized methods, rather than to generic, commercially applicable process enhancements. This may lead to savings in the short-run, but does little to expand US capability to surge production in a crisis.

Given the vicissitudes of the defense sector and the existing disincentives to long-term investment in productive capacity, however, there is a strong case for DOD to encourage defense-dependent contractors to adopt more advanced, yet proven, process technologies. Through technical extension services, tax credits, and depreciation allowances, DOD could help overcome existing barriers to such investments and upgrade the production processes of America's defense industries.

In the final analysis, declining defense spending must force DOD to concentrate its research efforts on defense-specific technologies and applications. Attempts to broaden the defense research agenda to achieve economic objectives will divert DOD's attention

---

37. For a discussion of these disincentives, see US Congress, Office of Technology Assessment, *Redesigning Defense: Planning the Transition to the Future US Defense Industrial Base* (Washington, D.C.: US Government Printing Office, July 1991), 67-68.

away from its central, national security mission, despite claims that "economic security" is America's primary security challenge. At the same time, this focus on defense-specific R&D must encompass efforts to identify and exploit privately funded technological developments to meet military requirements.

National Interests in a Global Economy

The globalization of the world's technology markets greatly complicates the issue of defense funding for dual-use technologies. To leave the development of dual-use products to commercial market forces risks possible domination of these sectors by foreign-owned or foreign-based firms. Such monopolies could theoretically endanger national security if the United States lacked alternative suppliers for critical defense components and technologies. This argues for a revision of the basic calculation of military payoffs from support for dual-use technologies to incorporate an estimate of the value of the freedom from foreign dependence.

But, as we have already seen, the United States no longer has a real choice between autarky and interdependence; foreign dependence at some level is an irreversible fact given the growing technological capabilities of East Asia and the European Community.[38] Certain technologies simply are not available from US-based suppliers, nor does the US military have the buying power to press foreign-owned firms to locate production facilities within the United States. Regardless of US policy initiatives, the importance of foreign technologies to US military capabilities is likely to increase. For example, in 14 of the 21 critical technologies identified by the Department of Defense, Japan and/or the European Community is expected to make "important" or "major" contributions. Rising foreign technical capabilities render the relative economic and military costs of autarky prohibitive. The task thus becomes one of managing the risks associated with foreign sourcing rather than trying to extricate ourselves from long standing trends in the global economy.

Theodore Moran of Georgetown University has developed the most analytically elegant method for addressing the foreign dependence challenge.[39] Borrowing from anti-trust theory, Moran

---

38. For a discussion of US policy responses to this development, see Andrew Freiberg, "The End of Autonomy: The United States After Five Decades," *Daedalus* (Fall 1991):69-90.
39. Theodore H. Moran, "Globalization of America's Defense Industries," 57-99.

suggests that foreign sourcing, even dependence, need not constitute vulnerability so long as the United States has access to a variety of suppliers. He suggests that the relevant concern is the concentration of foreign control, not the extent of foreign dependence. If a vital technology is widely available from a number of producers physically located in a number of different countries, then the United States is relatively invulnerable to foreign manipulation. Thus, dependence on South Korea, Japan, Singapore, and Thailand for commodity memory chips poses little threat to US security. By combining economic theory with national security concerns, Moran offers one approach to making the necessary trade-offs between economic efficiency and national security.

While Moran's approach bounds the problem of foreign sourcing, it does not eliminate it. In fact, unilateral alternatives to the risks of foreign sourcing are severely limited, making it effectively impossible to guarantee that the United States will not face supply difficulties during a crisis.[40] Confronted by a foreign vulnerability deemed dangerous enough to warrant US response, America's choices are essentially two, neither of which guarantees a lasting solution to the problem. First, the United States could, at considerable expense, stockpile the required components. Alternatively, it could fund the creation of new sources of production.

Stockpiling has been the traditional US response to foreign supply vulnerabilities, as in the case of oil or certain strategic metals. Should tightly controlled foreign high-technology components be judged vital to the nation's defense, suitable stockpiles of such items as advanced semiconductors, machine tools, precision optics, or silicon wafers could be established. Stockpiling offers a number of advantages. First, the existence of an adequate reserve of vital defense goods would reduce the US sensitivity to foreign supply disruptions and foreign attempts to influence US actions. For some items, it might be possible to develop sufficient reserves to meet all US wartime requirements even under the most demanding scenarios. Alternatively, smaller stocks might be sufficient to meet US military needs until domestic production capability is developed. In any case, stockpiling efforts should concentrate on those components for which vulnerabilities are most pronounced (e.g., single sources in non-allied, neutral sup-

---

40. Indeed, monopolistic domestic producers might also represent a serious challenge to DOD's ability to increase defense production rapidly. See James Miskel, "Thin Ice: Single Sources in the Domestic Industrial Base," *Strategic Review*, Vol. 19 (Winter 1991): 46-53.

plier nations), the need for rapid production is most critical (e.g., expendable systems—missiles and munitions), and the time necessary for developing suitable alternatives is extensive (e.g., certain electronic components, high-technology products).

Second, stockpiling is relatively inexpensive, especially when compared to the imposition of trade restrictions designed to preserve domestic production capacity.[41] For example, a National Defense University study found that emergency production of 17 precision-guided munitions could be ensured with a stockpile of foreign components costing only $15 million.[42] Given DOD's contention that cases of foreign vulnerability are exceedingly rare, the cost of a prudent stockpiling program for key high-technology components would appear reasonable. This is particularly the case given the long period of time that weapon systems remain in the US inventory. Although technologies may change rapidly, the components embedded within weapon systems are often years, or even decades, old.

Finally, stockpiling offers a hedge against supply disruptions over the long-term. Foreign dependency changes over time, with technical capabilities migrating overseas or disappearing completely over the 10 to 30 year lifespan of fielded weapon systems.[43] With careful monitoring, stockpiles could be adjusted to take these changes into account.

The second approach, development of alternate sources, could take a number of forms. As suggested by Moran's analysis, diversification of suppliers offers one means to reduce one's vulnerability to foreign supply cutoffs. These suppliers need not be located within North America, however. This would suggest that the United States should open its defense market, at least at the component/subsystem level, to even greater foreign participation. While this might seem counterintuitive if the objective is seen as preserving the US defense industrial base, it is in fact a sensible solution to the real challenge of ensuring secure supplies of vital defense goods.

---

41. Preserving inefficient industries through trade restrictions (e.g., voluntary export restraint agreements, tariffs, etc.) imposes costs on the entire economy. This is especially true if the industry has strong links to other sectors, whose competitiveness will necessarily suffer so long as it is forced to support an uncompetitive supplier.
42. Cited in Brian McCartan, "Defense or Opulence: Trade and Security in the 1990s," *SAIS Review* (Winter-Spring 1991): 139.
43. See Institute for Defense Analyses, *Dependence of US Defense Systems on Foreign Technologies* (Arlington, VA: Institute for Defense Analyses, December 1990).

In selected cases, diversification of suppliers could also dictate a strategy of developing domestic production capacity. This could be achieved most directly by stockpiling the requisite machine tools and supplies to ensure that the United States has sufficient idle production capacity to meet its surge/mobilization requirements. Indeed, the current shakeout in the defense industry may offer an ideal opportunity for the United States to purchase spare productive capacity to be held in reserve. Although starting such cold production lines may take some time, the cost of requiring only sufficient stockpiles to maintain production in the interim would be relatively modest. The alternative—maintaining low-rate, inefficient production as a means of preserving capacity—would prove substantially more costly.

Under a mobilization or reconstitution scenario, it might be possible for the United States to build production capacity for advanced technologies from scratch. While this option is dismissed by those who argue that the United States will irrevocably lose the requisite skills and technical know-how, it is difficult to predict with such certainty what would be possible in a national crisis. The speed with which new technologies spread among the industrialized world suggests that a nation with a technologically sophisticated workforce and sufficient capital can, with determined effort, enter new technical fields relatively quickly. Given a dire defense need, the United States might very well be able to build the necessary production capacity in sufficient time to counter any new threat. This is particularly true since the United States enjoys, and will continue to enjoy, world-class technological capabilities across the broad spectrum of technologies. Without question, any potential adversary, even including Europe or Japan, would face greater technological challenges than those confronted by the United States. While the resulting industry might not be as efficient as foreign commercial firms, it could nevertheless satisfy US defense needs.

As suggested previously, greater reliance on commercial technologies is likely to lead to greater foreign sourcing. This same reliance, however, could produce less dependency. As commercial manufacturing technologies become more flexible and the pace of technological change and diffusion accelerates, the opportunities for finding alternate sources or for bringing domestic production capacity on-line will become more prevalent. In contrast, failure to fully exploit commercial technologies virtually guarantees that DOD will become increasingly dependent on sole-source producers in the United States and abroad.

The second foreign dependency problem—assured access to leading-edge technologies—offers fewer unilateral solutions. Obviously, improvements in DOD's procurement practices that encourage greater use of commercial technologies would give it access to a wider range of technologies within the United States. In addition, heavy US investment in defense-specific technologies and applications at a time of declining worldwide defense spending will ensure that America remains the world leader in defense technology. However, the rapid advance of foreign capabilities means that foreign companies (and US-owned foreign subsidiaries) could make substantial contributions to the US defense effort provided the Pentagon has timely access to these new technologies.

Advocates of an American industrial policy suggest that the United States can preserve its access to cutting edge technologies without resorting to dependence on foreign firms. By imposing trade restrictions and funnelling defense spending to specific industrial sectors, the government could potentially create domestically based, leading edge industries capable of meeting US military requirements. As noted elsewhere, the obstacles to the successful implementation of such policies are substantial. Preserving or promoting commercial industries through trade protection and subsidies would impose significant costs to the nation while offering no assurance that the resulting firms would be able to stand on their own. Moreover, failure of such efforts would drain not only scarce defense resources, but also represent a net drag on the economy as a whole. Such policies would likely cost the United States more than simply stockpiling or building production capacity directly.

Left without a unilateral solution to the problem of assuring the Pentagon's access to certain leading edge technologies dominated by foreign firms, the United States must confront the fact that, in a global economy, its security depends on greater cooperation with the other industrialized democracies in the realm of defense procurement. While the United States and its allies have engaged in cooperative ventures previously, including technology-sharing agreements, the results to date have been disappointing. For much of the postwar period, policies have been premised on US technological superiority and the belief that the United States had little to gain from foreign research efforts. Moreover, cooperation has been hindered by Washington's willingness to use technology as a carrot or a stick to influence its allies' actions. Indeed, the primary examples of how technological dependence can limit a nation's freedom of action are drawn from US policies toward its allies.

Now that US policies designed to rebuild the economies of Europe and Japan have borne fruit, it is time to reexamine American attitudes toward technology-sharing and cooperation. In order to prevent economic concerns from undermining broader national security objectives, we and our allies must develop consistent policies governing the political/military uses of trade and investment in the context of a long-term objective of establishing a unified defense market.

Technological Superiority

Underlying much of this discussion has been the assumption that the United States will seek to maintain military forces that are technologically superior to any potential foe. This objective guided much of US defense planning during the cold war and, with the success of US forces in the Persian Gulf War, appears to be a reasonable goal for future defense planners. With the collapse of the Soviet Union (and its military R&D and production system), however, the technological challenges facing US armed forces are substantially changed. Despite much discussion of the proliferation of advanced weaponry to the Third World, changes in military technology suggest that the spread of individual weapon systems poses little threat to the United States. Instead, military power is increasingly dependent on the integration of a broad range of forces, on the creation of "systems of systems." The war with Iraq demonstrated not simply the military gains to be had through incremental improvements in military platforms and subsystems, but the exponential increases in military power achievable through the complete integration of all combat systems. Despite being the largest Third World importer of modern weapons prior to the war, the Iraqi military was completely overwhelmed by the Western onslaught. Third World countries cannot hope to make up for their poverty by arming vast numbers of troops. Trends in military technology dictate that technical sophistication and wealth are more important than ever before.[44]

---

44. A survey of existing military capabilities suggests that the prewar Iraqi military was the most capable (outside of China) in the entire Third World. Indeed, only US friends and allies (e.g., Israel, Egypt, Saudi Arabia) possess advanced military systems in any number. See US-CREST, *Cooperative Strategies: High-Technology Security Cooperation: A Transatlantic Industrial Perspective* (Arlington, VA: US-CREST/Hudson Institute, 1991), 7. This says nothing about the proliferation of

Superiority, however, is a relative measure. If the Third World offers no plausible technological threat that justifies continued heavy US investment in military technology, the question arises as to which countries possess the capability to seriously challenge the US military lead. The obvious answer is Japan and the advanced nations of the European Community. Simply stated, no other nations come close (or will come close) to having the technological and economic resources to mount a serious threat to US military superiority for the foreseeable future. Even if current trends in Russia are reversed, its military forces would take years to rebuild, and would never reach the comparable levels of sophistication unless it achieved substantially better economic performance. More importantly, the growing role of commercial technologies in military systems guarantees that even heavy Russian investments in military R&D would be unable to match Western capabilities for decades. (Provided, of course, that strict export controls were maintained.)

Posing Europe and Japan as potential military adversaries is distressing, to say the least. However, much of the current discussion on foreign dependency implicitly assumes that a major break between the United States and its allies is not only possible, but likely enough to justify substantial spending to prepare for it. In the field of militarily-relevant high-technology, Japan and Europe represent the United States' largest suppliers. This relationship has developed as a result of conscious American policies: US policymakers have sought to build up our allies and bind them to the United States. That such an outcome has in fact occurred hardly seems reason for concern.

Nevertheless, the United States has had little recent experience with foreign dependence in military systems.[45] Without question, the United States' ability to act unilaterally and influence the actions of its allies will be constrained as a result of our growing reliance on foreign suppliers and our declining defense spending.[46] This argues for finding cooperative solutions to mutual challenges, rather than for creating new sources of tension.

---

weapons of mass destruction, however. In this area, the technological challenges remain formidable and the risks enormous, justifying heavy US military R&D investments.

45. This is not the case with Europe and Japan, which have had considerable experience with US controls on their access to military technology. See Moran, "The Globalization of American Defense Industries"; and Andrew Moravcsik, "Arms and Autarky in Modern European History," *Daedalus* (Fall 1991): 23-46.

46. In truth, the collapse of world communism will also undermine US

A Defense Technology Agenda

The changes in the security and technology environments afford US defense forces significant new opportunities, but carry with them new constraints and potential vulnerabilities. Declining defense budgets, the rising sophistication of commercial technologies, and the increased technical competence of America's allies will make it more difficult to maintain previous rates of military innovation. In fact, attempts to sustain the previous forced pace will likely exhaust much needed political and economic energies. Fortunately, the collapse and dissolution of the Soviet Union offers a respite from constant pressures to develop and field the next generation of military technology. Emerging threats in the rest of the world are of a very different nature, with the most dangerous scenarios—the proliferation of weapons of mass destruction—presenting quite a different challenge than that which the vast majority of today's defense technology base is geared to address.

To an unprecedented degree, the United States and its allies now hold the keys to world-class military technologies. Although arms production is growing throughout the rest of the world, the sophistication of these systems will not soon match even that of the weapons produced by the former Soviet Union. As a result, any American effort to preserve its technological edge must focus as much on constraining Western exports of advanced weaponry as on our own development programs. In an era of declining defense spending, when defense companies are looking increasingly to the international market as their salvation, placing serious constraints on export sales will prove politically challenging, to say the least. However, attempts to preserve national defense industrial bases through arms exports could do more harm to the national interest than good.

Turning to more narrow issues of the US defense technology program, ongoing trends suggest the following broad areas for policy action.

---

freedom of action. As the leader of the free world engaged in a life-and-death struggle with the Soviet Union, the United States could justify many actions that might otherwise have raised objections both at home and abroad. Without the Soviet threat, American citizens, and the world community at large, are likely to scrutinize US military actions abroad far more closely.

Defense Research and Development

Military requirements will continue to demand that defense research be highly focused on unique DOD requirements. Declining defense spending and reduced opportunities for defense contractors to profit from large procurement contracts will reduce incentives for these firms to invest in defense-specific technologies. Moreover, recent proposals to shift away from mass production toward R&D and prototyping will likely require a significant increase in R&D spending to make such work sufficiently profitable for defense firms.

Consequently, the Department of Defense must be far more selective in determining where its R&D dollars are to go, concentrating its efforts on defense-specific technologies unlikely to be developed by the commercial market alone. Despite calls for DOD to become an engine of commercial competitiveness through the sponsorship of generic commercial or dual-use technology research, DOD's first obligation must be the defense of the nation. DOD has neither the expertise nor the resources to assume the additional obligation of promoting economic growth at a time when defense budgets are falling substantially. Moreover, narrow emphasis on the development of defense technologies will likely yield greater military benefits, particularly since defense research, unlike commercial R&D, remains largely subject to national controls. DOD-funded advances in defense-specific technologies are more likely to produce an edge over any potential adversary than DOD-funded advances in generic commercial technologies that are traded freely across borders.

A decision to retain a narrow focus for military R&D should not, however, constrain the search for high-risk, high-payoff technologies. In particular, funding for DARPA (now ARPA) should be protected from raids by the services to ensure that it remains a hothouse for ideas not usually supported within the individual military branches. ARPA performs an important mission, serving as an early warning device for new technological opportunities, as well as potential threats.

In a fiscally constrained environment, however, the Congress and the Pentagon must take care to ensure that declining defense spending does not result in abandonment of certain basic research endeavors. The military has served as an important supporter of key research areas, particularly computer science. These research programs should be protected, either by fencing off fundamental research funding or, better still, by transferring the associated funding to the federal agency directly charged with supporting basic research, the National Science Foundation. At the same time, and reflecting the recommendation that DARPA concentrate on military technologies, congressionally instigated dual-use technology development efforts should be transferred gradually to the Department of Commerce to preserve the clear distinction between economic and military research objectives. Finally, policymakers should refrain from assigning new, commercial technology development missions to the national laboratory system. Although efforts to make federally funded technologies more available to the private sector should continue, national laboratories should continue to focus primarily on serving specific government mission needs. Obviously, with the end of the cold war, research priorities can and should change. However, excess capacity in the labs should be dealt with through privatization rather than the assignment of commercial technology missions.

Exploitation of Commercial Technologies

The recommendation that DOD should maintain a narrow focus within R&D does not suggest that the Department should ignore the R&D work of the private sector. Rapid advances in commercial technologies will present tremendous opportunities for military applications. These opportunities will only be realized, however, if DOD both undertakes the necessary reforms in its procurement practices to gain access to these technologies on a timely basis, and invests in applied research to identify, modify, and incorporate commercial components into military systems. Consequently, the major new mission of the military research establishment must be the aggressive scanning of commercial technology markets and the rapid adaptation of relevant technological advances.

Exploitation of commercial technologies will become increasingly important as the composition of American military forces changes over the coming decade. Falling defense spending will result in smaller forces and will increase the relative importance of so-called "force multipliers"—surveillance, intelligence, command and control, and information systems. These are precisely the areas where commercial technologies offer the greatest promise. Commercially developed computers, communication systems, and software have already made major contributions to US military capabilities. If properly applied, future breakthroughs could offer similar payoffs.

Commercial technologies cannot simply be purchased off the shelf and inserted into military systems. The DOD research program must develop comprehensive receiving mechanisms, involving extensive monitoring of commercial R&D and limited in-house R&D to understand and apply technologies as they are introduced. The main purpose of this in-house work would not be the development of new technologies. Instead, it would provide the underlying technical resources necessary to identify the potential military value in private sector inventions. Moreover, DOD's work would concentrate on developing applications, not new generic technologies.

This recommendation would require a substantial shift in DOD acquisition procedures to better deal directly with the commercial market. In the past, many firms have chosen to avoid doing business with the DOD rather than submitting to its complicated and costly acquisition procedures. The shrinking defense market will only increase the disincentives for many commercial firms, making it even more difficult for DOD to obtain the latest technologies. Numerous valuable proposals have been offered in recent years for simplifying DOD contracting law, reforming data rights provisions, and eliminating unique military specifications. Now is the time to pursue such reforms, not just in the name of economic efficiency, but for the sake of military expediency. In short, the Congress and DOD must strike a more workable balance between the public's insistence on fairness and the market's demand for efficiency.

To the extent that DOD succeeds in speeding its application of commercial technologies, it may even contribute positively, albeit indirectly, to the nation's commercial competitiveness. The military could serve as an important early buyer of new developments, making more rapid production increases and product improvements possible.

Managing Foreign Dependence

Expanded use of commercial technologies will necessarily loosen the Pentagon's control over the sourcing of components and subcomponents, leading perhaps to greater reliance on overseas suppliers. If DOD and the Congress hope fully to exploit commercial technologies, it must recognize that private sector moves toward global sourcing and the growing dispersion and integration of the world's technical talent makes the goal of national autarky unachievable. Consequently, in all but a narrow range of very specific defense technologies, the task becomes one of management of foreign sourcing, rather than prevention.

At the very least, DOD must undertake a systematic effort to identify the extent and nature of its current dependence on foreign suppliers. At present, DOD maintains no comprehensive database of the national origins of its defense goods, particularly beyond the major contractor level. Not only does this greatly hinder debate on this subject, but it also leaves military officials without any clear direction of how to proceed. The first step must be to conduct a systematic survey of different types of military hardware (e.g., missiles, communications systems, avionic subsystems) to identify common instances of foreign sourcing, dependence, and vulnerability. Additionally, foreign sourcing should be tracked over time to determine how the level of foreign content and sourcing varies during a weapon system's lifespan. Finally, DOD, in conjunction with the Department of Commerce, will have to improve its ability to track technological developments and productive capacities around the world to facilitate the rapid identification of alternative suppliers of key technologies. The purpose of these exercises should not be to identify every instance of foreign sourcing, or even of foreign vulnerability, but to identify generic vulnerabilities affecting a number of different systems.[47]

In cases of foreign dependency, DOD faces few attractive options. All will require balancing theoretical security threats stemming from supply disruptions against increased costs. This suggests that, over the long-term, the primary course of action should be cooperative, diplomatic action rather than unilateral efforts designed to achieve complete independence. Any proposal to manage foreign dependence will raise costs and produce uncertain military benefits. While such measures may be necessary, they will inevitably prove cumbersome, technologically limiting, and ultimately only partially effective.

As a result, the primary objective of US policy should be to establish clear rules and procedures governing defense trade with the European and Asian allies. At a minimum, the United States should seek agreements limiting extraterritorial controls on corporations operating abroad. This would allow US officials to plan

---

47. According to one Department of Commerce official, their study of foreign sourcing in only three navy systems took three years to complete. He estimated that a new study of one system could be completed in roughly one year. Obviously, attempts to identify every case of foreign sourcing and dependency would be prohibitively costly, if not impossible.

for the use of the productive capacity of foreign firms operating within the United States (or friendly countries abroad) during times of crisis. While this would deny the US one instrument for influencing its allies' actions, it would also serve to remove a source of occasional tension between the United States and its allies and make it easier for US affiliates abroad to obtain national treatment.

A more ambitious policy would seek to develop comprehensive rules and dispute resolution procedures on the accepted political uses of trade, creating a presumption that allied nations have an *obligation* to trade in certain goods without political interference. Such negotiations would probably prove more difficult than those on extraterritorial controls, requiring that leaders agree to foreswear export restrictions as a policy instrument among allies. While defense-specific technologies might be excluded from such agreements, the sale of commercial technologies used in weapon systems should be covered. National governments would not be obliged to compel domestic manufacturers to sell to allied militaries, even in times of crisis. However, they would agree not to interfere with the fulfillment or negotiation of contracts between allied governments and domestic manufactures. Arrangements on surge or emergency production could then be dealt with through contractual agreements.

In the past, the United States has exploited its technological superiority to accomplish foreign policy objectives at the expense of its European and Japanese allies, sometimes with disappointing results, both economically and diplomatically. Denials of approvals to export European aircraft containing US components to third countries are one example of this type of behavior. As America's relationship with its allies becomes more balanced, its ability to exercise such influence is declining. Consequently, the United States now has a real opportunity to both contribute to its military capabilities and remove a potential source of tension.

Regardless of the success of such efforts, lingering concerns about foreign dependency will no doubt still require some unilateral actions. For absolutely essential defense goods, where disruptions of supply could severely affect the national interest, DOD should either stockpile the requisite number of systems and subcomponents or build domestic production capacity by offering incentives for foreign firms to locate within the United States. While either alternative is expensive, it is still less costly than trying to sustain an inefficient domestic producer, particularly if that producer is in an important industry for the economy at large. The cost of such programs, however, will dictate that the list of absolutely vital items be limited.

For the broader range of components and technologies which may not be crucial to the nation's security but do contribute significantly to the fighting ability of US forces, a strategy aimed at diversifying the location and ownership of suppliers, as described by Professor Moran, probably offers the most realistic means of balancing the opportunities and risks of foreign sourcing. These risks should be evaluated not only in terms of the location of production facilities for components of one weapon system, but for alternative systems capable of accomplishing the same military mission.

Requirements that components be available from several different companies with production facilities in a number of countries may make it difficult for DOD to utilize some technologies whose production is concentrated within a single country. As time passes and the technology matures, this should be less of a problem as even the most advanced technologies tend to disseminate throughout the industrialized world. Still, efforts to cope with foreign sourcing and dependency require continual monitoring of this dissemination process to determine the risks posed by foreign dependency.

6

Setting the Goals for a
Federal Technology Policy

While the objectives of defense research and development are relatively straightforward, the proper goals for federal efforts to promote commercial technologies are more ambiguous. Over the past several years, studies of American technological competitiveness have suggested a number of possible goals for US technology policy, including enhancing American industrial competitiveness, reducing the trade deficit, developing critical commercial technologies, and boosting US productivity growth. While these are all laudable goals, only improved productivity growth stands as an appropriate objective for US technology policy. Concerns about the American trade position, the health of particular industrial sectors, and the relative US position in certain key technologies are certainly understandable and well placed. However, the connection between these particular symptoms and the nation's overall well-being is not always direct, nor is technology policy the appropriate tool for addressing these problems that derive from broader macroeconomic forces.

Establishing Objectives

This chapter examines four basic goals that technology policy might serve: (1) improved US industrial competitiveness; (2) an enhanced US trade position; (3) commercial competitiveness in selected high-technology industries; and (4) improved US productivity growth rates. Selecting the appropriate objective for policy dictates how success can be measured and helps define both priorities and limits for federal action.

Improving Industrial Competitiveness

Although a popular goal, industrial competitiveness is a particularly difficult objective to define, offering few firm markers by which policymakers can measure the need for, or success of, various technology policy alternatives. The 1985 President's Commission on Industrial Competitiveness defined competitiveness as "the degree to which a nation can, under free and fair market conditions, produce goods and services that meet the test of international markets while simultaneously maintaining or expanding the real incomes of its citizens."[1]

Others have gone beyond this, defining competitiveness as the situation in which (1) US goods and services are of comparable price and quality to those produced abroad; (2) the sale of these goods and services generates sufficient economic growth to increase the income of all Americans; (3) investment in the necessary labor and capital is financed through national savings; and (4) the nation is able to sustain this position on a continuing basis.[2]

Even with these extensions, competitiveness remains a vague objective for guiding a long-term technology policy. Most often, the competitiveness of the US economy is defined as the competitiveness of the US manufacturing sector. The focus on manufacturing is understandable. During the 1980s, imports of goods manufactured abroad hit many US companies particularly hard. Moreover, over the past century, the US manufacturing sector has been better able to apply new technologies than most of the service sector, making substantial improvements in productivity more readily achievable in the industrial sector.[3] However, while the manufacturing sector is essential to America's economic future and the link between its health and technological progress clear, there are serious problems with making industrial competitiveness the primary focus of federal policy.

First, to the extent that improving competitiveness means creating comparative advantages in key industries, it need not necessarily translate into real improvement in the economic health of the United States. Certainly, if the US determined that it wished to be competitive in a set of export industries, it could perhaps achieve that goal by heavily subsidizing particular sectors and erecting barriers to foreign competition. Theoretically, this might make the United States more competitive in selected market segments, but it might do so only at a cost to the overall health of the economy. European support for the Airbus Industrie consortium is a case in point. Clearly, government subsidies for

---

1. As cited in Office of Technology Assessment, *Competing Economies: America, Europe, and the Pacific Rim* (Washington, D.C.: Government Printing Office, October 1991), 3.

2. Competitiveness Policy Council, *Building a Competitive America: First Annual Report to the President and Congress*, March 1, 1992, 2.

3. For a discussion of the productivity of services and their ability to apply new technologies, see James Brian Quinn, Jordan J. Baruch, and Penny Cushman Paquette, "Technology in Services," *Scientific American*, Vol. 257, No. 6 (December 1987): 50-58.

aircraft development projects such as the Airbus AS300 helped create a globally competitive firm capable of challenging America's Boeing and McDonnell Douglas commercial aircraft businesses. However, even accounting for the lower prices paid for new aircraft by European airlines, the beneficiaries were neither the Europeans nor the United States, but the rest of the aircraft-consuming world.[4]

More importantly, a policy aimed at improving manufacturing competitiveness would leave unaddressed the major challenges facing service-sector industries. Indeed, the MIT Commission on Industrial Competitiveness recognized this limitation:

> Manufacturing may be essential, but it accounts for less than a fourth of the GNP and for less than a fifth of all employment. Further, manufacturing is certainly not the only troubled sector of the economy,... productivity growth in many non-manufacturing industries has been significantly worse. Since these other segments now account for such a large part of the economy, progress in them is essential; the nation cannot sustain an overall improvement in its standard of living without them, no matter how well manufacturing performs.[5]

Finally, even if one accepts industrial competitiveness as an appropriate policy objective, one is still left without any explicit means to evaluate the nation's performance. Policymakers would be forced to rely on a composite of sometimes conflicting, industry-specific data. Without a coherent methodology for weighing the relative importance of trade shares, productivity, and GDP growth rates, decision-makers would be left vulnerable to the special pleadings of particular industries with no clear vision of the correct balance to strike.

---

4. Richard Baldwin and Paul Krugman, "Industrial Policy and International Competition in Wide-Bodied Jet Aircraft," *Trade Policy Issues and Empirical Analysis* (Chicago: University of Chicago Press, 1988), 45-71. The issue of strategic trade policy and the possible dynamic benefits of such a strategy is discussed below. Even if the Europeans did sustain a net loss because of their subsidy of the AS300 project, the United States by no means benefitted. By subsidizing an industry in which the US was a net exporter, European policy hurt Boeing and the welfare of the United States. The prime beneficiaries of the lower prices caused by the Airbus-Boeing competition were the consumers (i.e., airlines), and, at the national level, countries that did not participate in the competition (i.e., the rest of the world).

5. Michael L. Dertouzos, et al., *Made in America: Regaining the Productive Edge* (Cambridge, Mass.: The MIT Press, 1989), 41.

Enhancing the US Trade Position

Using technology policy to reduce the trade deficit also misses the mark. America's aggregate trade problems have little to do with its technological capabilities. Rather, as discussed in chapter two, America's current trade deficit is mainly the product of larger macroeconomic forces, particularly US savings and investment patterns. Consequently, a more effective approach to solving them should address their root causes directly. This would entail a substantial reduction in US government deficits, as well as other programs to increase domestic saving rates. Beyond these first-order solutions, continued pressure on foreign nations to open up their domestic markets is certainly appropriate. In contrast, technology policy is too slow an instrument to make a significant contribution to the current trade situation. The process of technological development and diffusion, though accelerating, remains a long-term phenomenon when compared to other, more direct macroeconomic instruments. Political leaders who undertake technology initiatives in order to redress adverse trade conditions are likely to be disillusioned by the meager short-term results.

Moreover, attempts to focus on "high-technology trade" also raise a number of difficult and politically charged questions. Among other things, they leave unanswered the question of what qualifies as a high-technology industry. For example, the automobile industry, which accounts for between one-half and three-quarters of the US trade deficit with Japan, is not usually considered a high-technology business. More generally, should unsophisticated products manufactured by high-technology processes be eligible for special attention? Do sophisticated products produced inefficiently also qualify? Undoubtedly, some sectors employ more sophisticated methods and produce more advanced products than others. But there is no politically satisfying rule to distinguish one industry from another. But without a clear definition, decision-makers lack a usable measure for evaluating the effectiveness of policy. Even more damaging, an emphasis on foreign trade diverts political attention to other nations' practices rather than America's own. With imports accounting for only 13 percent of GNP, and exports 12.3 percent in 1990, an overemphasis on foreign trade as the locus of policy is clearly undesirable. Current US economic difficulties are more pervasive and must be addressed across the board.

Stimulating Development of Critical Technologies

At the other end of the spectrum of potential policy goals are narrowly defined technical objectives. Under this approach, technologies would be selected for support on the basis of their expected market size, their perceived influence on other industries, or their anticipated effect on American competitiveness. This approach essentially equates the development of key technologies with economic growth, making them, by definition, of vital interest to the nation.

Politically and bureaucratically, the "critical technologies" approach vastly simplifies the problem of defining an effective federal technology policy. The federal government has a long history of selecting and developing specific technologies in order to fulfill vital mission requirements. Presumably, the practices developed for funding defense technologies could be transferred to the funding of appropriate commercial technologies. Moreover, measuring the technical success or failure of government efforts would be simpler than trying to determine how such policies affect US industrial competitiveness, the trade balance, or productivity growth. Delineating explicit technical goals establishes clear yardsticks for measuring the federal government's performance, providing a means of ensuring accountability and control.

Yet the very simplicity of the critical technologies approach is precisely its greatest drawback. Although selecting, prioritizing, and supporting particular technologies for development is well within the federal government's capabilities, creating new technologies, even commercially successful technologies, need not improve US economic performance. As with support for specific industries, by establishing a set of explicit technical goals the critical technologies approach risks encouraging policies that detract from US welfare, as much as they contribute to it.

Clearly, the detailed and analytically rigorous critical technologies reports prove that the bureaucracy *can* develop a coherent picture of tomorrow's leading technologies. The real question is whether the government can act upon this portrait in a manner likely to yield real benefits for the economy. To implement a critical technologies strategy, the government would have to know when and when not to invest. It would also have to have an adequate mechanism for realigning its priorities in the face of technological and economic obstacles. Technological breakthroughs achieved at exorbitant costs could reduce US economic welfare as often as they contribute to it. Similarly, what might be lauded as a long-term perspective on the part of federal program managers could be nothing more than an unwillingness to abandon economically infeasible lines of research. Finally, all-out efforts to surmount major technological obstacles may obscure economically superior alternative paths *around* such obstacles, thereby wasting public resources.

While technical breakthroughs are easily observed, their economic consequences are more difficult to measure. Calculating the *national* rewards of subsidies for critical technologies is complicated by the fact that the benefits of new technologies increasingly flow across national borders, making it difficult for the originating nation to reap the full rewards of its investment. Moreover, without firm criteria for making trade-offs between economic and technological objectives, a technology policy aimed at producing specific technological objectives cannot also be expected to achieve economic payoffs greater than would have been produced by the market on its own.

There are other pitfalls associated with a critical technologies approach. Technology investments do not take place in a vacuum. Public investment in government-designated critical technologies constitutes a powerful signal to the investment community. Investors, starved for information, will likely view the government's selection of key technologies or companies as authoritative, diverting funds from other potentially valuable areas. This diversion would be beneficial if the government possessed a superior method for determining which technologies are most promising. However, it is far from clear that the methodologies employed by the Office of Science and Technology Policy or Commerce Department would be substantially better than those used by the much larger number of private market analysts already at work.[6] Moreover, when making choices about what is and is not critical, it is important to remember that, except at the margin, investment decisions concern where and when to invest, not whether to invest. In a real sense then, the selection of critical

---

6. Obviously, the critical technology reports of the Department of Defense are based on better information than is available to the private sector. As the buyer of military hardware, DOD transmits information about its own future buying intentions through the critical technology reports. The private sector does not have any other equally reliable source for this information. In contrast, the Department of Commerce can only provide its interpretation of the buying intentions of the commercial market, intentions that are already subject to a great deal of speculation by a multitude of private market analysts.

technologies constitutes a zero-sum game, with as many losers (in terms of their ability to attract funding) as there are winners. Inevitably, the critical technologies approach uses extrapolations of current knowledge to predict which technologies will be most important in the future. This approach is satisfactory for evolutionary technologies whose future importance can be safely predicted. However, the risks and benefits of revolutionary technologies are far more difficult to predict. Consequently, a critical technologies approach may direct funding to those areas where the risks and uncertainty is *lowest*, while leaving research efforts outside the technological mainstream underfunded.

As this study suggests, technology policies that focus on technology, rather than on economics, miss the point. From a public policy perspective, the task of "picking winners" is far more complicated than simply choosing commercially viable technologies. That task is already performed adequately by the private market. For the government, picking winners means selecting commercially viable technologies that yield greater net social benefits than market-driven investments. As now defined, a critical technologies approach would produce explicit technological successes (and failures), but can rightfully promise nothing in terms of real *economic* benefits.

Increasing Productivity Growth

The most appropriate objective of federal technology policy is to foster increased US productivity growth. The slowdown in American productivity growth that began in the early 1970s has resulted in significantly lower real incomes in the United States than might otherwise have been achieved. If US labor productivity growth had continued at its pre-1973 level over the subsequent 20 years, for example, real hourly wages would be 25 percent higher today than they actually are.[7] In fact, over the long-term, there is simply *nothing else which affects the nation's economic well-being as significantly as does productivity growth*. It is the most important factor in producing sustained growth in real wages and income. Increases in the productivity of labor ensure continually rising real wages, while growth in capital productivity rates guarantees greater returns to investors. Nor are the benefits of productivity growth limited to the sector in which it occurs. While productivity levels help to determine relative wage rates, the benefits of productivity growth accrue to all workers in the

---

7. William A. Cox, *Productivity, Competitiveness, and US Living Standards* (Washington, D.C.: Congressional Research Service, 1990) 2.

economy. The salaries of highly skilled, highly productive workers grow at approximately the same rate as those of workers in less productive fields.

Moreover, productivity growth provides an expanding, though not necessarily more burdensome, tax base for the fulfillment of society's other objectives. Indeed, productivity growth is essential to the preservation of social peace. By the late nineteenth century, many were predicting the imminent decline of industrial capitalism as a result of the steady impoverishment of the masses. Instead, the vast increases in manufacturing productivity made possible by Taylorism and scientific management at the end of the nineteenth and beginning of the twentieth centuries, and the consequent rise in real wages, allowed the United States to avoid many of the nightmares of industrialization predicted by Marx and others.

Differences in national labor productivity rates largely distinguish high-wage societies from low-wage societies. They also exercise a profound influence on the composition of a country's international trade. Highly productive nations can export products based primarily on their superior productivity levels, whereas less productive countries must rely on relatively low wages to compensate for lagging efficiency.

Absolute increases in productivity rates are essential for improvement of a country's economic well-being. The importance of relative gains, however, is less definitive. If the country's productivity rates continue to improve, then its economic situation will also improve regardless of what occurs in other countries. If productivity growth in one country consistently falls behind that of its trading partners, however, the lagging country will become a source of relatively cheap labor, and its exports will shift toward relatively more labor-intensive goods. While the mechanism of international trade ensures that trade balances will eventually tend toward equilibrium, the process by no means can assure lagging countries that their living standards will rise in concert with the rest of the world.[8]

In its simplest form (and holding capital markets stable), the process works as follows. As productivity growth lags, a country's exports become more expensive to produce relative to other

---

8. The following is drawn from William J. Baumol, Sue Anne Batey Blackman and Edward N. Wolff, *Productivity and American Leadership: The Long View* (Cambridge, Mass.: The MIT Press, 1989), 15-23. See also Paul Krugman, "Myths and Realities of US Competitiveness," *Science* (November 1991): 811-815.

countries, which, by definition, are able to produce more with fewer inputs. As the prices of a country's products rise, foreign demand will naturally fall. Falling foreign demand for exports also means that foreigners will demand less of the lagging country's currency since they need less to purchase the desired level of exports. Declining demand for currency translates to a drop in its price—in other words, the currency will depreciate. Moreover, the lagging country's currency will continue to depreciate until its exports are once again competitive and its trade balance moves toward equilibrium.

This would appear to indicate that competitiveness can be achieved simply by adjusting a country's exchange rate. However, this brief description masks the longer-term implications of relatively slow productivity growth for real wages. As the lagging country's currency depreciates, foreign products and internationally mobile inputs become more expensive. Even if nominal wages remain fixed, real wages will decline relatively because workers are able to purchase fewer goods than before. In effect, workers are forced to sell their labor at cheaper and cheaper rates on international markets to remain competitive. Finally, as labor becomes relatively less expensive, the composition of the country's exports will also tend to shift away from products with a high capital-to-labor ratio to more labor-intensive goods.

It is important to recall that all of these changes are *relative*, however. As long as productivity is increasing absolutely, the well-being of the nation is also increasing. The higher the growth rate, the better off the lagging country will be, even if foreign growth rates exceed those of the lagging country. Still, this is by no means reason for complacency. Indeed, as a lagging country (in relative terms), the United States should be attentive to the productivity growth of its trading partners if only to identify means by which the productivity of the US economy could benefit from foreigners' experiences.

An American Productivity Strategy

Enhancing US productivity growth rates must serve as the overarching economic objective for all long-term US economic policies, and for technology policy in particular. Improving productivity is the only long-term goal worth pursuing—all others are either symptoms of disappointing US productivity performance or short-term macroeconomic phenomena.

Unfortunately, to establish sustained productivity growth as the object of policy goes against the grain of much of the current thinking about technology policy. First, policymakers should be less concerned about which sectors of the economy are aided by technology policy, and certainly about which specific industries are helped, since any increase in productivity will contribute to the national welfare. Despite the rhetoric about how much manufacturing matters, the country benefits equally whether productivity increases occur in manufacturing or services. Indeed, as the service sector grows, improvements in its performance will become even more important than comparable improvements in manufacturing. The situation is analogous to that of agriculture. With only three percent of the population involved in farming, even large increases in productivity can have only a minor effect on national labor productivity rates. Increases in manufacturing productivity will have a greater effect, but not so great that the United States can rely exclusively on manufacturing to pull the entire nation along given the sector's modest size.

In working to improve the efficiency of service workers, America faces an entirely new productivity challenge, however.[9] Nor does productivity growth depend solely on so-called "high-tech" industries, especially when the distinction between high-tech industries and other industries is rapidly becoming meaningless. All industries must become high-tech if the country hopes to improve its productivity growth, and, as a corollary, firms whose productivity lags behind national and international standards inevitably hurt the rest of the country. Efforts to sustain such firms through subsidies or trade protection retard efforts to increase the overall productivity of the country and must be phased out.[10]

Finally, an emphasis on productivity makes it obvious that the development of new technologies, no matter how revolutionary, is of secondary concern. What matters is the application and commercialization of new techniques and technologies throughout the economy. Even a widget that doubles productivity rates will have a negligible effect if only one percent of industry is

---

9. See Peter F. Drucker, "The New Productivity Challenge," *Harvard Business Review* (November-December 1991): 69-79. It is worth noting that US manufacturing productivity has actually grown substantially over the past decade. National productivity rates have lagged because of the relatively low growth rates of many service industries.
10. Michael E. Porter, *The Competitive Advantage of Nations* (New York: Free Press, 1990), 7-8.

applying it to their operations. The diffusion of technologies is what is crucial. In this light, finding technological opportunities overseas is as important as developing new technologies at home, provided they are disseminated throughout the American economy at similar rates.

A few notes of caution are in order. *First*, productivity growth fluctuates widely from year to year. As a result, short-term trends will provide little insight into how well any particular policy is performing. Moreover, temporary improvements in productivity are practically meaningless; the real power of productivity growth results from compounding returns over the longer term. This makes formulation of effective policy extraordinarily difficult, as it is practically impossible to evaluate the results over the short-term. Past experience suggests that the US political system is ill-equipped to pursue consistent policies over the length of time necessary to meaningfully evaluate them. Without immediate, tangible results, American voters may soon tire of initiatives. Sustained support by better informed political and business elites is essential, as was the case for US defense policies during the cold war.

Second, although technological progress is a key component of productivity growth, other factors are also important. In particular, education and capital investment levels play a vital role in improving productivity. Indeed, investment, education, and technology interact to drive productivity growth. Much of Japan's impressive gains over the past forty years are attributable to its substantially higher savings and investment levels, rather than to its ability to develop new technologies. Higher savings rates allowed Japan to apply new technologies on a broad scale as it upgraded production capabilities. Concentration on technology development alone is not enough.

These two caveats notwithstanding, productivity growth represents the most appropriate goal for any federal technology policy designed to yield real economic benefits. Such a focus offers three primary advantages. *First*, it dictates that policies be formulated with the long-term firmly in mind. This is appropriate, since the pace of technological change and diffusion is more in line with the relevant time frames for changes in productivity growth than for other short-term goals. *Second*, a focus on productivity growth helps policymakers to avoid becoming overly fixated on particular technologies or industries. The development of technologies per se would be an inappropriate objective of policy; instead, policy should attempt to develop an environment that promotes technological progress in general. *Third*, an emphasis on productivity as the critical component of US competitiveness focuses attention on the underlying national economy, wherein exchange rates and trade balances are of secondary importance. The productive capacity and well-being of the nation and, in particular, of the American worker, is central.

7

Seeking Solutions:
Systemic Constraints on
Technology Development

During the past decade, the debate over an American technology strategy has too often focused on the wrong issues, leading to prescriptions for change that addressed the symptoms of America's technology problems rather than the underlying causes. Indeed, there has been a common tendency to proceed directly from a laundry list of the competitive weaknesses of US industry to plans of action designed to remedy specific perceived ailments. While a great deal of time and effort has been invested in assembling evidence of America's economic decline and devising programs to counteract obvious deficiencies, relatively little effort has been devoted to categorizing systematically the weaknesses of the American technical enterprise.

This inclination to treat symptoms has manifested itself in a number of forms. As noted earlier, the compilation of lists of important or "critical" technologies by teams of technologists from government and industry became quite the vogue for a brief period, with the Department of Defense, the Department of Commerce, and the Office of Science and Technology Policy (all at Congress' direction) preparing lists of those technologies that would be most important to an advanced industrial economy in the next century. The Europeans and Japanese also busied themselves producing similar lists. Meanwhile, private business groups joined in this list-making frenzy on their own, with the Council on Competitiveness' report, *Gaining New Ground*, setting the high water mark for this genre.

There were very few real differences between these various lists. While the Department of Defense emphasized some defense-specific technical areas in which the commercial world has little interest, by and large industry representatives and government officials agreed on the broad areas of technology that were most promising. Moreover, they tended to agree on the relative position of US industry compared to its counterparts in Japan and Europe. At most, however, this consensus about *which* technologies should be developed indicates more about what the real problem with US industry is *not*, rather than what it is. Clearly, American business executives—and even government civil servants— know, in general terms, which technologies are important. The problem remains, however, to identify the reasons that companies are apparently not acting on that knowledge to a sufficient degree to sustain American productivity growth.

The emphasis on treating symptoms instead of causes has shaped the legislative initiatives on technology policy during the late 1980s and early 1990s, as well. Rather than looking for systemic failures, policymakers and analysts have spent their time constructing programs and doling out funding to whichever high-technology industry was most capable of capturing lawmakers' imaginations. Congressional earmarks for research on x-ray lithography, high resolution displays, and multichip modules all seek to inject funding into technical areas that legislators believe are being underfunded by the private sector. Similarly, the congressionally established Advanced Technology Program (ATP) within the Department of Commerce has been busily providing funding to industry for various commercial research and development projects, without any clear statement of the program's overarching objectives or the problems it seeks to address. While such efforts may very well develop some interesting, and perhaps even commercially successful innovations, they cannot hope to redress the systemic problems experienced by US companies when developing and applying new technologies.

The proper point of departure for any discussion of a new American technology strategy, therefore, is to focus on why US industry is apparently failing to develop and apply technologies that most observers agree are essential to the long-term economic well-being of the nation. As chapters two and three highlighted, the contours of America's competitive challenges are well known, if sometimes misinterpreted. Designing a coherent strategy, however, requires that they not be treated as isolated phenomena, but recognized as products of specific failures of the American system. These flaws fall into three distinct categories:

- Underinvestment in new technologies because of the unique characteristics of the R&D process, characteristics that result in a disjuncture between private rewards and social returns;

- Failure to develop or apply technologies because of implicit or explicit barriers, imposed either by the firm itself, by market conditions, or by governmental regulations and operations; and

- Under- or over-investment in certain areas because the prevailing incentive structure in the United States inappropriately values various types of activities, and specifically discourages investment in "intangibles" such as R&D and training.

This chapter seeks to clarify these three underlying causes and to demonstrate how the various observed problems derive from one or more of these failures. Chapter eight will move beyond this task and begin to define, in general terms, the proper public policy responses to each problem and to identify the most appropriate policy instruments for attacking these shortcomings.

Problem One: The Nature of the R&D Process

In theory, the returns to society of investment in research and development will be greatest when the last dollar invested yields a dollar return. Left to their own devices, however, markets are incapable of achieving this ideal outcome: on average, the private returns from research and development are substantially less than the returns to society as a whole. Benefits from research are transferred to other firms, consumers, and society at large, making it impossible for the originating firm to capture the full rewards of its R&D investments. Consequently, private firms can be expected to undervalue these "external" returns during their capital allocation process, leading them to underinvest in research and development from society's perspective. This will occur even as firms act in a manner that maximizes their private returns.

This difference between private and public returns is perhaps the most widely accepted rationale for government intervention to promote commercial research and development.[1] Economists have described this case of market failure as a problem of appro-

---

1. The theoretical foundations for this argument were laid in R. R. Nelson, "The Simple Economics of Basic Scientific Research," *Journal of Political Economy*, Vol. 67 (1959): 297-306; and Kenneth J. Arrow, "Economic Welfare and the Allocation of Resources for Invention," in Universities-National Bureau Committee for Economic Research, *The Rate and Direction of Inventive Activity* (Princeton, NJ: Princeton University Press, 1962), 609-625.

priability: firms cannot appropriate all of the returns to their investment and therefore underinvest in research and development. A number of studies have attempted to calculate the average societal returns from investments in research and development (see Table 7.1).[2] Although estimates of total social returns from R&D vary substantially between different studies, they generally exceed the average private returns on other types of investments. This difference suggests that firms invest enough in R&D to maximize their private gains, but not enough to maximize society's returns. In other words, additional R&D investments in excess of those undertaken by industry acting alone can be expected to yield significant benefits to society at large.

There are a number of reasons why private inventors may be unable to reap all of the benefits of their R&D investment. For example, basic scientific research at the forefront of knowledge may yield information that is not easily controlled, making it impossible for firms to license or otherwise benefit from the diffusion of such basic knowledge to others.[3] Predictably, company investment in basic research has been limited, amounting to roughly five percent of all company-funded R&D spending and only 16 percent of all basic research conducted in the United States.[4]

The difficulty of controlling the spread of information also affects applied research and development work. Innovations may be quickly copied at less cost by the firm's competitors and introduced before the originating firm has time to capture the full benefits of its invention. One study estimated that to imitate a

---

2. For a brief, current discussion of the issue, see Edwin Mansfield, "Estimates of the Social Returns from Research and Development" in Margaret Meredith, Stephen Nelson, and Albert Teich, eds., *Science and Technology Policy Yearbook* (Washington, D.C.: American Association for the Advancement of Science, 1991), 313-320.

3. Some reject the assumption that information transfer costs are zero. Instead, they suggest that the costs of transferring information and technologies are significant, meaning that firms must invest a substantial amount of money in research and development simply to be able to take advantage of outside sources of technical knowledge. See David C. Mowery and Nathan Rosenberg, *Technology and the Pursuit of Economic Growth* (New York: Cambridge University Press, 1989).

4. National Science Foundation, *National Patterns of R&D Resources: 1990 (NSF-90-316)* (Washington, D.C.: NSF, May 1990), 43-44. What basic research is conducted is usually done so that a company has the "receiving mechanisms" necessary to exploit scientific research conducted elsewhere.

new technology, rival firms on average spend only 65 percent of the cost of the original innovation.[5] As a result, some of the benefits of private R&D investments flow to imitators, just as benefits flow to consumers through competition and lower prices. At times, the mere knowledge that something can be accomplished is sufficient to simplify vastly the task of imitation. In software design, for example, the introduction of new products immediately notifies competitors of functions and features that can be incorporated into their own designs, even if no code is actually copied.

Additionally, some of the potential returns to R&D are lost because companies tend to invest in areas they know and exploit only those results that support their existing business focus. As a result, some of the knowledge gained by a firm through its R&D investments cannot be exploited, nor can the company otherwise benefit from it because there is no ready market for the sale of such "residual" knowledge to other potentially interested firms.[6] If such knowledge does leak out of the firm—through professional exchanges or the movement of workers, for example—the benefits of the original R&D are captured by outside firms.

Individual firms obviously do not consider these external social benefits when evaluating the profitability of prospective R&D investments. This disjuncture has long been recognized as justification for government intervention. Patent laws are an obvious example of how the government attempts to stimulate additional private investment in innovative activity. By giving companies a temporary monopoly on a new technique or product, patents offer a means for firms to realize a greater return on R&D investments through monopoly profits. Additionally, the large federal investment in defense technology reflects the conclusion that private firms could not expect to recover enough of their research costs in the defense market to justify heavy investment in advanced military technologies.

---

5. Edwin Mansfield, "Microeconomics of Technological Innovation," as cited in Congressional Budget Office, *Using Federal R&D to Promote Commercial Innovation* (Washington, D.C.: Government Printing Office, April 1988), 13.
6. The reasons why no such market exists are relatively easy to understand. To sell a product, sellers must disclose enough information to convince buyers of its value. In the case of a product consisting of pure information, disclosure of enough data to sell the product would result in disclosure of the product itself.

Table 7.1. Selected Studies of Estimated Returns to R&D Expenditures.

Author	Rate of Return on R&D	Object of Study	Years	Notes
Mansfield (a)	40-60 30	Petroleum Industry Chemical Industry	1945-1958	Technology change assumed to be embodied in capital
	7	Chemical Industry		Technology change assumed to be organizational
Minasian (b)	54	Chemical Industry	1938-1957	Gross social return
Fellner (c)	31	Macroeconomy	1953-1966	High-range estimates of R&D costs
	55	Macroeconomy		Low-range estimates of R&D costs
Griliches (d)	93	Chemical & Petroleum	1957-1965	Based on confidential census data
	25 2 23 5 17	Metals & Machinery Electrical Equipment Motor Vehicles Aircraft Manufacturing average		
Terleckyj (e)	29	Macroeconomy	1948-1966	Return to firm-financed R&D
	78			Return to R&D embodied in purchased inputs
Scherer (f)	70-104	Macroeconomy	1973-1978	Internal process R&D and input-embodied R&D
Nadiri (g)	20	All Manufacturing	1958-1975	
	12 86	Durables Nondurables		

Table 7.1. Selected Studies of Estimated Returns to R&D
Expenditures. (continued)

Author	Rate of Return on R&D	Object of Study	Years	Notes
Link (h)	51	Chemical Industry	1975-1979	Rate of return increased by
	34	Machinery Industry		roughly 15 to 85
	21	Petroleum Industry		percent if environmentally mandated R&D is excluded.

(a) Edwin Mansfield, "Rates of Return from Industrial Research and
Development," *American Economic Review*, Vol. 55(2) (May 1965), 310-322.
(b) Jora Minasian, "Research and Development, Production Functions, and
Rates of Return, " *American Economic Review*, Vol. 59(2) (May 1969), 80-85.
(c) William Fellner, "Trends in the Activities Generating Technological
Progress," *American Economic Review*, Vol. 60(1) (March 1970), 1-29.
(d) Zvi Griliches, "Returns to Research and Development Expenditures in the
Private Sector" in John W. Kendrick and Beatrice N. Vaccara, eds., *New
Developments in Productivity, Measurement and Analysis* (Chicago:
University of Chicago Press, 1980), 419-454.
(e) Nestor Terleckyj, *Effects of R&D on the Productivity Growth of Industries:
An Exploratory Study* (Washington, DC: National Planning Association, 1974).
(f) F.M. Scherer, "Inter-industry Technology Flows and Productivity Growth,"
Review of Economics and Statistics, Vol. 64 (November 1982), 627-34.
(g) M. Ishaq Nadiri, "Contributions and Determinants of Research and
Development Expenditures in the US Manufacturing Industries" in G. von
Furstenberg, ed., *Capital, Efficiency and Growth* (Cambridge, Mass.:
Ballinger, 1980), 361-92.
(h) A.N. Link, "Productivity Growth, Environmental Regulations and the
Composition of R&D," *The Bell Journal of Economics*, Vol. 13 (Autumn 1982),
166-69.

Source: Congressional Budget Office, *Federal Support for R&D and
Innovation* (Washington, D.C.: CBO, April 1984), 30-31.

Models of Innovation

Government investment in basic scientific research also stems from a recognition of this spillover phenomenon. Because no firm can expect to recover sufficient benefits to justify substantial investments in basic scientific research, the government has sponsored the vast majority of this work since World War II. For much of this period, policy and analysis of research and development activities have been dominated by the "pipeline" model of innovation.[7] This abstraction portrays innovation as proceeding through a series of well-defined stages, from basic research to applied research to development. In this view, investment in basic research at one end of the pipeline inevitably leads to products being developed and marketed at the opposite end. This model engendered the belief that so long as the pipeline is continuously fed with new injections of basic scientific knowledge, it could be counted on to produce a steady stream of new technologies.

Under this model, spillover effects and externalities are thought to be especially pronounced at the early stages of the process, thereby justifying government subsidies for basic research work. In contrast, externalities are thought to be less significant during the development stage when companies are focusing on product design and manufacturing. Accordingly, government intervention at this point of the process is not thought to be required, and the expected private gains are considered sufficient stimulus to generate the required level of investment.

The rigidity and predictability suggested by the pipeline model of innovation provided a convenient tool for the formulation of policy. While government support for basic scientific research was fully justified by using the model, policymakers could also find ready justification for resisting calls by private corporations for federal support for specific industries. So long as the federal government pursued a sufficiently rich and diverse scientific research agenda, it could be argued that it had done enough to promote technology development in the commercial sector.

More recent work, however, suggests that innovation progresses in a more iterative manner, with the creation of new technologies beginning not with the creation of some new piece of basic knowledge but with the design of a new product to meet

---

7. See Congressional Budget Office, *Using R&D Consortia for Commercial Innovation: SEMATECH, X-ray Lithography, and High-Resolution Systems* (Washington, D.C.: US Government Printing Office, July 1990), 5-10.

a recognized need. This model, sometimes referred to as the "chain link" model, holds that as obstacles are encountered during the design of a new product, inventors will search out the necessary information to overcome each barrier. As a result, the process moves back and forth between development work, applied research, and, at times, basic scientific exploration. As designers encounter obstacles and seek solutions, they are forced to tradeoff cost and performance goals, modifying the design as required.

In this view, the impact of information costs is substantial. Given the expense involved in obtaining and applying technical knowledge, researchers will tend to seek solutions to any particular problem first by tapping the resources available within their immediate environment. Firms with broad research and development programs and highly developed lines of communication between their various activities will therefore have a distinct advantage over specialized firms or companies that have imposed artificial barriers to the free flow of technical information across organizational lines.

This model also predicts that if developers are unable to find an adequate solution to their problem from within the company itself, they will search for answers from other resources in a steadily expanding circle. Suppliers, customers, local researchers, data banks, and technical journals may all be contacted during this search for the required information. To the extent that these resources are readily available because of their geographic proximity, the costs to developers will be reduced. In any event, this iterative process will continue until the barrier is overcome, either by the discovery of a solution or by product redesigns.

The implications of the chain link model for government policy are less clear-cut than those offered by the traditional pipeline conception. In both models, the greatest spillovers are derived from basic scientific research, arguing for federal support for a broad basic science agenda. However, the new model also suggests that federal efforts to stimulate product design and development are also appropriate, insofar as they stimulate demand for new information and fundamental research.

Geographically Specific Spillovers

In general, spillover benefits are thought to flow relatively easily throughout the economy and even across national borders. However, the greater importance of spillovers in constrained geographic regions has recently attracted increased attention.[8]

---

8. See, for example, Michael Porter, *The Competitive Advantage of Na-*

Innovative firms tend to encourage competitors and suppliers to innovate at a higher rate, particularly if they are in geographical proximity. Consequently, a firm's investment in R&D not only promotes its own competitiveness, but also the competitiveness of its neighbors. This positive feedback among innovating firms can lead to the almost spontaneous creation of industry clusters that facilitate the easy exchange of ideas, resources, and even people, thereby accelerating the rate of technological progress. Moreover, the clustering of related companies in turn creates a highly competitive climate that further promotes innovation. As the chain-link model would predict, the creation of industrial environments rich with relevant technological and scientific resources vastly simplifies the task of the product designer, reducing the costs of searching out required information and stimulating rapid transfers of technology among companies.

The rise of California's Silicon Valley and Boston's Route 128 are perhaps the two most prominent examples of such clustering. Industry clustering is common in a wide variety of other high technology industries as well. For example, Sematech, the Microelectronics & Computer Technology Corporation, Dell Computer, and CompuAdd Corporation have combined to stimulate a center for computer and semiconductor manufacturing around Austin, Texas. In all, roughly 450 related companies have located in the area, employing 55,000 workers. Similarly, laser manufacturers and electro-optics companies are heavily concentrated around Tucson, Arizona and Orlando, Florida. Finally, drawn by market leaders WordPerfect and Novell, approximately 175 software companies employing 12,000 workers are clustered in Utah around Provo, Orem, and Salt Lake City.[9]

Clustering of innovative companies is by no means strictly a feature of high-technology industries. Less prominent but no less competitive industries also demonstrate clustering patterns, such as the carpet manufacturers around Dalton, Georgia, insurance companies in Hartford, Connecticut, and the tile industry around Sassuolo, Italy, all of which are the products of similar spillovers from innovation.[10]

---

tions (New York: The Free Press, 1990); W. Brian Arthur, "Positive Feedbacks in the Economy," *Scientific American*, Vol. 262 (February 1990): 92-99; and Paul Krugman, *Rethinking International Trade* (Cambridge, Mass.: MIT Press, 1990).

9. Kevin Kelly, "Hot Spots: America's New Growth Regions Are Blossoming Despite the Slump," *Business Week*, October 19, 1992, 80-88.

10. Paul Krugman, "Myths and Realities of US Competitiveness," *Sci-*

The formation and growth of such reservoirs of technical knowledge feed on themselves, attracting investment from other innovative firms as they seek to harvest some of the benefits of their competitors. For example, Motorola established a Unix software development center in Urbana, Illinois, to draw on the resources of the University of Illinois' computer science department and the skills of the 60 software companies located in the area.[11] Such clusters of companies attract investment by foreign companies as well. Both Toshiba and Kyocera Corporation have established facilities in upstate New York to take advantage of the innovative climate created by roughly 110 advanced ceramics companies located around Alfred, Cornell, and Binghamton Universities.

Federal and state governments obviously have a strong incentive to encourage the creation of spillovers that promote clustering of innovative industries. Government encouragement of industry clustering offers the most direct method of ensuring that the nation benefits preferentially from its investment in commercial R&D. Whereas dispersed government funding of basic research and development is as likely to benefit foreign nations as it would the United States, government investments in the technological infrastructure of communities around the nation could create geographically confined benefits that would, by contrast, disproportionately benefit the United States.[12]

While the growth and creativity of such centers seems to feed on spillovers from the business environment itself, their creation appears to depend on the existence of a technical infrastructure sufficient to attract firms to the area. Such highly specific infrastructure elements include the presence of an established industry leader or university laboratories engaged in advanced research, the availability of venture capital, and support from

---

ence (November 1991): 811-815; and Michael Porter, *The Competitive Advantage of Nations*, 213. Despite the heavy emphasis on high-technology in the policy debate, innovation occurs throughout the economy and often outside of the structures normally thought to comprise the R&D infrastructure. Nevertheless, productivity will grow most rapidly if innovative activity and technological progress are encouraged *throughout the entire economy*.

11. Kelly, "Hot Spots," 81.

12. This is not to say that spending on basic R&D is unjustified. Additional R&D spending in the United States *or* abroad will produce benefits for the United States. However, they do not necessarily have to benefit one country preferentially over another, given the ease with which new technologies flow across international borders.

local governments. State programs, such as Pennsylvania's 10-year-old Ben Franklin Partnership, have also helped start-up companies and stimulate the creation of industry clusters. Close partnerships between educators, businessmen, and government leaders appear to be crucial to all of the efforts.

Spillovers and Targeted Government Support

Despite the fact that most federal efforts to redress the spillover problem have been applied indiscriminately across industries, there is no a priori reason to suppose that all industries and activities suffer from identical spillover problems. At the very least, the wide range of study results shown in Table 7.1 suggests that different industries and technologies may be more or less affected by under-investment by the private sector. For example, returns from investment in production technology research, including innovations in production methods, may be relatively difficult for other firms to duplicate, both because firms have no need to inform others of their manufacturing techniques and because spending on such "industrial infrastructure" is difficult to duplicate.[13]

It may not be possible to realize a full return on some process technology breakthroughs, because such concepts travel as freely as basic scientific data. However, implementing such procedures as "just-in-time" production is expensive, ensuring that firms will capture the majority of the benefits from their investment. Similarly, science-based industries may find it harder to reap the benefits of their research than industries where applied research is key, simply because basic scientific information is more difficult to control. The emphasis on secrecy over patent protection in capturing the benefits from R&D investments in such industries as chemical processing would tend to confirm this observation.[14]

Ideally, government efforts to redress the spillover problem, therefore, would be targeted on specific industries and activities.

---

13. One exception is firms engaged in defense manufacturing, which must not only inform the government of manufacturing techniques and procedures, but are sometimes compelled to share such developments with competitors when technologies result from government-funded work. This levy against industrial secrecy is an important reason why companies may prefer, all else being equal, not to work for the government.

14. Richard Levin, Alvin Klevorick, Richard Nelson, and Sidney Winter, "Appropriating the Returns from Industrial Research and Development," *Brookings Papers on Economic Activity* (3:1987), 783.

The great difficulty, however, is determining which industries and technologies are more prone to spillover problems than others. Even within a particular industry, some technologies may provide substantial spillovers, while others produce none at all. At present, there are no practical criteria for making this determination. Though some progress has been made in identifying the spillovers from past innovations, this work is not readily applicable to the problem of forecasting which technologies are most likely to suffer from underinvestment in the future. Neither industry size, nor the potential financial returns from new technologies, is a sufficient basis for making these judgments. Moreover, even if a technology has a broad impact on the economy and serves as an input to other industries, it may suffer relatively less from spillover problems.[15] Likewise, the identification of certain technical fields as "critical" does not establish them as technologies with particularly severe spillover problems. As a result, the most fruitful strategy will likely remain one which supports R&D broadly, relying on substantial average returns to the government's investment, as opposed to a riskier, targeted approach which offers no assurance that the resulting gains will outweigh the potential losses. Where support is targeted, it should focus on generating and capturing geographically specific spillovers through the creation of centers for innovation.

Problem Two: Barriers to Innovation

US companies may also be pursuing inefficient or counterproductive technology strategies due to implicit or explicit barriers to the development and application of new technologies. For example, legal restrictions on cooperation between firms, certification requirements, barriers to entry for new markets, or the lack of a supporting network of suppliers might all serve as barriers to technological advancement. Such barriers may make it impossible for a company to develop certain types of technology or make it exceedingly difficult to transfer technologies between separate organizations or industrial sectors. Not only can barriers prevent firms from realizing the full benefits of their own tech-

---

15. For example, recent work on the appropriability of semiconductor R&D suggests that it is more appropriable than average, indicating that public support is unjustified. Richard C. Levin and Peter C. Reiss, "Cost-reducing and Demand-creating R&D with Spillovers" as cited in Theodore H. Moran, "The Globalization of America's Defense Industries," *International Security*, Vol. 15, No. 1. (Summer 1990): 80.

nology investment, they can restrict opportunities for beneficial spillovers between firms.

It is important to note, however, that some barriers are appropriate and desirable. For example, restraints on the development of dangerous technologies or the pursuit of corporate strategies that could prove detrimental to the interests of employees or consumers may be socially undesirable. Additionally, the market forces that render certain technologies commercially nonviable are perhaps the most common, and appropriate, types of barriers to technology development. The task then is to identify and eliminate barriers that exist unnecessarily, either because they were created without due consideration of their negative consequences or evolved over time in manners inconsistent with today's market realities and technological possibilities.

While there are many forms of barriers, they generally fall into three broad categories depending on their origins. First, barriers can be imposed by companies themselves through either the pursuit of inappropriate business strategies and poor technology management structures or by their own resource constraints. Second, barriers can be imposed by the government, in the form of outright prohibitions against certain types of activities or through more subtle constraints created by federal regulation, particularly government procurement regulations. Finally, barriers to technology development and application can be imposed by the structure of the market itself. Each of these types of barriers has been identified as a partial cause for American industry's failure to compete internationally in key market sectors. Each is analyzed below.

Barriers Established by Firms

A company's management practices, organizational structure, previous experience, institutional philosophy, or simple ignorance can all serve as effective barriers to innovation. While such firm-specific limits can sometimes be the product of outright poor management, they often derive from the persistence of practices that are no longer appropriate given a changed market environment. For example, Henry Ford dramatically reshaped the early automobile industry with the introduction of new manufacturing technologies that allowed Ford to mass produce automobiles at a significant cost advantage over its rivals. By the late 1920s, however, the automobile market had changed substantially as a result of increasing wealth and the advent of the two-car family. Consumers were less sensitive to cost, preferring instead to pay a premium for additional features and more stylish designs. This time, General Motors was in position to remake the industry through its product innovations, while Ford remained constrained by its strategy of mass production of identical products. The persistence of corporate strategies long after they have become irrelevant continues to haunt many segments of US industry. Firms which grew prosperous during an era of mass production of homogeneous products have often found it difficult to adopt the methods and technologies required to be competitive in a market characterized by changing patterns of demand, and diverse, dynamic product lines. According to the MIT Commission on Industrial Productivity,

In industry after industry the Commission's studies have found managers and workers so attached to the old way of doing things that they cannot understand the new economic environment. Challenged by stronger foreign competition and stagnant productivity, they respond by clinging more tenaciously to the patterns of production and organization they associate with the heyday of American economic primacy. To some extent, it is the magnitude of past successes that has prevented adaptation to a new world.[16]

The troubles of the US auto industry in the late 1970s and early 1980s are attributable to such a failure to respond to a changing market and the challenges posed by Japanese imports, higher fuel costs, and customer demands for quality over novelty. Despite fundamental changes in the marketplace, companies are often unable to readjust their strategies without a major crisis or other corporate upheaval.

Alternatively, firm-specific barriers may be the product of judgments about the relative costs and benefits of expanding into other market segments, judgments that might be based on incomplete or incorrect information. Companies that focus exclusively on their traditional markets and customers may not recognize opportunities to adapt and apply their technologies to other market segments. Although other forces are clearly at work, a major part of the problem facing defense companies in their attempt to enter civilian markets is their lack of sufficient market knowledge and their unfamiliarity with commercial sector practices.

Large firms may have pursued a decentralized management strategy that severely limits the flows of information between

---

16. Michael L. Dertouzos, et al., *Made In America: Regaining the Productive Edge* (Cambridge, Mass.: The MIT Press, 1989) 46.

business units. In the case of widely diversified corporations that grew up during the 1960s through the acquisition of businesses in unrelated markets and product areas, companies may be unable to produce or capture potential spillovers from their other operations, resulting in the relatively inefficient use of technology expenditures.

Companies may also lack the requisite technology and competitor monitoring systems required to stay abreast of the latest developments in their industry and to identify potential applications of their existing technical resources. This problem can be particularly severe among smaller firms that do not possess the resources to investigate adequately new process and product technologies, markets, or management techniques. While larger firms may be able to amortize such information search costs over a larger business base, obtaining such information for smaller firms may simply be beyond their capabilities. Instead, small companies are often dependent on incomplete or self-serving sources of technical information.

Because such firm-specific barriers to technology development and application derive either from the structure of the firm or from internal managerial decisions, outsiders, including public officials, have few levers to shape companies' behavior, structure, or operations in order to eliminate these barriers. Eliminating inappropriate barriers arising from a firm's behavior will require that management innovations be suited to specific market circumstances and individual firms. However, management can be influenced by outsiders through education, information-exchange, and example. Management consultants, business educators, trade associations, industry journals, competitors, customers, suppliers, and, at times, even government officials, can help firms adjust their internal strategies to align better with market realities. Much of this education process can be accomplished by existing mechanisms already operating in the private sector. However, as we will see in chapter eight, modest government efforts to stimulate greater attention to technological opportunities and achievements, particularly among smaller firms, could yield positive rewards.

Barriers Imposed by Government

A second major source of barriers to innovation are governmental regulations and controls. In pursuit of a variety of objectives, federal, state, and local governments impose legal and regulatory constraints on firms' behavior, limiting market opportunities and, in some cases, barring development of certain technologies altogether. In fact, federal regulations and tax laws have been blamed as partial causes of America's competitive ills. While there are undoubtedly cases where federal regulations impose inappropriate constraints on technical advancement, there are also many instances where government-imposed limits serve important societal objectives and actually improve the competitiveness of American industry.

Government-imposed barriers fall into two broad categories. First, they include explicit regulations that discourage or prohibit certain types of activities or research in order to promote some social objective. Second, they derive from inefficient or ineffective government operations that impede technological progress.

Examples of regulatory limits on technology development and diffusion are plentiful. In order to encourage technology development, the government constrains the rapid diffusion of new technologies by granting and enforcing patents. Even when government regulations do not specifically bar technology development, they can at times discourage innovation. To the extent that government regulation of the telecommunications industry has been outpaced by technological developments, the regulations serve to slow or stop progress. The overhaul of America's telecommunications sector in the early 1980s, for example, unleashed a wave of technological innovation not matched by the state-owned monopolies of Europe. A restructuring of competition in the US cellular phone or cable television industries could be expected to result in a comparable burst of innovative activity.

US liability laws and the threat of exorbitant damage awards may inhibit private investment in certain technical areas that carry high liability risks. For example, concerns about potential liability have served to discourage defense firms from aggressively investing in certain technologies required to cleanup hazardous waste at Defense Department and DOE facilities. Other regulations, such as US export controls—particularly controls on so-called "dual-use" technologies—limit the potential market for such technologies and consequently discourage or prevent private investment.

Many have also argued that US antitrust laws limit the ability of US firms to cooperate effectively with other firms on the development and application of technologies. This argument proved persuasive on Capitol Hill, where the Congress passed the Cooperative Research Act in 1984 that greatly reduced the potential liability of firms engaged in cooperative research. Indeed, the Congress has been a strong advocate of greater cooperation among US firms in high-technology industries, enacting numerous programs designed to promote the formation of research and development consortia. Sematech is perhaps the best-known example of this drive to counteract the reputed negative effects of US antitrust laws. Similar efforts to relax antitrust limits on joint production have also received consideration.

Ironically, the *absence* of government regulations can also hinder the development and diffusion of new technologies. Firmly established government regulations provide a stable and predictable environment for private investment, thereby allowing firms to plan long-term development efforts without fear that the value of their investments will be negated by subsequent regulatory or legal developments. The reluctance of firms to engage in waste cleanup activities reflects the absence of a clear federal policy on long-term liability for environmental technologies as much as the threat posed by current American liability regulation. The slow development of a legal framework for the products of the biotechnology industry has similarly impeded that industry's development.

Barriers to Civil-Military Integration One oft-noted and costly case of government-imposed barriers to technology development and diffusion is the artificial separation of civilian and military markets. The unique administrative burdens imposed on defense contractors and research laboratories make it difficult organizationally to integrate civilian and defense research and development endeavors. In a 1991 Center for Strategic and International Studies report, for example, critics of DOD's procurement practices cited four key barriers to better integration of the civilian and defense technology bases: (1) unique accounting requirements and audits; (2) military specifications and standards; (3) technical data rights; and (4) unique contract requirements.[17] All of these barriers are products of the government's pursuit of conflicting public policy objectives under the unique conditions of the US defense market. Over the years, a forest of regulations have resulted from attempts to ensure that DOD contracting procedures were fair and open to all eligible participants, that suppliers were held accountable, and that the government paid a reasonable price for its military equipment. To some

---

17. CSIS Steering Committee on Security and Technology, *Integrating Commercial and Military Technologies for National Strength: An Agenda for Change* (Washington, D.C.: Center for Strategic and International Studies, March 1991), xii-xiii.

extent, these regulations achieved their purpose. However, most observers agree that they did so at a tremendous cost in terms of reduced efficiency, higher costs, and diminished access to the latest commercial technologies. Given the importance to the technology transfer process of direct interaction among researchers, this organizational separation erects a substantial barrier to exchanges of know-how between commercial and defense researchers.

By discouraging some companies from pursuing defense work and forcing others to separate their defense businesses from their commercial operations, DOD regulations have stifled the useful exchange of new technologies between the civil and defense sector and have artificially constrained the US defense industrial base. These regulations, combined with DOD's ignorance of the commercial marketplace, have effectively prevented DOD from exploiting many of the technological opportunities available in the commercial market. As a result, commercial components and technologies are often more advanced than those being fielded in military systems. This results in higher unit costs, longer development times, and less effective military systems.

This isolation has a number of other negative economic consequences as well. Most importantly, it greatly reduces the potential economic benefits deriving from defense research, thereby raising the relative cost of military R&D. Some have gone so far as to blame this military-civil divide for the declining competitiveness of the United States.[18] While such claims are perhaps overblown, the separation of the defense and civilian industrial bases clearly reduces the efficiency of the federal government's investment in military technologies. In fact, even with dual-use technologies, the existence of a large, isolated defense market may hinder commercial development by removing some of the incentive to exploit nondefense opportunities.[19]

For companies engaged exclusively in defense production, the regulatory limits imposed by Defense Department acquisition regulations have made it difficult for firms to transfer their military-technical know-how to commercial markets. While mili-

---

18. See the Carnegie Commission on Science, Technology and Government, *New Thinking and American Defense Technology* (New York: Carnegie Corporation of New York, August 1990), 12.

19. See, for example, the Office of Technology Assessment's discussion of the polymer matrix composites industry in *Holding the Edge: Maintaining the Defense Technology Base* (Washington, D.C.: Office of Technology Assessment, April 1989), 170-176.

tary contractors may possess the technologies needed for success in the commercial sector, they may lack other necessary business functions (i.e., marketing), which will prevent them from applying their technical knowledge to commercial applications. In such cases, military work has led companies to develop unique business strategies that are largely inapplicable to the private sector.

Similar constraints have made it difficult to transfer technologies from government laboratories to private corporations. Despite several legislative attempts over the past decade, including the Stevenson-Wydler Technology Innovation Act of 1980 and the Federal Technology Transfer Act of 1986, and the Bush Administration's National Technology Initiative, efforts to shift the focus of national laboratories toward developing commercially relevant technologies still suffer from a variety of regulatory and institutional barriers. While the legal mechanisms for such cooperation have, for the most part, been put in place, industry observers continue to complain that differences in organizational perspectives and incentive structures make cooperation difficult at best. Additionally, while technology transfer between different organizations has become more fluid, it remains a difficult process.

The Burden of Inadequate Government Performance

In addition to limits imposed by federal regulations, technological progress can also be impeded by inefficient implementation of existing regulations and responsibilities. An inefficient patent system and poor enforcement of intellectual property rights can undermine the effectiveness of these measures for promoting technology development. Similarly, the shortage of sufficient numbers of scientists and medical researchers with the Food and Drug Administration can slow the development and introduction of new medical technologies. The willingness of pharmaceutical companies to provide $300 million to the FDA in 1992 to fund the hiring of additional FDA scientists is indicative of the impact of government operations on the competitiveness of the private sector.

While an inefficient civil service can hinder technological progress, more disturbing are those instances where the government fails to perform its responsibilities at all. For example, as the previous discussion of spillovers suggests, competitiveness and technological progress can be impeded by the absence of a supporting structure of educational resources and public infrastructure. The weaknesses of the nation's school system, particularly those schools serving poor urban areas, will negatively affect the nation's long-term economic welfare. Similarly, insufficient public investment in infrastructure in the form of roads, bridges, and public facilities can raise costs for businesses and, in some cases, drive these businesses to invest where the supporting environment is more conducive. Given the increasing importance of information flow to the nation's future and the inherent difficulty involved in transferring technologies, government investments in a better information infrastructure are also justified.

Market-Imposed Barriers

Finally, barriers to technology development may be imposed by the structure of the market itself and the characteristics of the technologies involved. Most importantly, firms may be effectively barred from investing in some technologies because the barriers to entering a new market are overwhelming. Confronted with high start-up costs, steep learning curves, stiff competition, and concentrated markets, companies may simply choose not to pursue certain technological opportunities.

Barriers to entry are a common phenomenon. At the extreme, these barriers conspire to create "natural monopolies" that eliminate any possibility of new firms entering a market. Transportation, local telecommunications, and public utilities are typical of such natural monopolies. In these industries, technological limitations and the large initial capital costs make entry by competing firms virtually impossible. In these clear cases of market failure, government intervention is deemed essential and most nations maintain either direct ownership or strict regulatory controls over these industries.

Over the past decade, a body of economic thought has developed that suggests that certain high technology industries are typified by such large economies of scale and high up-front research and development costs that they effectively become natural monopolies on a global scale.[20] In other words, world markets for these high technology products are believed to be able to sustain only a very limited number of efficient manufacturers. Without effective competition in these market segments, these global giants could theoretically be able to reap monopoly profits.

The aerospace and microelectronics industries are two sectors often cited as industries with such high entry barriers. During the 1980s, producers of advanced semiconductors regularly cited the overwhelming cost of establishing a state-of-the-art semicon-

---

20. See Paul R. Krugman, ed., *Strategic Trade Policy and the New International Economics* (Cambridge, Mass.: The MIT Press, 1988).

ductor fabrication line as an insurmountable barrier to entry. It was argued that Japanese companies, buoyed by profits from high-volume production and vertical domination of key markets such as consumer electronics, were better able to afford these huge investments, locking US companies out of a strategic industry. Similarly, the commercial market for large commercial aircraft is commonly viewed as another example of a "strategic industry" where only very few producers can operate efficiently. Today, only three firms—Boeing, McDonnell Douglas, and Airbus—have the resources to produce large commercial transports. Indeed, McDonnell Douglas has found it increasingly difficult to remain competitive, while Airbus prospers only with generous help from European governments.

Theoretically, the nations in which these global monopolies are located could reap disproportionate benefits from their presence, offering a real incentive to policymakers to try to create competitive advantages for its firms through trade protection, subsidies, and export promotion. Ideally, the benefits from a "strategic" government support program for such industries would produce benefits in excess of the subsidy costs. In such cases, government assistance to overcome steep entry barriers could make economic sense for the well-being of the nation as a whole.

However, there are ample reasons to suspect that the outcome of such a strategy might prove disappointing, both because of the immense difficulties involved in determining which industries really fit the mold and because the reactions of foreign governments may ignite a "subsidy war" which could dissipate any of the expected benefits from the strategy.

Though theoretically valid, the precepts of strategic trade theories would engender a number of problems should policymakers attempt to apply it in the real world. In the words of Paul Krugman,

> an intellectually respectable argument can be made for government policies to create or preserve advantage. The fact that an argument is intellectually respectable does not mean that it is right. Concerns over competitiveness that are valid in principle can be and have been misused or abused in practice.[21]

While it may be possible to create competitive advantage in certain industries, it is not clear that the United States always has an economic interest in doing so. For one thing, the costs of

21. Paul Krugman, "Myths and Realities of Competitiveness," *Science* (November 1991): 254.

such intervention may offset the marginal benefits accruing to the United States. Likewise, a subsidy war between the US, Japan, and Europe could reduce the well-being of all countries as inefficient, protected industries and costly overcapacity are developed within each nation.

More importantly, as with other targeted technology development efforts, the central problem remains one of picking which industries to support and which to ignore. The government would require an immense amount of information regarding the market structure, profitability, and technologies of any target industry—information that is largely unknowable. Moreover, it would have to be able to predict how the industry will evolve over time to ensure that even selective government investments would offer better results than would have been produced by the market alone.

For noneconomists, the new theories supporting the pursuit of strategic trade policies are intuitively attractive. Correctly implementing such policies, however, is virtually impossible given the political environment in the United States. As Robert Lawrence has observed,

> In theory, economists may agree that market failures exist, resulting in rents and spillovers, which may justify government intervention. In the real world of scarce information, uncertainty, and pervasive rent seeking, policymakers will inevitably miss the crucial and subtle distinctions between profits that are high because of rents and those that are high because of risk; between wages that are high because of rents, and those that are high because of skills; and between sectors that provide inputs, and those that result in spillover externalities. Moreover, policymakers would find it extremely difficult to identify appropriate sectors and confine public largesse to sectors meeting such criteria.[22]

In short, without a clear, consistent and defensible method for choosing among competing claims for support, policymakers have no basis for selecting one technology over another, one industry in place of others, and, certainly, one company instead of its competitors.

---

22. Robert Lawrence, *An American Trade Strategy* (Washington, D.C.: The Brookings Institution, 1990), 21.

Problem Three: Misguided Incentives

Finally, there is a third possible explanation for American industry's perceived failure to invest adequately in research and development: inappropriate and counterproductive incentives. Unlike barriers to innovation that block or impede progress toward technological goals which companies might otherwise seek, inappropriate incentives push economic actors to pursue their perceived self-interests using strategies that are detrimental to the long-term health of the nation and its industries. In the case of technology development, misguided incentives discourage firms from investing in research and development even when such decisions could yield significant returns to the company and its owners.

Over the past several years, a consensus has emerged holding the US capital allocation system as partially responsible for the relatively lower levels of US investment in new technologies. Capital markets in the United States, it is argued, encourage "short-termism" in American management, making it exceedingly difficult for even the most forward-looking of managers to make the long-term investments crucial to a firm's continued success. In particular, profit-seeking stockholders whose only interests are near-term stock appreciation are blamed for heightening the incentives for maximizing current earnings, often at the expense of long-term competitiveness. Rapid trading of a company's stock, the pressure of quarterly earnings reports, and the lack of commitment by America's largest investors to the long-term are all blamed for the sensitivity of American managers to fluctuations in stock prices and the tendency to spend relatively less on long-term investments. Moreover, when such investments are undertaken, they are more likely to be directed toward activities readily valued by outside investors rather than toward "intangible" activities where results are less predictable or quantifiable. While heavy spending on capital goods like plant and equipment that yield relatively predictable returns was essential to the mass production era of the 1950s, there is evidence to suggest that more intangible investments—R&D, worker training, information systems, managerial innovations—are relatively more important to competitiveness in today's global economy.

A comprehensive study of the US capital allocation system cosponsored by the private Council on Competitiveness and the Harvard Business School suggests that the incentive structures confronting US managers and investors alike can work to undermine the competitiveness of American companies.[23] According to the report's author, Michael Porter, the diverse problems confronting American industry are not isolated phenomena, but constitute a systemic failure of the capital allocation process.

> Although critics frequently blame the shortcomings of U.S. industry on a "short time horizon," ineffective corporate governance, or a high cost of capital, these concerns are just symptoms of a larger problem. What is at issue is a much broader problem, involving the entire system of allocating investment capital within and across companies. This system includes shareholders, lenders, investment managers, corporate directors, managers and employees, who make investment choices in a context determined by government regulations and prevailing management practices.[24]

In brief, the American capital system is characterized by a divergence of interests between owners and corporations that hinders investments in those areas likely to yield the greatest returns. In contrast, Germany and Japan are beneficiaries of a system of patient, long-term capital investment that yields important competitive advantages in the global marketplace.

Evidence of America's investment problems is widespread. Aggregate US spending on all types of investment—plant, property, equipment, R&D, and training—is less relative to GDP than spending by Japanese and German industry. Moreover, even the leading US technology companies are often out-invested by their rivals in Japan. In computers, automobiles, construction equipment, and steel, Japanese market leaders spend relatively more on research and development than IBM, General Motors, Caterpillar, or USX.[25] US investments are also shorter-term in focus. According to one survey of chief executives, only 21 percent of US R&D projects were classified as long-term, whereas 47 percent of Japanese projects and 61 percent of European R&D were considered long-term in focus.[26] The same survey also found that US decision-makers were applying a higher hurdle rate when assessing investment projects than warranted by the cost of capital in the United States. Finally, American CEOs estimated that market pressures forced them to underinvest substantially.

---

23. Michael Porter, *Capital Choices: Changing the Way America Invests in Industry* (Washington, D.C.: Council on Competitiveness, 1992). The following section draws heavily on Porter's analysis.
24. Porter, *Capital Choices*, 20.
25. Porter, *Capital Choices*, 25.
26. J.M. Pterba and L. H. Summers, "Time Horizons of American Firms: New Evidence From a Survey of CEOs," Harvard Business School and Council on Competitiveness, 1992, cited in Porter, *Capital Choices*.

However, there are important qualifications to this picture of the US capital allocation system. Virtually all observers agree that the US system performs particularly well when investing in high-risk, start-up enterprises where profits may be years away. The US system is also particularly adept at shifting resources to emerging industries such as biotechnology and mobile communications, despite prospects of years of substantial losses. Moreover, in certain industries such as telecommunications, pharmaceuticals, software, chemicals and petroleum, American firms perform relatively well in comparison to their overseas counterparts in terms of investment levels. In fact, US industry appears to over-invest in some areas, such as corporate acquisitions and commercial real estate. Finally, there is a widespread consensus that the United States has the most efficient capital market in the world, characterized by low transaction costs, high liquidity, and rapid information flows.

In part, the problems with the US capital allocation system stem from macroeconomic problems in the United States. A stable and growing economy encourages investors to plan for the longer-term. Moreover, large pools of domestic savings facilitate productive investment. However, the looming federal budget deficits, which hold the prospect for higher long-term interest rates and higher inflation, combined with low national savings rates and a tax code and fiscal policy that encourages current consumption over longer-term investment, tend to undermine investment in the United States.[27]

As Porter points out, the problems with the US system go beyond macroeconomic considerations, however. First, the external capital market in the United States—the mechanism by which companies attract funds from outside investors—differs markedly from those operating in Germany and Japan. In the United States, roughly 60 percent of all equity in publicly traded corporations is held by transient owners such as pension funds, mutual funds, and money managers. In contrast, in 1950, only

---

27. US domestic savings rates plunged during the early 1980s. Whereas total domestic savings was roughly nine percent of US net national product during the 1960s, and eight percent during the 1970s, it fell to only 4.5 percent during the 1980s. Although non federal savings rates declined during the decade, the federal budget deficit was the primary cause for the sharp drop-off, absorbing nearly half of all US domestic savings over the decade. President George Bush, *Economic Report of the President* (Washington, D.C.: US Government Printing Office, February 1992), 328.

eight percent of total equity was held by such institutional investors.

The effects of the rise of institutional investors on corporate performance and valuation are substantial. Institutional investors are driven exclusively by near-term returns on their investments. Indeed, mutual and pension fund managers are evaluated explicitly on their performance relative to various stock indices. Moreover, the regulatory environment surrounding such money managers dictates that they diversify their portfolios extensively, investing only in high-liquidity instruments and holding only very small stakes in any one company. For example, the California Public Employees Retirement System reportedly holds stock in over 2,000 companies. Moreover, its largest holding was only 0.71 percent of the corporation's total outstanding equity.

More recently, institutional investors have eliminated company-specific information from their investment decisions entirely, shifting to greater use of index funds. In 1991, 12 percent of all institutional investment was in index funds, with some pension funds placing over 50 percent of their holdings in such funds. Moreover, because of their small stakes in any one company, institutional investors have little influence on company decision-making, further reducing their incentive to gather company-specific information and leaving them with only their ability to buy or sell a company's stock as a lever for affecting management decisions.

This pattern of ownership creates pressures on these investors that are unrelated to company-specific developments. Rapid trading and extensive diversification discourage these large investors from spending the time and money to gain an in-depth understanding of corporations and their industries. Moreover, because they are assessed on an ongoing basis with maximum emphasis on measurable results, money managers have little incentive to look for information on fundamental determinants of a company's long-term success. Instead, investors tend to use proxies, such as current earnings, to evaluate the worth of any particular firm. For established firms, this focus discourages actions such as long-term investment that undermine current earnings. Significantly, the US practice of treating research and development and training as expenses, rather than investments, penalizes spending on such intangible forms of investment even more severely. Investors also tend to prefer acquisitions over internal development efforts because these assets are more easily and inexpensively assessable.

In the case of new start-ups, however, investors generally recognize that current earnings are irrelevant to valuation of the company's prospects for rapid appreciation. As a result, they are forced to look for more fundamental information that better reflects the real value of new companies in emerging industries. However, the same lack of in-depth information can lead to overinvestment in new technologies and industries, particularly in forms readily understood by the market (e.g., plant and equipment).

In contrast to the United States, Germany and Japan have an external capital system characterized by large, semipermanent shareholders driven by a desire for both long-term appreciation and long-term relationships between investors and companies. As a result, extensive information on a company, its industry, and its long-term prospects is accumulated over time from both public and insider sources. Moreover, these shareholders have far more influence on management decisions than is the case in the United States. As a result, the incentives of German and Japanese owners are more in line with those of the company's management.

The external capital markets have a direct impact on the forces driving the internal capital allocation procedures of US companies. The importance of stock prices in shaping corporate decision-making (and in setting executive compensation), combined with the tendency to constitute corporate boards from industry outsiders who have little understanding of either the company or its markets, tends to push harmonization of internal and external goals. As a result, US firms concentrate on achieving measurable, near-term results that will positively affect their current earnings. Moreover, the decentralized structure of many US firms and the emphasis on financial control and standardized, impersonal reporting mechanisms has limited information exchange between line and upper management. This, combined with the tendency to fill the highest ranks of management with nontechnical personnel, limits the availability to key decision-makers of more nuanced information on any particular investment opportunity. It also shifts the internal incentives toward near-term investments with clearly predictable and measurable results, further undermining support for investment in areas such as research and development.

Again, the German and Japanese systems create very different incentive structures consistent with the forces operating in the external capital market. The goals of these German and Japanese managers and directors tend toward perpetuation of the enterprise over the long term. Moreover, they invest heavily in facilitating information flows between different management levels and between the firm and its suppliers and customers. Diversification is also more limited than in the United States. As a result, upper management is relatively more likely to have a clear understanding of the industry and key competitive forces. Finally, technical criteria are given relatively more weight in investment decisions than are strict financial measures of return.

Correcting the shortcomings of the US capital allocation process will require a major overhaul of US financial markets and the regulation governing institutional investors. While action in this area is sometimes beyond the more narrow scope of technology policy, it is essential if the United States hopes to achieve anything more than ad hoc solutions to specific technological challenges.

Conclusions

The United States suffers from three distinct constraints on technological progress that limit and redirect investment away from areas which offer substantial long-term benefits to the economic well-being of the nation. The first problem derives from the nature of research and development itself, whereby spillovers from innovative activities are undervalued by the market. This barrier to progress is universal, affecting US industry as much as it affects industries abroad that are engaged in research and development. The specific character of the other two inhibitors—inappropriate barriers to innovation and misguided incentives—are uniquely American. Redressing these problems will require unique solutions attuned to the specific circumstances prevailing in the United States.

The following chapter examines the range of policy choices available to overcome each of these impediments to technological progress. Any workable technology strategy must recognize the differing problems confronting American business and match the proper policy tool to the specific task to be accomplished. Most importantly, it must develop reasonable criteria and limits governing the use of public funding to encourage private technology development.

8

Policy Lessons from Theory and History

Given the variety of weaknesses in the process by which US companies develop and apply new technologies, any successful federal technology strategy will have to be carefully calibrated to meet the specific maladies it seeks to remedy. Unfortunately, technology policy discussions to date have tended to focus primarily on the most obvious—and controversial—solutions available to cure a wide range of very different problems. That is, proposals have focused on mechanisms for distributing federal monies to worthy private sector researchers and high-technology companies in order to overcome perceived weaknesses in the US system. This solution to the technology policy challenge offers considerable appeal: it is simple, direct, and can be expected to generate a strong and vocal constituency. What a technology strategy centered on public largesse cannot guarantee, however, is real progress in identifying and eliminating practices that undermine the technological competitiveness of American industry.

Instead, it is essential that any technology strategy carefully match the tools available to the underlying problem to be solved. Overcoming the distinct problems identified in chapter seven—spillovers, barriers to innovation, misdirected incentives—will require very different combinations of policy instruments. In a very few instances, these instruments will include federal funding of selected private sector research and development efforts. However, in most instances, what is required is not additional federal monies but a process by which relevant government regulations and operations can be improved to the benefit of US companies. In turn, devising such a process will require unprecedented cooperation between business and government so that public objectives *and* private sector growth can be accommodated in the most efficient manner possible.

This chapter addresses two critical dimensions of a workable technology strategy for the United States. First, it attempts to outline some general policy responses to address the three broad categories of problems outlined in the previous chapter. Second, it focuses on the most controversial aspect of any technology strategy—the direct subsidy of commercial technology development—and draws a set of pragmatic criteria for evaluating any proposed policy. Together, these two dimensions establish the framework for a workable American technology strategy.

Matching Tools to Tasks

Despite the United States' historical predilection for market mechanisms, the federal government has at its disposal a diverse set of policy instruments with which to influence the development and diffusion of new technologies. Perhaps the most important of these is the government's ability to affect, through fiscal and monetary policies, the macroeconomic environment within which US firms operate. To the extent that federal macroeconomic management establishes a predictable, growing economy, investment is encouraged and firms are more likely to fund long-term, high-risk technology development efforts. In an unstable, unpredictable macroeconomic climate with fluctuating growth, on the other hand, the very real possibility of high inflation rates and frequent changes in tax codes or regulations can be expected to impact negatively on investments in long-term research whose benefits might be nullified by changes in the external business environment.

Leaving aside federal control on macroeconomic policies, however, the levers available to the federal government for influencing commercial technology development and diffusion are still diverse. In general, they fall into five basic categories: (1) fiscal and tax measures; (2) trade policies; (3) regulatory policies; (4) changes in government operations; and (5) public awareness and educational efforts. Through changes in these areas, government decision-makers can directly support the attainment of specific technological goals, raise or lower barriers to innovative activities, or change the structure of incentives confronting corporate researchers and managers, investors, lenders and employees.

Each of these instruments has a role to play in the formulation of a coherent technology policy. However, they vary in terms of their effectiveness in addressing specific problems. For example, government subsidies for defense companies attempting to move into commercial markets could greatly facilitate this transition. With government monies, defense manufacturers may be able to overcome the artificial barriers imposed by government regulation and develop effective marketing and production techniques to compete in the commercial marketplace. Government subsidies may also encourage commercial companies to pursue long-term research and development efforts that they would not otherwise have undertaken due to the disincentives built into the US capital system. Similarly, changes in trade policy (e.g., a protective tariff) may stimulate or sustain domestic production of a particularly significant technology.

However, there are reasons to believe that such measures are less than ideal solutions to the underlying problem. Addressing the effects of the Defense Department's perverse acquisition regulations through subsidy programs may provide immediate relief for those companies fortunate enough to receive the subsidies, but such measures would do nothing to eliminate the causes for the barriers between military and commercial production. Similarly, attempting to correct for the effects of the misalignment of the incentive structure in US capital markets through government grants treats symptoms rather than causes. In both cases, a drive to eliminate the underlying causes of the problem, though more difficult, could be expected to have a more profound and lasting effect on the technological capabilities of US industries.

When devising a national technology strategy, it is also crucial to remain focused on the overall objective of US technology policy. As suggested in chapter six, technology policy must serve the goal of increasing overall productivity levels and national well-being. Policy changes designed to assist specific sectors of the economy, particularly when they involve the adoption of protectionist trade barriers, must be assessed in terms of their effect on the nation as a whole. While trade sanctions may benefit a particular sector or interest group, they will almost always lead to negative consequences for the economy at large.

As a general principle, the federal government has allocated funds primarily for the purpose of providing public goods—those goods and services that benefit society as a whole but which would be underfunded were markets left to their own devices. Government support for infrastructure development, health care, defense, social justice, law enforcement, and education all derive from the belief that these public goods are essential to a safe and well-functioning society *and* that they would be inadequately supported by private markets acting on their own.

Obviously, the question of what is and is not a public good suitable for government support is sometimes open to question. While most agree that government spending on infrastructure development, the armed forces, and education are clearly warranted, there is more debate on whether the government should support other activities. Throughout the technology policy debate, for example, there has been a great deal of discussion of

✳ "strategic" industries and critical technologies. Proponents argue that federal funding is justified in these areas because they are essential to the economic future of the country. If these sectors are failing, the argument continues, then there is clearly a failure of the private market to support these critical industries adequately.

However, there is no clear analytical definition of which industries are truly critical and which technologies are vital to the nation's future. Typically, lists of strategic industries encompass high-technology sectors such as microelectronics, computers, aerospace, communications, biotechnology and advanced materials. Why the health of these industries is more important than that of other manufacturing or service sectors is unclear, however. Even if the computer industry, for example, provides products that will fundamentally reshape the entire economy, it is uncertain whether the industry itself is critical, or whether the application of computer technology throughout all industries is key.

Fortunately, the taxonomy of technology-related problems outlined in the previous chapter suggests that only spillovers qualify as public goods deserving of government investment. Spillovers from privately funded research and development offer significant benefits for society at large, benefits that are not considered as firms make their individual investment choices. This difference between social and private returns from research spending clearly makes spillover effects a public good deserving of direct government support. Moreover, attempts to correct for the nature of the R&D process through other governmental policy changes (e.g., regulatory reform, etc.) would be ineffective, at best. Public goods are like any other good—they must be purchased. Of course, as is discussed below, there are many possible ways for the government to purchase these public goods. Direct grants, tax credits, and support for efforts to maximize the flow of spillovers between companies are all possible approaches to redressing the basic spillover problem.

The appropriateness of federal subsidies to address the other two basic causes of America's technological troubles—barriers to innovation and misguided incentives—is far less clear, however. Changing the incentive structure affecting technology choices in US companies, for example, does not require any government funding per se. Instead, what is required are changes in the regulatory environment to permit the alignment of shareholder and company interests. Certainly, changes in tax laws will be required to restructure the prevailing incentive system. However, these changes need not amount to a subsidy to US industry or investors. Unlike the spillover case, attempts to affect the system's incentives do not constitute a purchase by the government of some public good. As a result, tax law changes could, and perhaps should, be revenue-neutral, affecting corporate decision-making without redistributing wealth.

Overcoming the many different barriers to technological progress will require a somewhat more complex set of policy instruments. While the removal of inappropriate regulatory obstacles, such as unique government accounting and purchasing practices, will be difficult, it will require mainly political will rather than federal dollars. In contrast, measures to improve the efficiency and effectiveness of government operations, for example, by improving access to government-funded technical data or bolstering work on standards development, may require additional federal expenditures. In essence, such efforts are an extension of the government's function of providing public goods for the efficient operation of the economy.

Overcoming firm-specific barriers will be even more difficult. In part, obstacles to innovation within firms may be better addressed through changes in capital market regulations than through direct federal intervention. However, even with such changes, there is no guarantee that firms will update their corporate strategies or revamp their organizational structures as required. The appropriate government role in these circumstances is probably limited to an educational function—highlighting "best practices" within industry and providing assistance to companies trying to learn how to upgrade their operations and gain access to new technologies. The Malcolm Baldridge quality award program is one good example of how even modest government efforts can raise awareness in industry of new managerial techniques and quality control methods. In general, however, there appear to be adequate private sector mechanisms to promote awareness of new technologies and processes among larger corporations. A stronger argument can be made that such mechanisms appear to be underdeveloped for small and medium-sized firms, leaving these firms at the mercy of self-interested vendors and consultants as they seek out information on how to improve their operations. Modest federally funded efforts, administered preferably by state and local organizations, could make a substantial contribution to overcoming these problems.

Finally, federal attempts to help firms surmount market-imposed barriers should probably be even more limited. Obviously, where barriers to entry are so significant as to create natural monopolies, federal intervention to regulate such industries is appropriate. Moreover, where foreign practices, such as dumping, trade restrictions and government subsidies, conspire to create obstacles to US companies, trade policy remedies to remove these obstacles are in order. However, arguments that propose federal assistance to certain industries simply because they face unusually large barriers to entry are highly suspect. Simply because a new semiconductor fabrication line may cost upwards of $1 billion to construct does not establish a public obligation or public reason to fund such an endeavor. Unless a clear case of market failure is demonstrated, direct public support is unwarranted. Despite much discussion of "strategic" industries and strategic trade policy, proof that such industries are clearly identifiable and generate important public goods has been lacking.

In brief, we are left with a rather straightforward set of criteria for fitting the proper policy tool to the specific task. However, there remains considerable room for debate as to how the government should go about structuring and implementing such programs. As suggested, the most controversial aspect of these efforts has been the process by which the federal government distributes funds to promote technology development. The following section attempts to establish some broad criteria for formulating such policies and examines ongoing US government programs in light of these criteria.

Structuring Federal Assistance Programs

The analysis of the political forces at work in the formulation of any technology policy suggests that while there may be an abundance of policy proposals, many will be heavily motivated by private interests rather than public concerns. Sorting through them requires the application of a uniform set of criteria for assessing whether any particular policy is likely to achieve its objectives. The foregoing discussion of economic, technological, and political obstacles suggests the following basic principles for any technology development effort:

- **Additive.** Public funding should stimulate, not replace, private R&D spending. This automatically renders suspect any program that simply issues grants to selected companies, suggesting instead that mechanisms which produce additional R&D spending in industry at the margin (e.g., tax credits) are more appropriate.

- **Politically Resilient.** Programs should be able to resist or accommodate political pressures without subverting their basic purpose. Policies that rely on good faith and perfect execution are patently unrealistic. Instead, programs that accept the inevitability of calls for special treatment by congressmen, companies, and other institutions are likely to be more effective and sustainable over the long term.

- **Market-Sensitive.** Programs should contain clear mechanisms that can transmit market signals to relevant decision-makers and permit them to adjust smoothly over time to changing circumstances. In particular, decisions about the commercial relevance of any particular project should be delegated to those with the most direct information about market conditions.

- **Susceptible to Informed Government Decision-Making.** Government officials should have independent access to the requisite information to make necessary decisions. Selection criteria and decision-making should be tailored to ensure that government decision-makers have the resources to carry out their mission in a defensible manner, without relying on self-interested parties.

- **Targeted at Areas of Underinvestment.** Policies should be directed toward those activities where social returns greatly exceed private returns. There must be some assurance that a given policy will produce net benefits, economic or otherwise, which would not have been produced were private markets allowed to function on their own.

Obviously, this checklist poses a considerable challenge for designers of an effective technology program. While no policy should be expected to meet every one of these points definitively, serious questions should be raised about any proposal that fails to address at least a majority of these conditions. A brief analysis of four ongoing technology programs, using these criteria, highlights some of their strengths and weaknesses and helps to define the limits of a successful federal technology strategy.

The Research and Development Tax Credit

The research and development tax credit, enacted as part of the Economic Recovery Tax Act of 1981, is perhaps the most robust technology-promotion effort to date. In brief, the R&D tax credit allows firms to deduct 20 percent of the increase in their R&D spending over the average amount spent during the preceding three years. This effectively changes the cost-benefit calculation for all firms considering additional R&D expenditures. In theory, with a R&D tax credit, companies should increase their R&D spending to the point where the last dollar spent returns a dollar reward that *includes* the value of the tax credit. Consequently, projects that might have been considered economically unrewarding become more feasible when the tax credit is included.

Since 1981, the R&D tax credit has been modified and extended several times. Between 1982 and 1985, the value of the tax credit was set at 25 percent of the incremental R&D investment. The credit expired in 1985, but was reinstated in 1986 and extended annually in 1987 and 1988. However, upon renewal, the value of the credit was reduced to 20 percent. The R&D tax credit has since been extended again through annual congressional actions, and both former President Bush and President Clinton called for the credit to be made permanent.

Congressional actions over the past decade have served to steadily erode the value of the R&D tax credit. The change from a 25 to 20 percent deductible was compounded by the 1986 tax law that lowered corporate taxes and thereby reduced the value of the R&D tax credit. In addition, in 1988 Congress enacted a 50 percent deduction allowance, further diminishing the value of the tax.

Despite these changes, evidence indicates that the R&D tax credit has served as a powerful stimulus for increased private sector R&D. Early estimates of the amount of additional corporate R&D conducted for each dollar of foregone tax revenue range from $0.35 to $0.99.[1] One study estimated that between 1981 and 1985, the R&D tax credit boosted private R&D spending by roughly seven percent, resulting in an additional $3 billion increase in R&D spending.[2] A follow-up study confirmed these initial results. Moreover, it indicated that, after 1986, the stimulative effect of the tax credit declined substantially, reflecting the lower value of the credit following changes in the legislation and reductions to overall corporate taxes. Nevertheless, even after its

---

1. Congressional Budget Office, *Federal Support for R&D and Innovation* (Washington, D.C.: Congressional Budget Office, April 1984), 78.
2. Martin Neil Bailey and Robert Lawrence, "Tax Policies for Innovation and Competitiveness," study issued April 3, 1987.

value was reduced, it continued to have a strong positive effect on private R&D spending.[3]

The advantages of the program from a policy perspective are obvious. Most importantly, implementation required few bureaucratic innovations. Moreover, because it applies identical, mechanical standards to all industries, the implementation of the R&D tax credit program has been relatively immune to political pressures. It avoids entirely the need to select specific technologies or industries for support, opting instead to leave such decisions entirely to the market. By delegating these decisions to normal market forces, the tax credit approach places relatively few informational demands on policymakers beyond setting the overall deduction and developing an adequate methodology for determining which expenses qualify for the credit.

However, because it encourages research and development across the board, the tax credit makes no attempt to distinguish between activities that might suffer from high levels of underinvestment and those that do not. Consequently, even with the tax credit, some technologies may remain underfunded from society's perspective, while others might receive too much funding. Because the social returns to R&D investment, on average, significantly exceed private returns, however, the net result of even this blunt approach is positive. Essentially, the situation is analogous to picking stocks in the stock market. If one invests in a diversified portfolio, he or she is assured (usually) of a positive return. In contrast, picking and choosing among stocks raises the possibility of higher returns, but also carries a comparable risk of losses.

Despite considerable support, the program continues to be enacted on a temporary basis, requiring the periodic intervention of the Congress for its renewal. This susceptibility to the political process is perhaps the weakest characteristic of the program to date. While there is no firm analysis supporting raising or lowering the size of the credit, numerous observers have suggested that its temporary status has reduced its effectiveness. Corporate planners, they argue, will undervalue the credit when making long-term R&D investment decisions, unsure whether Congress will severely modify or even discontinue the credit in the future. Consequently, from a policy perspective, removing this uncer-

---

3. Martin Neil Baily and Robert Z. Lawrence, "Tax Incentives for R&D: What Do the Data Tell Us?" in US Congress, House of Representative, Committee on Ways and Means, *Permanent Extension of Certain Expiring Tax Provisions* Serial 102-83 (Washington, D.C.: US Government Printing Office, 1992), 393-408.

tainty is clearly desirable. In addition, eliminating other tax law provisions that undermine the effectiveness of the tax credit by encouraging firms to move their R&D operations offshore could make a real contribution to US competitiveness.[4]

The Advanced Technology Program

The Advanced Technology Program (ATP) within the Commerce Department's National Institute of Standards and Technology (NIST) takes a significantly different approach to promoting commercial technology development. Established by the 1988 Technology Competitiveness Act, the ATP program provides grants to individual companies, independent research institutes (non-university), and joint ventures for "precompetitive, generic technology" research. To ensure that companies are committed to the work, the ATP program strictly limits the government's share. In the case of individual companies, ATP will provide at most $2 million for direct research costs over three years. The program will provide less than 50 percent of the funding over five years for programs sponsored by joint ventures. ATP funding grew substantially during its first three years, from $10 million in 1990 to $63 million in fiscal 1993.

Unlike the R&D tax credit, which relies exclusively on the private sector for selecting which technological opportunities to support, the ATP program relies on a rigorous application procedure to determine which projects merit federal support. In an annual competition, ATP solicits R&D projects that show commercial and technological promise, demonstrate a high level of commitment by the sponsoring organization, and are "in the economic interest of the United States" because they offer "broad-based benefits" to the US economy. Although the initial awards have tended toward projects in material sciences, electronics, and information technologies, the program sets no specific target areas for research.

On the surface, the ATP approach seems to represent a workable compromise between broad, diffuse measures like R&D tax credits and more focused government-directed technology support programs. By soliciting proposals from industry and requiring a significant financial contribution by the private sector, the program ensures that projects remain sensitive to market conditions. Insisting that private corporations contribute some, if not most,

---

4. For a discussion of the damaging effects of regulation 861-8 and its unintended incentive to move R&D operations abroad, see Martin Neil Baily, "Tax Incentives for R&D."

of the funding for a particular project instills some additional market discipline in the technology selection process. Presumably, the greater the company's financial stake in a particular effort, the more thorough it will be in determining whether there is a market for the resulting technology and the more vigorous it will be in commercializing the final results.[5]

The openness of the ATP application process, with its loose definition of US "economic interest," also removes most of the difficulty surrounding government selection of technologies to support.[6] The task becomes one of ensuring that the "broad-based benefits" of the program appear legitimate, and that the proposals satisfy narrow technical criteria. This limits the informational demands on government officials, particularly since NIST has used a pool of qualified outside scientists, engineers, and businessmen to evaluate proposals. Moreover, the formality of the application and review process will probably help ATP avoid the most egregious types of political intervention.

Despite these strengths, ATP suffers from a number of serious drawbacks. The most significant involves the question of whether government funding is inducing additional research and development activity, or simply substituting public for private funds. By asking companies to submit proposals to be considered in a competitive process, ATP inevitably encourages them to submit their best proposals. Arguably, these would have been funded even if public support had not been forthcoming. Since this public windfall does nothing to change how recipients evaluate other possible R&D projects, there is little reason to hope that recipient companies will expand their overall R&D spending levels.

Secondly, despite attempts to include "broad-based benefits" in the selection criteria, the ATP evaluators still have no analytically sound method for determining whether a particular project suffers unusually from underinvestment. Federal support may

---

5. The validity of this approach is supported by Canadian experience; see "The Commercialization of Government-Sponsored Technologies: Canadian Evidence," *Research Policy*, Vol. 19, No. 198, 1990.
6. According to Public Law 101–515 Sec. 105, "A company shall be eligible to receive financial assistance from the Secretary of Commerce only if: (a) the Secretary...finds that the company's participation...would be in the economic interest of the United States, as evidenced by investment in the United States in research, development, and manufacturing...; significant contributions to employment in the United States; and agreement...to promote the manufacture within the United States of products that result from that technology (taking into account the goals of promoting the competitiveness of United States industry)."

yield some social benefits that would not have been produced otherwise, but if these benefits are less than the average benefits produced by all commercial R&D, then the ATP project approach could leave the nation worse off. Of course, this situation might be ameliorated somewhat if the commitment to pursue "broad-based benefits" and technology transfer agreements induced the firm to behave differently than it would have otherwise. Certainly, in the case of consortia, there is reason to believe that new technologies will spread to member companies more quickly than would otherwise have been the case. Moreover, in order to accept and apply new technologies developed in such consortia, private firms tend to undertake additional in-house research to complement their consortia efforts. Nevertheless, the basic problem remains that evaluators are forced to select the most meritorious proposals without any sound method for determining which might yield the highest social returns.

Thirdly, the strong signal produced by an ATP award could stimulate *overinvestment* in a particular technology or company by the private financial community. Government endorsement of any firm or technology could unduly effect the calculations of other market participants, making it easier for the firm in question to obtain additional funding while making it more difficult to obtain private capital for unselected firms. From the nation's perspective, the benefits of such a signal are ambiguous. Private funds flowing to an ATP recipient are inevitably flowing away from some other productive investment. If this other investment would have yielded higher social returns than the work of the ATP recipient, then the net effect of the government's signal could be negative.

A final problem with ATP stems from its strengths: by opening the competition to all areas of technology, it risks being perceived as scatter shot, particularly if its budget remains limited. Funding a handful of projects may achieve some technical breakthroughs, but it is unlikely to produce politically satisfying benefits. Given the minuscule number of companies that will receive ATP awards, their diversity and geographic dispersion, and the temporary nature of their association with ATP, the program may find it difficult to develop a committed constituency in the private sector. While the day-to-day operation of the program will probably remain resistant to undue political influence, pressures will likely grow over the long term for a more focused, results-oriented approach targeting specific technological areas.

Engineering Research Centers

The National Science Foundation's Engineering Research Centers (ERCs) offer another attempt to involve the private sector directly in the technology selection process. Established in 1984, the multidisciplinary ERC program seeks to strengthen ties between university research and industrial engineering challenges, while allowing engineering students to gain a greater understanding of real world manufacturing problems. Individual ERCs are co-sponsored by the NSF, universities, and industry (and, in some cases, by state and local governments). Currently, 19 ERCs are in operation with annual budgets of between $2.5 million and $8.0 million. Much of this funding comes from nonfederal sources, with NSF's contributions ranging from $2.0 million to $3.5 million per year. ERCs are selected on the basis of a national competition and are chartered for five years, with options to extend the program if warranted. The 1991 competition resulted in the creation of two new centers selected from a pool of 48 applicants. According to agency officials, well over 400 companies are currently participating in the ERC program.

In general, the program has received favorable reviews by industry representatives. In addition, most reviews seem to indicate that the ERCs have accomplished their objective of improving engineering education, although the number of students affected by the program remains small. Faculty members, however, have voiced some concerns relating to the short-term focus and unstable participation of the industry participants. Moreover, all of the centers have received far less funding than originally planned, which has restricted their activities and forced them to devote time to increasing industry participation.

Like the ATP program, the competitions for new centers are open to research in any technological area. The relevance of the project is guaranteed largely by the commitment of industries and universities to provide the requisite funding. In contrast to the ATP program, however, the ERC program emphasizes the creation of a process, rather than a specific technology. This further relieves the government of the need to select specific technologies to support. Moreover, the openness of American universities virtually guarantees that technologies will be "precompetitive" and "generic," at least from the participating firms' perspective.

Like the ATP program, ERCs are relatively immune to political interference in their day-to-day operations. Moreover, the competitive application process offers a reasonably sound method both for avoiding direct political intervention in technology choices and for limiting the informational demands on government policymakers. Determining whether an application meets the necessary program requirements in terms of industry and university participation, commitment, and representation is a far simpler task than evaluating which technologies are critical to the nation's future.

As with other targeted approaches, the ERC program offers little assurance that it will address technological areas with particularly high social returns (relative to private returns). However, by creating an environment in which innovating companies and researchers can come in close contact, the ERC program does promise to stimulate some of the "clustering" spillovers discussed previously. Moreover, the centers' dual role—to develop technologies while promoting education—ensures that additional spillovers in the form of a better educated workforce are created.

The Sematech Consortium and Support for Critical Technologies

Founded in 1987, Sematech is the most prominent example of a highly targeted federal research effort. Established in part on the basis of national security concerns about US dependence on foreign semiconductors, the non-profit consortium receives $100 million annually from the Defense Department and is dedicated to improving US semiconductor manufacturing technologies. The 11 remaining members of the consortium, representing the largest US merchant and captive producers of semiconductors, provide an additional $100 million to the consortium. Although the establishment of Sematech was a highly political process, and although DOD was extensively involved in helping to organize the new consortium, the federal government has generally limited its involvement in day-to-day operations and in setting the research agenda. Approximately 700 people are employed at the consortium's Austin, Texas research center, 200 of whom are on loan from member companies.

In all, the federal government contributed $600 million by 1993 to Sematech. Despite widespread support for the program, its results remain open to question. Supporters claim that Sematech has made immense progress and has largely fulfilled its original technical objectives. Moreover, Sematech is sometimes credited with reviving the US semiconductor industry and reversing the slide in the US market position. They admit that the program's technical goals changed over the past five years, but argue that the technologies produced by the consortium will make US manu-

facturers more competitive in important emerging markets. De-
tractors argue that Sematech has done little to improve the
competitiveness of US semiconductor manufacturers and has
instead simply funneled money to industry giants while ignoring
the needs of smaller producers. Despite these criticisms, it appears that Sematech has made a positive contribution to the
competitiveness of the US semiconductor industry.

Applying the five criteria outlined above to Sematech at best
produces a mixed evaluation. On the positive side, Sematech has
evolved over time to take account of changing market conditions
and has demanded little in the way of government decision-making regarding which specific research projects to support. Moreover, despite the initial considerable controversy surrounding the
effort, Sematech has consistently received the full funding
amount requested and has generated a broad, bipartisan constituency on Capitol Hill.

However, by no measure has the Sematech experiment been
free of political manipulation. The process by which Sematech
was originally founded was highly political, resulting more from
congressional action than any rigorous analysis of the relative
contribution of the semiconductor industry to America's long-
term productivity growth. Once the original five-year charter
expired in 1992, moreover, the political battle to continue the
program began again. Though the Bush administration sought to
cut Sematech's budget back to $80 million per year, lobbyists for
the consortium and supporters in Congress were able to restore
the program's funding levels to the $100 million level. Moreover,
congressional supporters have rejected DARPA's recommendations that the program be phased-out in favor of a competitively
awarded semiconductor research program.

Such a process opens the door to whichever industry happens
to capture the public ear. Several years ago, the demand for an
all-out government effort to develop high-definition television
(HDTV) technology reached a crescendo, before the emergence of
new technologies (digital television) and more rigorous market
analyses threw some cold water on the original enthusiasm. In
retrospect, most observers agree that the decision not to fund
HDTV research was probably a wise one, allowing sufficient time
to pass for researchers to develop a better standard. However, the
decision not to fund HDTV research was not motivated by pre-
scient analysis of the possibilities offered by digital television, but
by the ardent resistance of the Bush Administration to any thing
resembling industrial policy. With the Bush Administration gone,
gone too may be a sufficient counterweight to oppose self-inter-

ested industry groups looking for government assistance. As Robert Lawrence has observed, when it comes to industries in Washington, they are "like children in Lake Woebegon—they are all above average."[7]

The politicization of Sematech was probably inevitable, both because of its origins and its size. Whereas the ATP effort will likely create only a modest constituency, the political strength of Sematech is considerable. This virtually guaranteed continuation of the program, regardless of whether it was meeting any socially desirable objectives. Moreover, its exclusive structure and bias toward the industry's largest players virtually guaranteed that those firms left outside would complain, raising issues of fairness and accountability. In addition, the attempt to combine the largest manufacturers with more modest companies in a single consortium no doubt made Sematech *less* sensitive to the specific market conditions confronting individual firms. The defections of Micron Technologies and LSI, both of which complained that Sematech's agenda was incompatible with their own commercial needs, illustrates how an industry's competitive environment can vary substantially across companies. Harris Semiconductor's departure from the group demonstrates a similar divergence of interests among industry players.

There is also a real question whether federal funding stimulated additional private R&D or simply substituted public monies for private. In general, cooperative research does tend to encourage firms to undertake additional in-house research, both to create receiving mechanisms for consortium-developed technologies and also as a hedge against their competitors' activities (of which, through participation in the consortium, companies now have a better understanding). Public funds probably did help overcome some of the companies' original suspicions of cooperative research. Whether this required a $500 million commitment is questionable, however. Notably, Sematech officers have admitted that the consortium would continue its operations even if federal funds were withdrawn, suggesting that the original barriers to cooperation have long-since been overcome.

Critical Technologies and a Civilian ARPA The approach taken in the Critical Technologies Reports represents one possible means of overcoming the ad hoc process that has characterized

---

7. Robert Lawrence, "Innovation and Trade: Meeting the Foreign Challenge," in Henry J. Aaron, ed., *Setting National Priorities: Policy for the Nineties* (Washington, D.C.: The Brookings Institution, 1990), 169.

Sematech's foundation. These reports represent legitimate attempts to identify objectively those technologies which could prove significant to the country's economic future. By balancing industry perspectives with those of a host of experts from inside and outside the government, a more accurate picture of the technological horizons should be obtainable than that available through the political process alone.

Although this approach has made considerable progress in identifying technical objectives, it has yet to be translated into a formal program to achieve specific technological objectives. Many have suggested that either a separate, civilian agency be developed specifically to use federal dollars to support the development of commercial technologies, or that the research agenda of the Department of Defense's Advanced Research Projects Agency (ARPA) be expanded to encompass commercial technology development. With the Clinton administration's decision to remove the "Defense" from DARPA's name, it appears that the later approach will be given a try.

Founded in 1958, ARPA proved to be a highly effective supporter of crucial defense technologies. ARPA concentrates on identifying and promoting high-risk, high-payoff technologies that promise to revolutionize the conduct of warfare. The agency has gained a reputation as a flexible, forward-thinking elite organization that has made substantial contributions to America's defense. Its lean, expert staff, streamlined organizational structure, and bureaucratic independence has allowed ARPA to pursue innovative ideas that might have stood little chance of being supported by the individual military services. In short, it has been characterized as "85 venture capitalists linked together by a travel office."[8] While some of these investments have failed, and others have taken a very long time to pay off, ARPA's overall record is impressive.

The effectiveness of a civilian ARPA intended to develop a set number of critical technologies would depend greatly on how it pursued its work. Presuming that it would follow procedures roughly akin to those used in the past by ARPA, issuing contracts to specific companies and research institutes to achieve particular technical objectives, a civilian critical technologies agency could encounter significant obstacles.

Most obviously, a civilian ARPA would suffer from the problem of acquiring independent access to unbiased market information

---

8. Quoted in Burton Edelson and Robert Stern, "The Operations of DARPA and its Utility as a Model for a Civilian ARPA," (Washington, D.C., Foreign Policy Institute, November 1989), 5.

(and discipline). ARPA, with its exclusive focus on military technology, its ready access to military designers and service laboratories, and the requirement that the technologies it develops
eventually be accepted by the services, gains intimate knowledge
of what its customers are interested in. This almost always
ensures that technologies developed by the agency will find a
market in the military. Even with the insights offered by the
critical technologies approach, however, program officials at a
civilian ARPA would have only limited information on the actual
dynamics of the market, particularly as it concerned very narrow
technological choices. Companies wedded to outmoded technologies may nevertheless exercise strong influence in the setting of
a civilian ARPA's research agenda, particularly if the potential
competitors were small and politically unorganized.

Moreover, a civilian ARPA would likely encounter considerably
more political pressure than its military counterpart. Because of
its small size, bureaucratic location, and military mission, ARPA
has been largely shielded from excessive public attention and
relatively immune to political pressures. However, this immunity
is by no means complete. In the fiscal 1992 defense budget, for
example, Congress appropriated additional funding for ARPA to
cover a range of unrequested programs. These included every-
thing from high-definition displays to nonacoustic antisubmarine
warfare technologies to x-ray lithography. A civilian ARPA, unpro-
tected by the cloak of national security, would be subject to even
greater political pressures from various groups that might argue
that a particular sector or technology was vital to the nation's
economy. This situation would grow in severity as the agency's
budget grew. It seems improbable that members of Congress and
their constituents would keep silent for long if their favored
technologies were consistently passed over by the civilian ARPA's
staff.

While the process of devising a comprehensive list of critical
technologies would limit such interference, the narrow technical
choices remaining within the discretion of program officers would
still have enormous consequences for the markets and companies
involved. Without a consistent set of principles for promoting one
technology over another, even the most expert and well-inten-
tioned individual would be reduced to subjective judgments and
personal biases. Even if broad decisions are carried out within an
organized structure involving government and industry, specific
project judgments may end up unduly favoring one company or
technology path over another. Such favoritism could have an

extreme distortionary effect, particularly during the early phases of a technology's development.

The current ARPA effort to support the development of massively parallel supercomputers is a good example of how technology decisions can reverberate throughout the political system, as well as the market. Efforts to perfect massively parallel computer architectures enjoy widespread support, but ARPA has been accused of favoring technical approaches being pursued by two companies at the expense of other promising alternatives. This has led competing manufacturers to complain that ARPA is driving viable technologies out of the market. These complaints reached such a pitch that Congress directed ARPA to review its supercomputer regulations to eliminate any such bias. Although regulatory safeguards (multiple review processes, contract audit procedures, etc.) could be established to prevent the most egregious trespasses, such regulations could in the end deprive a counterpart civilian agency of the flexibility that has made its military counterpart so successful.

The critical technologies approach engenders another political challenge. The formulation of an explicit list of technologies inevitably results in a strong political emphasis on US performance in those areas. Just as the formulation of Sematech made the US share of world semiconductor output a measure of the country's well-being, listing other technologies as "critical" lends their development greater political importance than their economic significance might warrant. As these issues become salient, the arguments of companies in technical fields where the United States is behind will grow in resonance.

Finally, the contracts/grants approach offers no assurances that federal monies will be used to stimulate additional research. Even if matching grants are involved, there is no assurance that the private sector will spend more on R&D than they otherwise would. Nor do the criteria employed in the critical technologies report ensure that federal investments are directed at redressing particularly severe cases of private underinvestment. Instead, the criteria would be purely technical, leaving questions of economic return unanswered.

Establishing A Civilian Technology Agency

These criticisms of a civilian ARPA do not constitute a rejection of the notion that the federal government should develop a single agency to oversee implementation of its various commercial technology programs. Rather, it reflects concerns about the specific approach taken by ARPA, with its heavy involvement in technology decision-making and its emphasis on contract research projects. While such procedures may be appropriate for the development of military technology, there seems little reason to hope that they would be equally effective in promoting beneficial commercial innovations.

Turning the Department of Defense's ARPA into a civilian technology agency presents a number of organizational difficulties as well. The Congressional Research Service (CRS) has warned that ARPA has neither the personnel nor the expertise required to implement successfully the range of technology programs advocated by the new Clinton administration and members of Congress. In particular, CRS noted that despite the fact that the agency's budget had more than doubled in five years—soaring from $880 million in 1988 to $2.2 billion for fiscal 1993—the number of technical personnel at DARPA had remained flat. According to the report, "Current and former DARPA employees argue that the agency is a victim of its own success. DARPA's expanding responsibilities and special contract authorities have bogged down the agency with additional bureaucratic red tape." CRS also warned that were DARPA to follow Congress' recommendations and begin supporting commercial technology development for its own sake, the agency could lose track of its mission while becoming a lightning rod for "pork barrel politics."[9]

The formation of a separate Civilian Technology Agency, however, perhaps within the Commerce Department, does make political and bureaucratic sense. The present funding of civilian technology projects through NIST, DOD, the National Science Foundation, and NASA guarantees that program implementation will be fragmented, with multiple congressional committees having opportunities to influence the process. More damaging, it can detract from these agencies' primary missions. While NSF, DOD, and NIST have often done an adequate job of initiating and sustaining the various programs now underway, civilian technology development is not their primary mission. As a result, expanding the functions of these agencies risks either diverting their attention away from their central tasks or having the purposes of any particular civilian technology program subverted to serve the agencies' primary mission. In tight budget times, in particular, new civilian technology efforts are likely to face stiff competition within established agencies.

---

9. "Broader role may overextend DARPA, CRS says," *Aerospace Daily*, January 11, 1993, 44.

Implications for Policy

The preceding discussion suggests a number of prescriptions for policy:

First, to ensure that federal support induces incremental research, policies that rely on direct grants to individual companies or closed consortia should be avoided. Tax credits, which affect decisions at the margin, are generally preferable to outright grants. Where use of such credits is unrealistic, the programs themselves should be structured in such a manner that firms are likely to undertake incremental R&D. This argues for relatively open research forums that stimulate competitors to undertake complementary research within their own labs, as is the case with NSF's Engineering Research Centers.

Second, political resilience requires that program structures accept the need for formal, explicit selection procedures open to public inspection. The formal application procedures used by ATP and the ERCs provides a useful hedge against pernicious government decision-making and undue political influence on specific technology choices. In contrast, a decision process that relies heavily on subjective evaluations, even if conducted in good faith, will be more prone both to capture by private interests and to protest by excluded parties. In this case, the procedures used by ARPA to establish technical objectives do not serve as good models for future programs.

In addition, programs should be constructed so that they can resist or channel political pressures for special treatment into socially useful forums. This calls for disbursing benefits widely in order to balance the narrow interests of particular groups against one another. Obviously, the R&D tax credit is the program most resistant to this sort of political manipulation. But, such programs as the ERCs and technology extension services also offer some protection by holding out the possibility that any interested group, regardless of congressional district, has an equal chance in a formal, merit-based application procedure.

Third, mechanical methods for ensuring that policies remain relevant to the private sector are preferable to ones based primarily on the technical expertise of government decision-makers. Again, widely disbursed tax benefits offer the ideal example, but financing arrangements that require considerable private matching investment have also proven effective. In any case, detailed technical and program decisions should be delegated to the private sector to the maximum extent practical.

Fourth, government program managers should not be required to make decisions that are beyond their capabilities. This is the converse of the finding that authority over market-oriented decisions should be left to market participants. At the same time, it suggests that proposals which call on officials to identify industries and technologies which are especially deserving of public support (a challenge economists have yet to conquer) are doomed to failure. Instead, government decision-makers should limit themselves to more narrow issues concerning the suitability of a particular organization to undertake research, the compliance of applications with standard requirements, and the evaluation of accountability and control methods.

Fifth, commercial technology development efforts should avoid selecting particular areas for development on the basis of claims that they are especially critical to the economy's future. As has been argued before, problems of appropriability, higher-than-average spillovers, and dynamic trade effects are interesting in theory, but no defensible methodology has been developed for identifying which technologies are more susceptible to these problems than others. Consequently, broad, general support measures are the most appropriate.

However, while the analytic tools do not exist for deciding which technologies are especially deserving, there is considerable reason to believe that particular *activities* produce greater social returns. Specifically, programs which help to increase the interchange of ideas, the education of workers and students, and the diffusion of new technologies will probably yield greater social returns than would efforts simply to develop new technologies within private corporate laboratories.

Consequently, the primary focus of any targeted effort should be the creation of such centers for innovation. Federal and state technology extension services programs and localized research and development efforts tied to universities and other R&D centers offer perhaps the best chance for improving American industry's technological capabilities through a sustainable process. Combined with an enhanced R&D tax credit, this two-prong approach could serve to stimulate increased R&D throughout the country while creating additional geographically specific spill overs from innovative activity.

Selected Bibliography

Aaron, Henry J., ed. *Setting National Priorities: Policy for the Nineties.* Washington, D.C.: The Brookings Institution, 1990.

Aerospace Education Foundation, *Lifeline Adrift: The Defense Industrial Base in the 1990s.* Washington, D.C.: Air Force Association, September 1991.

Aerospace Industries Association. *The US Aerospace Industry and the Trend Toward Internationalization.* Washington, D.C.: AIA, March 1988.

———. *The US Aerospace Industry in the 1990s: A Global Perspective.* Washington, D.C.: AIA, September 1991.

Alic, John M., et al. *Beyond Spinoff: Military and Commercial Technologies in a Changing World.* Boston, Massachusetts: Harvard Business School Press, 1992.

The Analytic Sciences Corporation. *Foreign Vulnerability of Critical Industries.* Arlington, Virginia: The Analytic Sciences Corporation, March 1, 1990.

"Army Information Systems Plan Targets Off-the-Shelf Hardware." *Defense Electronics* (May 1991): 8.

Arrow, Kenneth J. "Economic Welfare and the Allocation of Resources for Invention." In *The Rate and Direction of Inventive Activity,* 609-625. Universities-National Bureau Committee for Economic Research. Princeton, New Jersey: Princeton University Press, 1962.

Arthur, W. Brian. "Positive Feedbacks in the Economy." *Scientific American* 262 (February 1990): 92-99.

Atwood, Donald, Deputy Secretary of Defense. Speech to the National Security Industry Associations, Washington, D.C., July 17, 1989.

Baily, Martin Neil and Robert Z. Lawrence. "Tax Incentives for R&D: What Do the Data Tell Us?" in US Congress, House Ways and Means Committee. *Permanent Extension of Certain Expiring Tax Provisions,* 383-408. Washington, D.C.: US Government Printing Office, 1992.

Baldwin, Richard and Paul Krugman. "Industrial Policy and International Competition in Wide-Bodied Jet Aircraft." In *Trade Policy Issues and Empirical Analysis,* 45-71. Chicago, Illinois: University of Chicago Press, 1988.

Baumol, William J., Sue Anne Batey Blackman and Edward N. Wolff. *Productivity and American Leadership: The Long View.* Cambridge, Massachusetts: The MIT Press, 1989.

Blechman, Barry M. *Worldwide Defense Electronics Market: Outlook 1992–1993.* Washington, D.C.: International Defense Technology, Inc., 1992.

Bollinger, Martin J. and John R. Harbison, *Consolidation in Aerospace/Defense: What's Next?* Bethesda, Maryland: Booz Allen & Hamilton, Inc., 1992.

Bush, George. *Economic Report of the President.* Washington, D.C.: US Government Printing Office, February 1992.

Camm, Frank. *How DoD Policy Affects Private Expenditure on Independent Research and Development: A Comparison of Empirical Studies.* Santa Monica, California: The RAND Corporation, April 1989.

Carnegie Commission on Science, Technology, and Government. *In the National Interest: The Federal Government in the Reform of K-12 Math and Science Education.* New York, NY: Carnegie Commission, September 1991.

——. *New Thinking and American Defense Technology*. New York, NY: Carnegie Commission, August 1990.

——. *Science and Technology in US International Affairs*. New York, New York: Carnegie Commission, January 1992.

——. *Science, Technology, and Congress: Analysis and Advice from the Congressional Suppport Agencies*. New York, New York: Carnegie Commission, October 1991.

——. *Technology and Economic Performance: Organizing the Executive Branch for a Stronger National Technology Base*. New York, New York: Carnegie Commission, September 1991.

Case, John. *From the Ground Up*. New York, New York: Simon & Schuster, 1992.

Chapman, Robert E., Marianne K. Clark, and Eric Dobson. *Technology-Based Economic Development: A Study of State and Federal Technical Extension Services*. NIST Special Publication No. 786. Washington, D.C.: US Department of Commerce, National Institute of Standards and Technology, June 1990.

Cohen, Linda R. and Roger G. Noll. *The Technology Pork Barrel*. Washington, D.C.: The Brookings Institution, 1991.

Cole, Lt. Col. Willie, Lt. Col. Richard Hochberg, and Commander Alfred Therrien. *Europe 1992: Catalyst for Change in Defense Acquisition*. Defense Systems Management College, September 1992.

Competitiveness Policy Council. *First Annual Report to the President & Congress: Building a Competitive America*. Washington, D.C.: Competitiveness Policy Council, March 1, 1992.

Computer Systems Policy Project. *Perspectives on US Technology and Trade Policy: The CSPP Agenda for the 103rd Congress*. October 1, 1992.

Congressional Budget Office. *Federal Support for R&D and Innovation*. Washington, D.C.: Congressional Budget Office, April 1984.

——. "Measuring the Distribution of Income Gains," CBO Staff Memorandum, March 1992.

——. *Using Federal R&D to Promote Commercial Innovation*. Washington, D.C.: US Government Printing Office, April 1988.

——. *Using R&D Consortia for Commercial Innovation: SEMATECH, X-ray Lithography, and High-Resolution Systems*. Washington, D.C.: US Government Printing Office, July 1990.

Council on Competitiveness. *Competitiveness Index*. Washington, D.C.: Council on Competitiveness, 1992.

——. *Gaining New Ground: Technology Priorities for America's Future*. Washington, D.C.: Council on Competitiveness, 1991.

Cox, William A. *Productivity, Competitiveness, and US Living Standards*. Washington, D.C.: Congressional Research Service, 1990.

CSIS Steering Committee on Security and Technology. Integrating Commercial and Military Technologies for National Strength: An Agenda for Change. Washington, D.C.: Center for Strategic and International Studies, March 1991.

Daniel I. Okimoto. *Between MITI and the Market: Japanese Industrial Policy for High Technology*. Stanford, California: Stanford Univerity Press, 1989.

Denison, Edward F. *Accounting for United States Economic Growth 1929-- 1969*. Washington, D.C.: The Brookings Institution, 1974.

Dertouzos, Michael L., Richard K. Lester, and Robert M. Solow. *Made in America: Regaining the Productive Edge*. Cambridge, Massachusetts: The MIT Press, 1989.

Destler, I.M. *American Trade Politics*, 2nd Edition. Washington, D.C.: Institute for International Economics, June 1992.

Drucker, Peter F. "The New Productivity Challenge." Harvard Business Review. (November-December 1991): 69-79.

Edelson, Burton and Robert Stern. "The Operations of DARPA and its Utility as a Model for a Civilian ARPA." Washington, D.C.: Foreign Policy Institute. November 1989. Mimeograph.

Electronic Industries Association. *1992 Electronic Market Data Book.* Washington, D.C.: Electronic Industries Association, 1992.

Flamm, Kenneth. *Creating the Computer.* Washington, D.C.: The Brookings Institution, 1988.

Freiberg, Andrew. "The End of Autonomy: The United States After Five Decades." *Daedalus* (Fall 1991): 69-90.

Fuchs, Peter. "Strategic Alliances: How US Start-Ups are Tapping into Japanese Capital, Markets and Technologies." *Business Tokyo* (April 1991).

Graham, Edward M. and Paul R. Krugman. *Foreign Direct Investment in the United States.* Washington, D.C.: Institute for International Economics, 1989.

Guile, Bruce R. and Harvey Brooks, eds. *Technology and Global Industry: Companies and Nations in the World Economy.* Washington, D.C.: National Academy Press, 1987.

Hall, Bronwyn. "The Impact of Corporate Restructuring on Industrial Research and Development." *Brookings Papers on Economic Activity: Microeconomics: 1990,* 85-136.

Herbert, Evan. "Japanese R&D in the United States." Research and Technology Management (November-December 1989): 11-20.

Institute for Defense Analyses. *Dependence of US Defense Systems on Foreign Technologies.* Arlington, Virginia: Institute for Defense Analyses, December 1990.

Kapstein, Ethan B. "Losing Control—National Security and the Global Economy." *The National Interest* 18 (Winter 1989-90): 85-90.

———. "We are Us: The Myth of the Multinational." *National Interest* 26 (Winter 1991-92): 55-62.

Kelly, Kevin. "Hot Spots: America's New Growth Regions Are Blossoming Despite the Slump." *Business Week* October 19, 1992: 80-88.

Kenney, Martin, and Richard Florida. "How Japanese Industry is Rebuilding the Rust Belt." *Technology Review* (February-March 1991): 25-33.

Kester, W. Carl, and Timothy A. Luehrman. "The Myth of Japan's Low-Cost Capital." *Harvard Business Review* (May-June 1992): 130-138.

Kolata, Gina. "Japanese Labs in US Luring America's Computer Experts." *New York Times* November 11, 1990: A-1, 24.

Koonce, David M. "Current Trends in the Defense Industry: A Financial Overview." unpublished paper, Martin Marietta Corporation, May 1992.

Krugman, Paul. "Myths and Realities of US Competitiveness" *Science* (November 1991): 811-815.

———. *Rethinking International Trade.* Cambridge, Massachusetts: MIT Press, 1990.

Lawrence, Robert Z. and Charles L. Schultze. *An American Trade Strategy: Options for the 1990's.* Washington, D.C.: The Brookings Institution, 1990.

———. "Innovation and Trade: Meeting the Foreign Challenge." In *Setting National Priorities: Policy for the Nineties,* Henry J. Aaron, ed., 145-184. Washington, D.C.: The Brookings Institution, 1990.

Lee, Thomas H., and Proctor P. Reid, eds. *National Interests in an Age of Global Technology.* Washington, D.C.: National Academy Press, 1991.

Levin, Richard, Alvin Klevorick, Richard Nelson, and Sidney Winter. "Appropriating the Returns from Industrial Research and Development." *Brookings Papers on Economic Activity* 3 (1987): 783.

Lohr, Steven. "High-Tech Goliaths, Taking Pains to Act Small." *New York Times* December 30, 1992: D1.

Lundquist, Jerrold T., "Shrinking Fast and Smart in the Defense Industry," *Harvard Business Review*. (November-December 1992): 74-85.

Maddison, Angus. *Dynamic Forces in Capitalist Development: A Long-Run Comparative View*. New York, New York: Oxford University Press, 1991.

Mansfield, Edwin. "Estimates of the Social Returns from Research and Development." In *Science and Technology Policy Yearbook*, Margaret Meredith, Stephen Nelson, and Albert Teich, eds., 313-320. Washington, D.C.: American Association for the Advancement of Science, 1991.

———. "Industrial R&D in Japan and the United States: A Comparative Study." *American Economic Review* 78, No. 2 (May 1988).

McCartan, Brian. "Defense or Opulence: Trade and Security in the 1990s." *SAIS Review* (Winter-Spring 1991).

McKinsey Global Institute. *Service Sector Productivity*. Washington, D.C.: McKinsey & Company, October 1992.

Miskel, James. "Thin Ice: Single Sources in the Domestic Industrial Base." *Strategic Review* 19 (Winter 1991): 46-53.

Moran, Theodore H. "Globalization of America's Defense Industries: Managing the Threat of Foreign Dependence." *International Security* (Summer 1990): 57-99.

Moravcsik, Andrew. "Arms and Autarky in Modern European History." *Daedalus* (Fall 1991): 23-46.

Mowery, David C. *The Growth of US Industrial Research*. CEPR Publication No. 182. Stanford, California: Center for Economic Policy Research, January 1990.

Mowery, David C. and Nathan Rosenberg. *Technology and the Pursuit of Economic Growth*. New York, New York: Cambridge University Press, 1989.

———. "New Developments in US Technology Policy: Implications for Competitiveness and International Trade Policy." CEPR Publication No. 166. Stanford, California: Center for Economic Policy Research, July 1989.

National Science Board Committee on Industrial Support for R&D. *The Competitive Strength of US Industrial Science and Technology: Strategic Issues* NSB-92-138. Washington, D.C.: National Science Foundation, August 1992.

National Science Foundation. *International Science and Technology Data Update: 1991* NSF 91-309. Washington, D.C.: National Science Foundation, April 1991.

———. *National Patterns in R&D Resources: 1990* NSF 90-316. Washington, D.C.: National Science Foundation, May 1990.

Nelson, R. R. "The Simple Economics of Basic Scientific Research." *Journal of Political Economy* 67 (1959): 297-306.

North Atlantic Council. "Conference of National Armaments Directors Group on NATO Defence Trade: Key Areas Affecting Defence Trade Among the Allies," Unpublished paper, January 17, 1992.

Office of Management and Budget. *The Budget of the United States: Fiscal 1992*. Washington, D.C.: US Government Printing Office.

Office of Science and Technology Policy. *Grand Challenges: Higher Performance Computing and Communications, The FY 1992 US Research and Development Program*. Washington, D.C.: Committee on Physical, Mathematical, and Engineering Sciences, 1992.

——. *US Technology Policy*, September 26, 1990.
Organization for Economic Cooperation and Development. Department of Economics and Statistics. *National Accounts: Main Aggregates* 1. Paris: OECD, 1992).
——. *The Newly Industrializing Countries: Challenge and Opportunity for OECD Industries*. Paris: OECD, 1988.
Passell, Peter. "Is G.M.'s Fate Still Crucial to the US?" *New York Times*, November 6, 1992,: D-1.
Phillips, Kevin P. "US Industrial Policy: Inevitable and Ineffective." *Harvard Business Review* (July-August 1992): 104-112.
Pilat, Dirk and Bart van Ark. "Productivity Leadership in Manufacturing: Germany, Japan and the United States, 1973-1989." University of Groningen, March 1992.
Pollack, Andrew. "'Fifth Generation' Becomes Japan's Lost Generation." *New York Times*, June 5, 1992,: D1, 3.
Porter, Michael. *Capital Choices: Changing the Way America Invests in Industry*. Washington, D.C.: Council on Competitiveness, 1992.
——. *The Competitive Advantage of Nations*. New York: Free Press, 1990.
Prose, Michael "Is America in Decline?" *Harvard Business Review* 70, No. 4 (July-August 1992): 34-45.
Pterba, J.M. and L. H. Summers. "Time Horizons of American Firms: New Evidence From a Survey of CEOs." Harvard Business School and Council on Competitiveness, 1992.
Quinn, James Brian, Jordan J. Baruch, and Penny Cushman Paquette. "Technology in Services." *Scientific American* 257, No. 6 (December 1987): 50-58.
Reed, Carol, "Hughes: No Longer Business As Usual." *Janes Defense Weekly*, August 1, 1992,:27, 30.
Reich, Robert B. "Does Corporate Nationality Matter?" *Issues in Science and Technology* 7 (Winter 1990-91): 40-44.
——. "Who is Them?" *Harvard Business Review* 69 (March-April 1991): 77-88.
——. *The Work of Nations: Preparing Ourselves for 21st-Century Capitalism*. New York, New York: Alfred A. Knopf, 1991.
Rutter, John. *Trends in International Direct Investment*. Staff Paper No. 91-5. Washington, D.C.: US Department of Commerce, International Trade Administration, July 1991.
Smith, Bruce L. R. *American Science Policy Since World War II*. Washington, D.C.: The Brookings Institution, 1990.
Sullivan, Paul R. "Strategies for Global Aerospace Companies." Boston, Mass.: Global Partners, November 20, 1990.
"Thomson-CSF and City of Dallas Plan to Fight Back on LTV Buyout." *Defense Marketing News*, May 29, 1992, 3.
Thurow, Lester. *Head to Head: The Coming Economic Battle Among Japan, Europe, and America*. New York, New York: William Morrow, 1992.
Tyson, Laura D'Andrea. "They Are Not Us: Why American Ownership Still Matters." *American prospect* No. 4 (Winter 1991): 37-38, 40-53.
Uchitelle, Louis. "US Businesses Loosen Link to Mother Country." *New York Times*, May 21, 1989,: A-1.
US Congress. Senate. Committee on Armed Services. *National Defense Authorization Act for Fiscal Years 1992 and 1993*. (Report 102-113). Washington, D.C.: US Government Printing Office, 1992.
US Congress. Office of Technology Assessment. *After the Cold War: Living with Lower Defense Spending*, OTA-ITE-524 Washington, D.C.: US Government Printing Office, February 1992.

——. *Arming Our Allies: Cooperation and Competition in Defense Technology*. Washington, D.C.: US Government Printing Office, 1990.

——. *Building Future Security: Strategies for Restructuring the Defense Technology and Industrial Base* OTA-ISC-530. Washington, D.C.: US Government Printing Office, June 1992.

——. *Competing Economies: America, Europe, and the Pacific Rim*. Washington, D.C.: US Government Printing Office, October 1991.

——. *Holding the Edge: Maintaining the Defense Technology Base* OTA-ISC-420. Washington, D.C.: US Government Printing Office, April 1989.

——. *Making Things Better: Competing in Manufacturing* OTA-ITE-443. Washington, D.C.: US Government Printing Office, February 1990.

——. *Redesigning Defense: Planning the Transition to the Future US Defense Industrial Base* OTA-ISC-500. Washington, D.C.: US Government Printing Office, July 1991.

US-CREST. *Cooperative Strategies: High-Technology Security Cooperation— A Transatlantic Industrial Perspective*. Arlington, Va.: US-CREST/ Hudson Institute, 1991.

US Department of Commerce. *Emerging Technologies: A Survey of Technical and Economic Opportunities*. Washington, D.C.: Department of Commerce, 1990.

US Department of Defense. *Critical Technologies Report*. Washington, D.C.: US Department of Defense, May 1, 1991.

——. Defense Science Board. *Report of the Task Force on Defense Semiconductor Dependency*. Washington, D.C.: US Department of Defense, 1987.

——. Undersecretary of Defense (Acquisition) and Assistant Secretary of Defense (Production and Logistics). *Report to the Congress on the Defense Industrial Base*. Washington, D.C.: U.S Department of Defense, November 1991.

US General Accounting Office. *European Initiatives: Implications for US Defense Trade and Cooperation* GAO/NSIAD-91-167. Washington, D.C.: US General Accounting Office, April 1991.

——. *Foreign Investment: Analyzing National Security Concerns* GAO/NSIAD-90-94. Washington, D.C.: US General Accounting Office, March 1990.

——. *High Technology Competitiveness: Trends in US and Foreign Performance* GAO/NSIAD-92-236. Washington, D.C.: US General Accounting Office, September 1992.

——. *Industrial Base: Significance of DOD's Foreign Dependence*. Washington, D.C.: US General Accounting Office, January 1991.

——. *Japanese-Affiliated Automakers: Management Practices Related to Purchasing Parts* GAO/T-NSIAD-92-5. Washington, D.C.: US General Accounting Office, November 14, 1991.

——. *Technology Transfer: Federal Efforts to Enhance the Competitiveness of Small Manufacturers*. Washington, D.C.: US General Accounting Office, November 1991.

Vernon, Raymond. "International Investment and International Trade in the Product Cycle." *Quarterly Journal of Economics* 80 (May 1966).

White, Robert M. "Science, Engineering, and the Sorcerer's Apprentice." *Science and Technology Yearbook: 1991*. Washington, D.C.: Association for the Advancement of Science, 1991.

Wolff, Edward. "The Rich Get Increasingly Richer: Latest Data on Household Wealth During the 1980s." Economic Policy Institute, October 1992.

Index